Commodity Markets and Latin American Development: A Modeling Approach

CONFERENCE ON COMMODITY MODELS IN LATIN AMERICA

Edited by
Walter C. Labys,
M. Ishaq Nadiri,
and
José Núñez del
Arco

Commodity Markets and Latin American Development: A Modeling Approach

Conference on
Commodity Models in
Latin America

Published for the National Bureau of
Economic Research, Inc.
by
Ballinger Publishing Company,
Cambridge, Massachusetts
A Subsidiary of Harper & Row
Publishers, Inc.

This book is printed on recycled paper.

International Standard Book Number: 0–88410–481–8

Library of Congress Catalog Card Number: 79–16533

Printed in the United States of America

Library of Congress Cataloging in Publication Data

Main entry under title:

Commodity markets and Latin American development.

Papers presented at a conference held in Lima, May 11–13, 1978, jointly sponsored by the Escuela de Administración de Negocios para Graduados (ESAN) and the National Bureau of Economic Research.
    1. Commodity control–Mathematical models–Congresses. 2. Commercial products–Latin America–Mathematical models–Congresses. 3. Latin America–Economic conditions–Mathematical models–Congresses.
I. Labys, Walter C., 1937–   II. Nadiri, M. Ishaq.
III. Núñez del Arco, José. IV. Escuela de Adminiatración de Negocios para Graduados. V. National Bureau of Economic Research.
HF1428.C62   330.9′8′003   79–16533
ISBN 0–88410–481–8

Contents

List of Figures

List of Tables

Preface

This book is a compilation of some of the papers presented at a conference sponsored jointly by the Escuela de Administracion de Negocios para Graduados (ESAN) in Lima and the National Bureau of Economic Research. The conference, entitled "Commodity Markets, Models and Policies in Latin America," was held at ESAN in Lima from May 11–13, 1978. The participants consisted of economists, planners, and policymakers from the United States and Latin America interested in commodity models and their use in planning. Unfortunately, not all of the papers presented in the conference could be included in this volume. Only papers dealing with modeling methodologies, particularly those related directly to Latin America's primary commodities, are included.

We thank all of the participants in the conference, and most particularly those who presented papers and the discussants and members of ESAN, especially Dean Lander Pacora Coupen, Tulio Camminati, Nissim Alcabes, Fernando Robles, Peter Wosner, and Alberto Zaqater.

The financial support of IBM World Trade Company to the National Bureau of Economic Research and the financial resources made available by the Escuela de Administracion para Graduados that made this conference possible are deeply appreciated.

Walter C. Labys, West Virginia University
M. Ishaq Nadiri, NBER and New York University
José F. Núñez del Arco, Interamerican Development Bank

1 | Introduction

There are a number of reasons for examining the role of commodity markets in the economic development of Latin American economies. The majority of Latin American countries are heavily dependent on primary commodities for the bulk of their export earnings, and this situation is unlikely to change significantly in the near future. While many of these commodities are of the "traditional" agricultural type, we are entering an era in which a foreseen relative scarcity of food resources will make many of these commodities extremely valuable. Industrial raw materials are also becoming more valuable as new scarcities arise. Dependence on these commodities, however, means suffering from frequent and wide price swings. This has led to recent action to consider forming producers' agreements among countries that export these commodities, for example, the Intergovernmental Council of Copper Exporting Countries (CIPEC) and the Bauxite Producers Exporting Committee (BAUPEC). In any event, studying commodity markets is essential to understanding and formulating Latin American policies on a domestic and international level.

Among problems that commodities have posed in planning for national growth in Latin America, the following can be cited. (1) The commodities involved make these countries dependent on industrialized countries for investment, technology, trade, and general know-how. (2) The trade dependence of any single country is often on one or two rather than a group of commodities. This dependence can become particularly difficult as it has in the past when commodity prices decline as a consequence of world recession. Indeed over the past two decades the terms of trade of their primary commodities have not increased. (3) The exported commodities are highly sensitive to substitution from synthetics produced within the importing countries. (4) Most of the industrial countries offer a degree of protection against these commodities. (5) The "new" export promotion policies being studied can only be effective if the future of "low" and "high" growth commodities is correctly assessed. (6) Little is known about the "mechanics" linking commodity exports and GNP growth in the various countries. (7) Up to now a clear picture has not emerged as to the potential impact of proposed international commodity stabilization schemes on Latin America.

The hope of solving some of these problems provides a need for a methodological approach that would examine the relation between commodities and growth and improve planning in this area. This book attempts to introduce to economists and planners some of the latest advances in commodity modeling methodologies that can help meet this need. While some of these advances relate to the basic commodity model, two others of interest deal with its application to trade and development processes. The first of these would employ commodity models as well as commodity sectoral models in conjunction with macroeconometric models. The second would transform commodity models to analyze and to predict the outcomes of commodity price stabilization schemes.

ORGANIZATION

The structure of the book is designed to provide a perspective on the relation between primary commodities and economic development in Latin America. The approach taken from a disciplinary point of view is basically a quantitative or modeling one. However, embellishments of a qualitative nature would seem necessary to make the examination of commodity impacts more comprehensive. The organization of the book is in four parts. The first part surveys Latin America's commodity markets from the point of view of policy planning needs and related modeling methodologies. The second part presents models of commodity markets of importance to Latin America. The third part studies the interrelationships between commodity markets and their dependent national economies with special emphasis on the mineral and agricultural sectors. Featured are the latest advances in models which analyze this interrelationship. The fourth part extends the modeling analysis by examining the international initiatives currently being taken in regard to stabilization and the related UNCTAD Integrated Program. For those readers less familiar with modeling methodologies, Chapters 2, 3, and 9 provide a general introduction to important policy issues concerning commodities and development. A brief account of the material presented in the four parts of this book is given below.

Part I

Modeling
Approaches to
Commodity
Planning in
Latin America

2

WALTER C.
LABYS

Commodity Models and Their Potential for Latin American Planning

This chapter examines the role commodity models can play in analyzing commodity markets and policies in Latin America. To show the importance of such models for planning, the strategic nature of primary commodities in Latin American development is first discussed. A perspective for planning featuring commodity models is presented next. The modeling methodologies employed in this context are discussed according to: (1) models of commodity markets, (2) models linking commodity markets and the dependent national economies, and (3) models designed specifically to analyze commodity stabilization. So that this chapter will help introduce the modeling methodologies of the other chapters, examples of commodity modeling studies related directly to Latin America's planning needs and policies are also presented. A full model's list appears in the bibliography.

IMPORTANCE OF PRIMARY COMMODITIES

Recent fluctuations in international commodity markets and their impacts on dependent national economies have been dramatic. From the fourth quarter of 1972 to the end of 1974, the prices of commodities important to Latin America such as maize, sugar, and copper doubled and quadrupled before they reached their peak as shown below.

	Price Increases	*Price Decreases*
Maize	1972–IV to 74–IV = 111%	74–IV to 76–II = 20%
Sugar	1972–IV to 74–1V = 490%	74–IV tn 76–II = 71%
Copper	1972–IV to 74–II = 175%	74–II t.o 76–II = 45%

From 1974 through 1976 they have tumbled almost as sharply. The price swings were also reflected in foreign exchange earnings. From a prospect for debt repayment capability in 1974, Latin American countries now find themselves again with balance of payments problems.

Among causes of price fluctuations during this period, Labys and Thomas (1975) cite real and anticipated scarcities of food, fuel, and other strategic commodities; responses of producers to years of declining income and prices; a shift in the technological-ecological availability of commodities; deviations in world weather patterns; shifts in speculative activity toward and away from commodity futures markets; use of the latter to hedge against exchange rate instability, rising inflation, and general monetary instability; and closer cooperation among nations leading to the formation of producers' cartels.

In addition, there are causes related to basic market forces. To begin with, the price adjustments needed to equate supply and demand in commodity markets are normally large. World supply of these commodities is limited by production conditions in exporting countries such as capacity or credit constraints, while many commodities are harvested only annually. World demand can also be relatively constant, because commodities normally represent only a small proportion of the value of the products for which they serve as inputs. Taken together, one finds that both supply and demand are relatively price inelastic, and, therefore, a given change in available or desired supplies causes a substantial price movement. In addition, a large share of this output derives from relatively few countries; excess supplies in only one of these countries can thus affect the market substantially.

Latin America suffers appreciably from fluctuations in commodity prices and earnings because of its position as a major commodity exporter.[1] Selecting a few examples from Table 2–1, Argentina provides 13.8 percent of the world's beef and 10.6 percent of the hides and skins; Brazil exports 30.1 percent of the coffee, 24.9 percent of the sisal, and 8.0 percent of the sugar; Ecuador supplies 18.0 percent of the bananas; and Peru 54.2 percent of the fish meal. These various commodities are also shown to exhibit substantial price instability. Of the eighteen commodities listed in Table 2–1, the ratio of the price variation to mean is above 40 percent for twelve of them. While the above commodity shares are substantial, their national impact is even greater, given the fact that these exports represent such a large proportion of each country's total earnings. Table 2–1 also indicates that copper accounts for 71.6 percent of Chile's total exports, coffee 59.5 percent of Colombia's exports, bananas 53.9 percent of Panama's exports, and tin 50.1 percent of Bolivia's exports.

With such a high degree of primary commodity dependence, we are justified in seeking planning approaches that invoke the latest advances in commodity modeling methodologies.

THE PLANNING PERSPECTIVE

The planning perspective developed concentrates initially on the role of economic analysis in the planning procedure and secondly on the contribution made by modeling to that analysis. Planning is widespread in both developed and developing countries. Not only are there ministries of planning and central planning boards, but there also are economic forecasting units and planning research departments. At one extreme, planning may consist of the normal tasks of government budgeting, the management of public enterprises, and the national time-phasing of certain public services.[2] At the other extreme, planning consists of preparing a detailed framework for the future economic structure and of implementing it through direct or indirect manipulation of government instruments. While in the former case market prices play a large role, in the latter case they are subordinate to overall plan goals.

The types of planning associated with commodity markets lie in between these extremes. Most typically they consist of forecasts of the prices, production, or exports of commodities; alternatively, they focus on the importance of nonprice factors in allocating scarce resources among competing commodities. Although planning varies considerably among countries, its character depends on considerations such as the degree to which the market mechanism pervades economic decisions or the extent of market imperfections and price distortions and their causes. Another complicating factor is the disequilibrium nature of commodity markets. Related market fluctuations cause development to slow down between periods of export revenue declines. Such "stop and go" phenomena require that commodity planning be pursued as intensely as planning in other sectors.

Although it is difficult to generalize about the nature of national, institutional, or even corporate planning processes, the example given in Figure 2–1 provides a starting point. Beginning at the top of the figure and following downward, the recognition stage views the planner as being confronted with certain policy problems. These problems

Table 2–1. Latin America: Characteristics of Primary Commodity Exports

Commodity	Average Export Value, 1970–1972	Major Exporting Countries	Country Share of World Exports 1970–1972	Commodity Share of Country Exports 1970–1972	Ratio of Price Variation to Mean 1960–1973
Beef	668.1	Argentina	13.8%	17.4%	43%
		Brazil	4.9%	3.5%	
Maize	335.2	Argentina	13.0%	14.5%	46%
Bananas	425.1	Costa Rica	13.0%	29.3%	26%
		Ecuador	18.0%	0.3%	
		Panama	11.3%	53.9%	
Sugar	1452.5	Brazil	8.0%	71.0%	129%
Coffee	1912.7	Brazil	30.1%	28.0%	31%
		Colombia	14.4%	59.5%	
Cocoa	126.6	Brazil	8.5%	2.1%	47%
Fishmeal	295.5	Peru	54.2%	28.0%	38%

Commodity					
Groundnuts	46.0	Brazil	5.3%	0.4%	54%
Cotton	488.1	Brazil	5.7%	5.0%	36%
		Mexico	4.6%	8.3%	
Sisal	29.2	Brazil	24.9%	0.6%	76%
		Mexico	13.7%	0.6%	
Hides	145.9	Argentina	10.6%	5.1%	29%
Copper	963.3	Chile	16.1%	71.6%	40%
Iron Ore	498.0	Brazil	8.5%	7.0%	22%
Lead	64.6	Peru	6.5%	3.3%	41%
Manganese Ore	35.8	Brazil	16.4%	1.0%	23%
Silver	109.8	Peru	10.0%	6.0%	42%
Tin	122.2	Bolivia	14.4%	50.1%	41%
Zinc	120.7	Peru	7.1%	5.7%	81%
		Mexico	6.4%	3.2%	
Petroleum	4245	Venezuela	9.9%	86.8%	—

Source: World Bank (1975).

```
┌─────────────────────┐
│ Recognition of Policy│
│ Problems to be Solved│
└─────────────────────┘
          │
          ▼
┌─────────────────────┐
│ Identification of    │
│ Decisions to be Taken│
└─────────────────────┘
          │
          ▼
┌─────────────────────┐        ┌──────────────┐        ┌──────────────┐
│ Evaluation of Impact │        │ Political     │        │ Strategic     │
│ of Alternative       │◄───────│ Considerations│◄───────│ Bargaining    │
│ Decisions            │        └──────────────┘        │ Power         │
└─────────────────────┘                                 └──────────────┘
          │                      ┌──────────────┐        ┌──────────────┐
          │                      │ Technological │        │ Capital/Labor │
          │                      │ Considerations│◄───────│ Requirements  │
          │                      └──────────────┘        └──────────────┘
          ▼                      ┌──────────────┐        ┌──────────────┐
┌─────────────────────┐          │ Institutional │        │ Ecological,   │
│ Acceptability of     │          │ Considerations│◄───────│ Social Legal  │
│ Foreseen Impact      │          └──────────────┘        │ Constraints   │
├──────────┬──────────┤                                   └──────────────┘
│ Non—     │          │          ┌──────────────┐        ┌──────────────┐
│ Acceptable│Acceptable│          │ Economic      │◄───────│ Export        │
└──────────┴──────────┘          │ Considerations│        │ Commodity     │
          │                      └──────────────┘        │ Market        │
          ▼                                              └──────────────┘
┌─────────────────────┐                                  ┌──────────────┐
│ Implementation       │                                  │ Domestic      │
│ of Policy            │                                  │ Commodity     │
└─────────────────────┘                                  │ Market        │
                                                         └──────────────┘
                                                          ┌──────────────┐
                                                          │ Linkages      │
                                                          │ Between       │
                                                          │ Commodities   │
                                                          │ and the       │
                                                          │ Economy       │
                                                          └──────────────┘
```

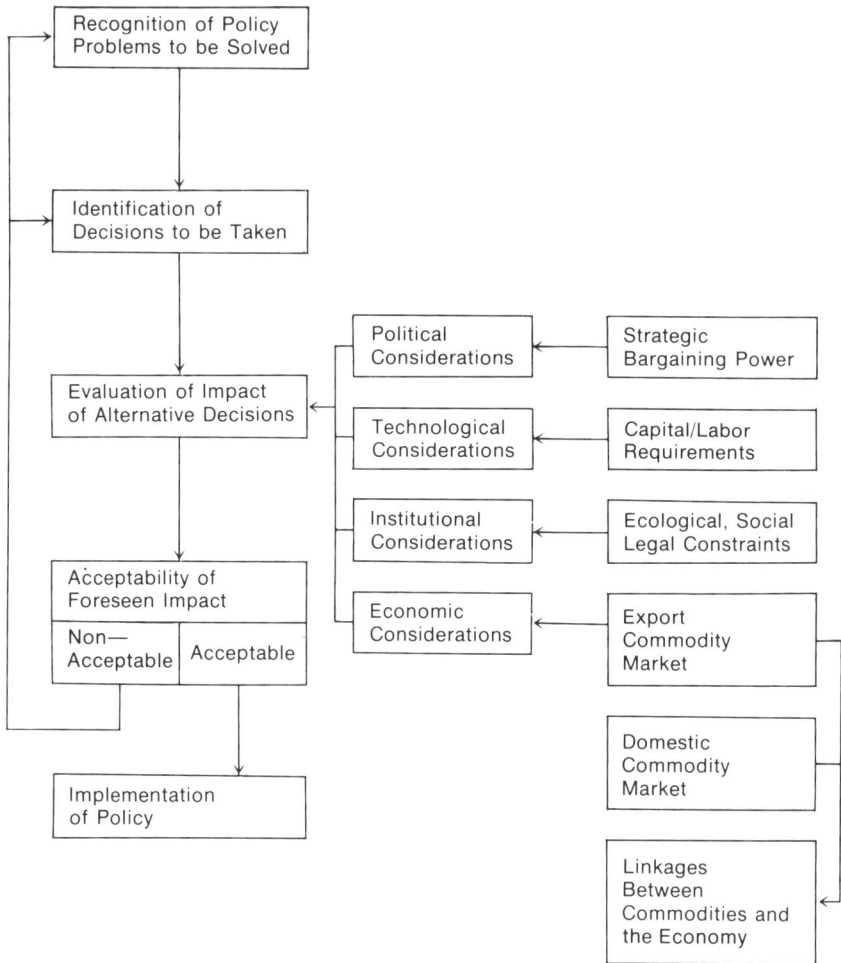

FIGURE 2-1. Commodity Policy Analysts and Planning

normally are concerned with relating commodity activity to specific planning targets or national objectives. At the identification stage, a number of alternative decisions or policies are proposed that could help solve the problems.

The most complex stage is the next one, that of evaluating the alternatives. Although most planners have a verbal or mental model of their evaluation process, they seldom are able to quantify it. We do know that it consists of assessing the relative welfare outcomes of alternative policies, each of which is influenced by economic, political, technological, and institutional considerations. Economic considerations, for example, might pertain to economic gains resulting from investment in the domestic or export commodity sector. Political considerations might refer to a commodity's importance in terms of bargaining strategies in contracting or trading. Technological considerations might relate to the level of capital intensiveness to be adopted in the production or extraction of the commodity. And institutional considerations might reflect ecological, sociological, or legal factors such as land distribution schemes.

Once the alternatives are examined, planners make decisions hoping the outcome will be politically acceptable. In some cases as shown, the decision may not be acceptable, and previously stated problems and alternatives will have to be reconsidered. The entire planning process can thus be described as requiring feedback to previous stages until an acceptable decision is reached. Once a decision or policy is deemed acceptable, it moves to the implementation stage.

A major concern in this book is the appropriate quantitative framework that will help planners analyze economic considerations in their evaluation of the impact of alternative commodity policies. The framework proposed is a modeling one.[3] Strictly speaking, a model embodies a hypothesis that involves a relationship between variables and that intends to explain and predict past, present, and future events or to describe policies and predict their outcome. For policy purposes, a model distinguishes between target variables that constitute the objectives of economic policy and controlled variables that are instruments affected by policies. Variations occurring in the levels of the controlled variables affect the levels of the target variables. In addition to specifying the economic relationship between variables, a model also attempts to incorporate technological, institutional and political relationships.

Figure 2–1 also shows commodity policies to be directed to either domestic markets or export markets. Domestic commodity policies normally are analyzed using a commodity model that interrelates factors inherent to domestic supply, demand, inventories, and prices. One can then demonstrate through simulations of the model how changing policies, for example, regarding employment or capacity adjustment, can influence quantities and prices. This dependence can be described according to how the market might have reacted historically or how it might react in the future. Essential to employing the model is that it be properly validated so that planners will have confidence in its explanation of market behavior or in its predictions.

Export commodity policies are analyzed with a similar modeling approach; only now the variables included relate to world commodity markets. As we shall see later, such models have been used to determine the impact of commodity stabilization schemes such as those proposed within the UNCTAD Integrated Program. One weakness of this approach is its limitations for explaining the impact of commodity exports on various sectors of the dependent national economy. Instead, the type of modeling exercise required involves linking one or more commodity models with a macroeconometric model or an equivalent computational model of the national economy. Let us now examine each of these modeling approaches more closely.

COMMODITY MODELS

Generally speaking, a commodity model is a quantitative representation of a commodity market or industry; the behavioral relationships included reflect demand and supply aspects of price determination as well as other related phenomena. Commodity models deal with foods and raw materials in an unprocessed and partially processed state. These commodities can be extracted from the land (fuel and nonfuel minerals), grown on the land (annual and perennial crops, including timber), raised on the land (cattle and poultry), or harvested from the water (fish, plants, and water itself). Recyclable and scrap materials are also included.

The most basic type of model from which other commodity methodologies have developed is the *market* model.[4] Focusing on the price mechanism that serves to clear the market, the rudiments of a market model·can be summarized in four equations, although much more complex structures are used in practice.

$$D = d(D_{-1}, P, P^c, A, T)$$
$$Q = q(Q_{-1}, P_{-\theta}, N, Z)$$
$$P = p(P_{-1}, D, \Delta I)$$
$$I = I_{-1} + Q - D$$

Demand (D) is explained as being dependent on prices (P), economic activity (A), prices of one or more substitute commodities (P^c), and possible technical influences (T) such as the growth of synthetic substitutes. Other possible influencing factors and the customary stochastic disturbance term are omitted here and elsewhere to simplify presentation. Accordingly supply (Q) would depend on prices ($P_{-\theta}$) as well as natural factors (N) such as weather, yields, and a possible policy variable (Z). A lagged price variable ($P_{-\theta}$) is included since the supply process is normally described using some form of the general class of distributed lag functions.

Prices (P) are explained by demand (D) and inventories (I), although this equation is sometimes inverted to explain inventory demand. The model is closed using an identity that equates inventories (I) with lagged inventories (I_{-1}) plus supply (Q) minus demand (D). Where the price equation is inverted to represent inventory demand, the identity can be recognized as the equivalent supply of inventories equation.

Market models have received considerable development in analyzing commodity policies in Latin America. Cocoa, coffee, cotton, rice, and wheat models have been constructed by Adams and Behrman (1976). Segura (1973) has studied the economics of anchovy exploitation and its relation to fish meal consumption patterns, including implications for Peru. Epps (1970) has evaluated the impact of alternative Brazilian coffee export policies on the world coffee market. And Fisher, Cootner, and Bailey (1972) have studied fluctuations in the world copper market in relation to Chilean export income.

In addition to the market model, there are a number of different modeling methodologies. Table 2–2 provides a summary of their basic characteristics: purpose of the methodology, quantitative method used, economic behavior specified, and examples of applications. Reviewing each of these briefly, models of the *process* type are also econometric in nature, but they deal with supply and demand within an industry rather than across a market. They thus focus on the transformation of commodity inputs into finished products. Whereas market models balance supply and demand to explain commodity prices, prices in a process model are normally a function of production and material costs, that is, markup. They are well suited for describing process industries dealing with petroleum, steel, or chemicals because they concentrate on the industrial production process, requirements for raw materials and labor, and plant capacity.

A recent extension of this approach has been to expand the description of the production process to include *linear programming* or *input-output* models that transform the raw materials inputs into intermediate and final products. Input-output models of commodity processes have also been developed independently of process models. Kruegar (1976) has shown how they can be used to explain intermediate and final demands for mineral commodities. Another use has been the disaggregation of the tables to analyze individual agricultural products. In relation to Latin America, Simpson in Chapter 7 employs disaggregated input-output models to determine output and income multipliers for agricultural product lines. The commodity principally studied is beef with implications for Argentina, Brazil, Paraguay, and Uruguay.

Optimization and programming methodologies have also proven

Table 2–2. Commodity Modeling Methodologies and the Modeling Process

Methodologies / Modeling Process	What is the purpose of the methodology?	What quantitative method is used?	What economic behavior is specified?	Examples of Commodity applications
Market Model	Demand, supply, inventories interact to produce an equilibrium price in competitive or noncompetitive markets	Dynamic microeconometric system composed of difference or differential equations	Interaction between decision-makers in reaching market equilibrium based on demand, supply inventories, prices, trade, etc.	Beef Wheat Cocoa Coffee Sugar Copper Tin
Process Model	Demand and production determined within an industry, focusing on transformation from product demand to input requirements	Dynamic microeconomic difference equation system suitable for integrating linear programming on production side	Interaction between decisionmakers in industries, markets, national economies based on demand, production, investment, capacity, commodity inputs, etc.	Petroleum Steel
Input-Output Model	System regarded as process that converts raw materials into intermediate and final products via intermediate processes	Input-output model operated separately or combined with macroeconomic framework or disaggregated raw materials balance framework	Interactions between inputs and outputs based on technical coefficients and demand permit computation of output and income multipliers for commodity sectors.	Energy Minerals Beef
Optimization and Programming Models: 1. Linear and Quadratic Programming Spatial Equilibrium	Spatial flows of demand and supply and equilibrium conditions assigned optimally in equilibrium depending on configuration of transportation network	Activity analysis of a spatial and/or temporal form. Degree of complexity depends on endogeneity and method of incorporation of demand and supply functions	Interaction between decision makers in allocating shipments (exports) and consumption (imports) optimized through maximizing sectoral revenues or minimizing sectoral costs	Wheat Sugar Livestock Petroleum Beef Cocoa

18

	Model			Commodities
2.	Recursive Programming	Production conditions and input revenue determined through primal/dual of linear program. Recursivity introduced through feedback component which includes profit, capital and demand	Activity analysis involving a sequence of constrained maximization problems in which objective function, limitation coefficients depend on optimal primal/dual solutions attained earlier in the sequence	Interaction between decision makers in reaching market equilibrium involves adaptive intertemporal processes related to production, investment and technological change	Coal Iron and Steel Wheat Corn and Soybeans
3.	Mixed Integer Programming	Size of firm, location, time phasing, technology and product-mix determined optimally	Activity analysis involving a maximization problem that combines a process component with a spatial or transportation component	Capital costs and transport costs minimized with respect to material balance in final products, intermediate products, capacity, investment and market requirements.	Fertilizers Copper Steel
	Trade Flow Model	Trade flows reflect not only resistance and potential but also policies relating to geography, contract arrangements and trade blocs	Structure of trade model which estimates trade flow matrix directly. Imports and exports follow from summation of trade flows.	Interaction between potential to import and to export limited by resistance to trade between countries.	Copper Iron Ore Tin Bauxite Lead Zinc
	Industrial Dynamics: Dynamic Commodity Cycle Model	Demand, supply, Inventories interact to produce an equilibrium price, emphasizing role of amplifications and feedback delays	Dynamic microeconometric differential equation system that features lagged feedback relations and variables in rates of change	Interaction between decision makers in adjusting rate of production to maintain a desired level of inventory in relationship to rate of consumption	Aluminum Broilers Cattle Copper Hogs Oranges
	Systems Model	Demand, supply and other major variables and objectives considered as a complete system rather than a single market	Dynamic microeconometric equation system which when formed into a simulation framework is coupled with activity analysis and/or decision rules	Interaction between decision makers belonging to the system environment based on performance variables such as revenues and costs as well as market variables such as demand, supply, prices, etc.	Beef Energy Fish Livestock Multicommodity Rice

Source: Labys (1975a).

useful. The linear and quadratic forms of *spatial equilibrium* models are popular in modeling international commodity markets. In particular, they can analyze spatial or interregional efficiency in the production, distribution, and utilization of commodities. Optimal patterns of commodity supply and demand can be determined subject to changes in trade policies such as tariffs and quotas as well as in domestic price support and acreage allotments. A recent application of spatial equilibrium with implications for Latin America given in Chapter 6 is Gemmill's model of the world sugar market. Among other studies are Brandt's (1967) analysis of Brazilian coffee policies, Kennedy's (1974) analysis of the world petroleum market with implications for Venezuela, and the Schmitz and Bawden (1976) analysis of the world wheat economy including Argentina.

The *recursive programming* variant of these models concentrates on the production side of the market, emphasizing the role of investment and technological change in allocating commodity production and omitting spatial allocation. These models relate more to investment behavior in a single nation because they are disaggregated below the market level, reflecting the behavior of individual decision makers. Within this context, they have been useful in analyzing diversification among agricultural crops as well as the impact of changing technologies on production in the steel and coal industries. The most noted application in Latin America has been that of Singh and Ahn (1973) analyzing agricultural development and crop investment patterns in the Rio Grande do Sol, Brazil.

A more recent development among optimization models is that of multiperiod *mixed integer programming*. Like recursive programming, which achieves optimization over time, this form of model emphasizes the impact of technological change on production processes. But it also combines a process component with a spatial or transportation component. Using an objective function that minimizes the total of capital costs, recurrent costs, and transport costs, the constraints reflect material balance for final products, intermediate products, capacity, investment, and market requirements. The resulting model permits size, location, time-phasing, technology, and product mix decisions to be made within its framework. An application of this type of model is described in Chapter 4 where Dammert analyzes investment planning in the Latin American copper industry.

Models of any methodology considered thus far can analyze trade patterns and trade policies for the commodity exporting and importing countries involved. However, trade patterns can also be considered in the context of traditional *trade* models such as that of Linneman (1966) and Taplin (1973). The actual tailoring of this approach to commodity markets has been performed by Tilton (1966). He explains variations in the trade flow matrix for a mineral commodity based on three factors: (1) the potential of country i to export a commodity; (2) the potential of country j to import the commodity; and (3) the resistance to trade between country i and country j. Policy applications of this approach relate to potential access to the mineral or potential access to foreign markets, as affected by geographic location, ownership ties, contracts, and preferential trade blocs. Examples of econometric studies related to Latin America include that of Whitney (1976) on copper, Dorr (1975) on aluminum, and Santos (1976) on iron ore. Chapter 5 by Demler and Tilton concentrates on a policy application to tin and zinc.

Both the *industrial dynamics* and *systems forms* of models deviate somewhat from the traditional market approaches; they describe commodity markets and industries as a complete system in which the impacts of objectives and decisions are viewed through adaptive and feedback processes. While the industrial dynamics model is preferable for dynamic analysis emphasizing feedback delays and cyclical processes, systems models typically incorporate biological or agronomic models with market models to emphasize the technical character of commodity production. Among commodities to which systems models have been applied in Latin America, the cattle industry in Argentina has received most attention. In particular Jarvis (1969), Yver (1971), and Nores (1972) have studied the cattle industry from the point of view of the optimal inventory of beef cattle.

MODELS LINKING COMMODITIES AND THE ECONOMY

The role of primary commodities in economic development has been emphasized mainly through linkages between the commodity export sector and the dependent economy.[5] Among the more important works in which this relationship has been studied are those of Singer (1950), Baldwin (1963), Reynolds (1965), and Maizels (1968). Statistical confirmation can be found in Baldwin (1966), Emery (1967), and Thoburn (1977). More recent investigations have centered upon the concept of domestic resource costs. Primary commodity studies of this nature include those of Pearson (1970) and Pearson and Cownie (1975).

Among reasons normally offered to support the argument of a linkage between exports and economic growth, Emery (1967;471) suggests the following: (1) an increasing level of exports generally implies that the country has the capabilities to step up its level of imports; (2) export development tends to concentrate investment in the most efficient sectors of the economy, those in which the country enjoys a comparative advantage; (3) the country also gains from economies of scale because the international market added to the domestic market increases the scale of operation possible; (4) the necessity of remaining competitive in international markets tends to maintain pressure on the export industries to improve efficiency; (5) for primary commodities, the country exports those goods most suitable to its natural resource, agricultural, and cultural base; and (6) secondary benefits are generated that result in increased investment, consumption, and flow of technology.

Underlying these reasons are several theories of trade and growth as recently summarized by Thoburn (1977). Export sector effects, particularly of primary commodities, are viewed as working through the impacts of export income flows and through externalities. This process has been viewed as following the theory of capital formation, based on a disaggregated multiplier-accelerator mechanism. Commodity export growth thus impinges on the economy through investment opportunities: (1) in the industry itself; (2) in industries supplying inputs to the export sector; (3) in industries employing the export as an input; (4) and in industries producing consumer goods for factors of production employed in the export sector. Hirschman (1958) has termed these additional investment opportunities as *linkages*. Where they are reasonably continuous and of sufficient duration, we should be able to detect and to study them.

The present relevance of the linkage concept depends on the particular growth of investment in the primary commodity subsector. Where foreign investment has been important in the launching of an industry, the focus on linkages is highly appropriate. The greater the proportion of intermediate to final purchases and of intermediate to final sales, the more can the local population participate as investors. Such opportunities would be over and above those resulting from direct participation in the industry. Where an investment in a commodity industry has been primarily domestic, linkage effects are not as notable, but linkage analysis still provides insight into the impact of the investment on the economy.

Linkage effects considered can generally be allocated into two groups. The first group relates principally to industry operations within the commodity subsector: *backward* linkages, *forward* linkages, and *technological* linkages. Backward linkages can be viewed to the extent that locally produced intermediate inputs and capital goods are used by the commodity industry. Forward linkages are found when the outputs of the export industry are used as inputs by other local industries. To these can be added technological linkages, which relate to different external effects imparted by the commodity industry on other industries in the economy, including the diffusion of new technologies, methods of organization, and so on. Depending on the magnitude of these linkages, the commodity subsector contributes to economic development by providing additional income and employment possibilities in the linked industries.

The second group of linkages results from expenditures of factor incomes and taxes paid by the commodity industry. The multiplier effects normally associated with macromodels embodying the accelerator operate through final demand payments by factors of production employed and by government expenditure of taxes gained from the industry. Such multipliers reflect the impact of a change in export income or commodity investment on domestic factor income. Of principal interest are the *final demand* linkages, in which purchases are made with incomes obtained from the employment opportunities. The proportion of such incomes spent on local products represents a second round of multiplier effects; investment in these products can thus be generated through the accelerator. Depending on the extent to which these incomes are saved, spent locally, or spent on imports, different income generation effects will result.

The tax expenditure component has been termed *fiscal* linkage, and these effects reflect the extent to which the government spends domestically the payments it receives from the commodity industry. In certain cases, these tax payments are substantial and thus highly important. Finally, the *external effects* or unpriced externalities are important. They can consist of social effects such as increased domestic savings and improved labor skills or environmental effects such as degradation of the land surface and water pollution.

Among analytical methods used to evaluate the impact of commodity linkages on the economy, one can cite works on returned value by Reynolds (1965), Mamalakis (1971), and Pearson and Cownie (1975) as well as studies on input-output linkages by Lydell (1975) and Panchamukhi (1975). Formal modeling systems derive from the early work on the use of macroeconomic models of trade and development.[6] In its simplest form, such a model system normally entails an elaboration of investment, effective demand, and income determination. This permits the tracing of the impact of policies on attaining full employment and can be implemented with existing forms of social accounting systems. The structure of such a system can be represented as follows:

$$C = F(Y)$$
$$V = f(Y, R)$$
$$Y = C + V + E - M$$
$$F = M - E$$
$$S = Y - C$$

Consumption expenditure (C) depends on the level of national income (Y). The investment (V) that would stimulate the correct level of income is influenced by the income level itself as well as the rate of interest (R). Where savings equals investment, national income is identical to consumption plus investment. However, such an identity fails to reflect the dependence of the economy on the rest of the world, particularly on the industrialized economies. Similar to the two-gap models suggested by Chenery and Strout (1966), the income identity contains in addition the balance of payments, exports (E) minus imports (M). This can also be interpreted as the net inflow of foreign capital (F), where E and M involve invisible payments and receipts including those on transportation, travel, banking, insurance, factor income payments and receipts, and other miscellaneous transactions. To insure that the savings and investment gap is identical with the foreign inflows gap, the savings identity (S) is included.

The impact of commodity exports on the macroeconomy is seen principally through E, which can be disaggregated into noncommodity E_{nc} and commodity E_c components:

$$E = E_{nc} + E_c$$

The value of commodity exports is determined from the previous commodity model considered at the county level:

$$E_c = PX \text{ where } X = Q - D \pm \Delta I$$

Exports are determined as a residual from the market equilibrium identity in the commodity model, although they also can be estimated from a behavioral relationship.

Of course such a model is weak in its inclusion of the various linkage effects mentioned. More complex models are used in practice that concentrate on the demand, investment, employment, wage and price, and fiscal and monetary aspects of the macroeconomy rather than on its two-gap character. *Econometric linkage* models of this type are just beginning to be developed. As explained by Adams and Roldan in Chapter 7, linkage models can assume either that the world commodity market impacts on the dependent economy without intervention or that domestic policy can be used to offset fluctuations on the world commodity markets. An important aspect of the Adams and Roldan model is that it contains both a coffee model and a model of the Brazilian economy. Thus, the possibility exists of analyzing feedback effects from country commodity policy to the world commodity market. A linkage analysis of a less elaborate nature appears in Chapter 8, where Lira measures impacts of fluctuations in the copper market on the Chilean economy.

One inadequacy of the above models is that they deal largely with final demand. To learn more about linkages between the export sector and the economy, one must also be concerned with intermediate demand. This can be analyzed by formulating a more general system encompassing a macrostructure plus an *input-output* structure. The latter is normally defined by

$$(I - A)\, Q' = D$$

Gross output of a sector (Q') when multiplied by the adjusted matrix of technical coefficients ($I - A$) gives the final demands of a sector (D). Technology that is embodied in the fixed input-output coefficients (A) determines what can be used in further production, while I is an identity matrix. At market price valuation, the elements of D satisfy

$$\sum_{i=1}^{n} D_i = \text{GNP} \approx \text{Y}$$

except possibly for the allocation of competitive imports to domestic producing sectors.

Input-output models that have been combined with macromodels for planning purposes fall in the class of *general equilibrium consistency framework* models. Such models, for example, as developed by Thorbecke and Sengupta (1972) for Colombia focus on the linkages between resource endowment, the structure of production, and the distribution of income. Recently, input-output models have been linked to macroeconomic structures that provide national and international product demands; they are also included in energy balance frameworks that feature supply-demand determination as well as ecological aspects of resource utilization, depletion, and waste. Possibilities for studying individual commodity impacts within the context of an input-output model are featured in Chapter 3 by Simpson

An alternative approach for combining commodity and country models is *commodity-link* models of the type originally suggested by Klein (1968) for improving the explanation of world trade patterns in the project LINK model. In his approach, the economic relationships between the developed and the developing countries depend largely on the quantities and price of commodities in world trade. Exports of commodities from developing countries depend on the income and activity variables represented in the models of the importing countries. At the same time, the income and activity variables represented by the models of the developing countries depend on the production and export of these commodities. The economies of the developed countries also depend on the supply of these commodities. Interaction between economic activity and world commodity supply and demand, which are balanced through an iterative process, results in the determination of commodity prices and other target variables.

While the LINK system features primarily country models, the SIMLINK system developed by Hicks (1975) explains trade and growth for developing regions principally using commodity models. In identifying certain commodities as a source of trade and growth for specific national economies, it utilizes economic activity in four developed economy regions to generate the demand for commodities and other exportable goods and services from eight developing economy regions. Volumes of commodity exports together with prices determine the export earnings of the developing regions, in which prices depend on world supply and demand conditions. Prices for all other sectors are introduced to derive import values. The supply of imports to each region is then compared with exports, and from the resulting terms of trade, the growth of domestic product is computed for each region. Both LINK and SIMLINK obviously are well suited for analyzing multi-commodity interactions and policies.

Analysis of the interaction of commodity markets with the economies of Latin America is possible with either model. Also of importance is the Latin American World Model that has been developed to aid integrated planning at a national and regional level in developing countries. As described by Chichilnisky (1977), the model emphasizes the role of food and energy commodities in analyzing basic needs strategies.

One final approach worth considering, which includes commodity-economy interaction, is that of a *multilevel, multisector* model; such a model consists of a system of optimizing models corresponding to different levels of aggregation. The principal application of this approach as described by Goreux and Manne (1973) has been in relation to the Mexican economy. The model features three levels of aggregation: (1) a multisector model of the Mexican economy; (2) two sectoral models—agriculture and energy; and (3) two regional models—agricultural district and electric power plants (including transmission lines). The type of planning intended relates to each of the three levels. At the central level, decisions may refer to the rate of domestic savings and the levels of borrowings from abroad. At the sectoral level, policies may relate to subsidies in fertilizer use or to pricing policies for industrial fuels. In this context, some thirty-two commodities are included in the agricultural submodel. At the regional level, policies can be analyzed related to specific investment projects, such as those dealing with irrigation or electric power.

MODELS FOR COMMODITY STABILIZATION

Recent studies of the impact of commodity stabilization on the economies of Latin America have dealt mainly with the issue of buffer stock stabilization policies as featured within the UNCTAD (1975) Integrated Program. Although that program includes possibilities for stabilization through compensatory finance, multilateral contracts, and processing and diversification as well as buffer stocks, the latter has received the most attention in policy modeling.

At this point there is no need to review the extensive works that have recently emerged regarding the likely impacts of buffer stock stabilization schemes. This has been well documented by Behrman (1977), by Adams (1978), and by Labys (1979a). In addition, Lord in Chapter 9 provides a further review with special reference to Latin America. Thus we turn directly to the particular role played by commodity stabilization models. Although the models analyzed are strictly commodity models, Klein (1971) has mentioned the possibility of analyzing stabilization with linkage models of the type described above. Adams (1977) has further shown how this could take place on an international level though including commodity models into the LINK framework.

The use of commodity models for stabilization analysis has most typically involved incorporating the model into a simulation framework that also includes buffer stocks as well as a buffer stock triggering mechanism. Economic analysis of buffer stock operation involves the computation of the value of buffer stock operations and of the revenue changes falling upon consumers and producers. An example of such a modeling exercise can be based on the previously given market model. Only now the level of inventories is adjusted to accommodate purchases or sales of stocks (S) by a buffer stock agency.

$$D = d(D_{-1}, P, P^c, A, T)$$
$$Q = a(Q_{-1}, P_{-\theta}, N, Z)$$
$$P = p(P_{-1}, \Delta I)$$
$$\Delta I = Q - D + S - S_{-1}$$

Stochastic disturbances that are among the destabilizing influences in commodity markets are omitted to help simplify the discussion.

The decision as to whether to make purchases or sales from the buffer stock depends on whether the market price falls to the floor price

(P^f) or rises to the ceiling price (P^c). The evaluation of economic benefits of the stocking operations begins with the computation of financial costs (B) for the stocking agency[7]

$$B = cS + (1 - ab)(S - S_{-1})P$$

where c is the cost of storage, a is the cost of moving the commodity in and out of the buffer stock, and $b = 1$ for $S > S_{-1}$ or $b = -1$ for $S \leq S_{-1}$. Since the benefits from buffer stock operation are usually considered over some period, it is necessary to discount the net worth of the agency at rate r and to value initial (S^i) stocks at some given value (P^i).

$$PVB = (1 + r)^{-T} S_T P_T - \sum_1^T (1 + r)^{-t} B_t - S^i P^i$$

To these financial costs must be added the "surplus" or "gains and losses" accuring to producers and consumers. The gains and losses of producers depend on whether the commodity is purchased for or released from the buffer stock. When purchases are made, producers sell the same amount as they would but at a higher price

$$PG = (P^* - P)Q$$

where P^* is the stabilized price and Q the quantity produced. When sales are made out of stock, producers receive a lower price and hence experience a loss

$$PL = (P - P^*)Q$$

Similar to the financial costs, it is necessary to state producers surplus in terms of net present value.

$$PPS = \sum_1^T (1 + r)^{-t}(PG_t - PL_t)$$

Consumer gains and losses similarly differ depending on whether purchases or sales are made. When sales occur, consumers gain by the reduction in price of the commodity demanded[8]

$$CG = (P - P^*)Q + \{(P^* - P)(S - S_{-1})/2\}$$

where Q is the quantity produced adjusted by buffer stock transactions. When purchases are made, the reduction in consumer surplus because of the higher prices becomes a loss.

$$CL = (P^* - P)Q^* + \{(P^* - P)(S - S_{-1})/2\}$$

The present value of consumers surplus is given by

$$PCS = \sum_{1}^{T}(1 + r)^{-t}(CG_t - CL_t)$$

The total economic benefits to be derived from the buffer stock operation are the sum of the present value of the financial costs and the producers and consumers surplus.

$$TEB = PVB + PPS + PCS$$

In the actual simulation of such a model a number of other factors enter that affect the outcome of the gains and losses, as explained by Goreux (1978). For commodity stabilization analyses conducted in relation to Latin America, Behrman and Tinakorn in Chapter 10 report on country earnings and financial costs of buffer stock operations for Latin American commodities considered within the UNCTAD integrated program: coffee, cotton, cocoa, copper, tin, and sugar. Other modeling efforts have dealt with individual commodities. Among studies of importance to Latin America are those of Ford (1977) on coffee, Kim et al. (1975) and Kofi (1972) on cocoa, Smith and Schink (1976) on tin, Chaipravat (1977) on rice, and Smith (1975) on copper.

Mentioned earlier was the fact that policy stabilization approaches other than buffer stocks exist. One approach where commodity modeling has been effective examines the likely impacts of the formation of commodity cartels in addition to OPEC. Pindyck (1976) uses a market model that includes commodity production by the cartel and by the fringe as well as net demand facing the cartel. The operation of the model involves feedback control that selects the price levels over time that will maximize the sum of discounted profits. Producer cartels studied include petroleum, copper, and bauxite.

Among other quantitative stabilization studies of interest, the use of commodity modeling has been minimal. Information derived from commodity models such as price elasticities of supply and demand has been employed, but the simulation methodology developed relates more to the direct computation of certain stabilization gains. For example, de Vries (1975) has analyzed the effects of different compensatory financing schemes, including those designed to stabilize earnings for individual commodities as well as total export earnings. In this regard, Goreux (1977) has recently analyzed the pattern of export shortfalls. Reutlinger (1976) has computed the impact of alternative buffer stock levels and storage policies in stabilizing world wheat supplies. This includes the valuation of economic benefits to the storage operation, producers, and consumers. Finally, Konandreas (1978) has analyzed the implications of a proposed world food reserve system on Latin America.

CONCLUSIONS

The extent of the primary commodity dependence in Latin America warrants more extensive commodity planning. Both coping with the commodity instability problem and developing the primary commodity subsector require that decisionmaking have a sound footing. The use of commodity models is not only indispensable, but it will also provide objective information to help reduce conflicts among policymakers as well as to help them shape the future more effectively.

To understand how commodity models can assist in planning, it has been necessary to define and explain a number of modeling methodologies and modeling approaches. An important element in using these models is the interaction between the modeler and the decisionmaker. Both sides have a responsibility toward each other. The modeler has the responsibility of clarifying the limits of the model and the degree of certitude to attach to the forecasts. The decisionmaker must select competent specialists who can help translate the technical information into useful policy inputs.

To improve decision making related to investment in minerals or other commodities, adequate knowledge of both the investment decision process and the market environment is necessary. Of particular importance is an understanding of the policy variables entering the decision makers' framework that come under government control, for example, taxation, export and import controls, mining laws, and exchange rates and controls.

For the market environment, a number of studies are available that provide information on commodities of relevance to Latin America. Also available are forecasts of government and private agencies as well as of other modelers. It is thus feasible for any government to expand its analysis of commodity markets with only a minimum of resources. This would furnish a background against which commodity planning and the formulation of commodity models could begin. It is hoped that this book will stimulate efforts in this direction.

NOTES

1. This problem is described more extensively in Chapter 9.

2. This view of planning is further developed in Yotopoulos and Nugent (1976) as well as in Pyatt and Thorbecke (1976).

3. The possibility of using models for planning has been discussed extensively. The modeling definition provided here appears from Islam (1970).

4. This introductory description appears from Labys (1978). The summary of modeling methodologies that follows appears from Labys (1976b): 36–45. A more complete description of the nature and use of commodity models can be found in Labys (1973a; 1975a).

5. The present modeling perspective has been developed by the author in several papers. See Labys (1978; 1976a); and Labys and Weaver (1973).

6. A review of this class of models appears in Dayal (1975).

7. This simplification is essentially that prescribed by Labys (1979b) and Goreux (1978).

8. The following expressions involve an adjustment factor of 1/2, which reflects surplus derived under a condition of an elastic demand curve but an inelastic (fixed) supply.

BIBLIOGRAPHY

Adams, F.G., ed. 1978. *Stabilizing World Commodity Markets: Analysis, Practice and Policy*. Lexington, Mass.: Heath Lexington Books.

——. 1977. "Commodity Prices in the LINK system: An Empirical Appraisal of Commodity Price Impacts." Conference on Stabilizing World Commodity Markets: Analysis Practice and Policy, Airlie, Virginia.

——. 1975. "Applied Econometric Modeling of Non-Ferrous Metal Markets: The Case of Ocean Floor Nodules." In W. Vogely, ed., *Mineral Materials Modeling*. Washington, D.C.: R.F.F. Working Paper EN-5.

Adams, F.G., and J.R. Behrman. 1976. *Econometric Models of World Agriculture Commodity Markets*. Cambridge, Mass.: Ballinger Publishing Co.

Adams, F.G., and A. Roldan. 1978. "Econometric Studies of the Impact of Primary Commodity Markets on Economic Development in Latin America." Conference of Commodity Markets, Models and Policies in Latin America, Lima, Peru.

Alejandro, F.; P. Clark; and A. Jul. 1973. "Projecting the Optimal Level of Copper Production in Chile." In R.S. Eckaus and P.N. Rodensteinrodan, ed., *Analysis of Development Problems: Studies of the Chilean Economy*. Amsterdam: North-Holland Publishing Co.

Assis, C. 1977. "A mixed integer programming model for the Brazilian cement industry." Ph.D. thesis, John Hopkins University.

Baanante, Carlos Arturo. 1975. "Andean Group Economic Integration: The Case of the Nitrogenous Fertilizer Industry." Ph.D. thesis, North Carolina State University at Raleigh.

Baby, V.J. 1973. "An Analysis of Economic Fertility and Recommendations for Increased Sorghum Production and Utilization in Colombia." Ph.D. thesis, University of Nebraska.

Bacha, E.L. 1968. "An Econometric Model for the World Coffee Market: The Impact of Brazilian Price Policy." Ph.D. thesis, Yale University.

Baldwin R.E. 1966. *Economic Development and Export Growth*. Berkeley: California University Press.

———. 1963. "Export Technology and Development from a Subsistence Level." *Economic Journal* 73, no. 289: 54–79.

Barreyro, H. 1971. "An Analysis of the Supply of Grains in the Pergamino Region of Argentina: A Dynamic Approach." Ph.D. thesis, Texas A & M University.

Bateman, M. 1978. "Analyzing and Forecasting World Sugar Prices." Conference on Commodity Markets, Models and Policies in Latin America, Lima, Peru.

Bates, L.W. 1975. "The Petroleum Industry in Brazil." Ph.D. thesis, University of Texas at Austin.

Bates, T., and A. Schmitz. 1969. "A Spatial Equilibrium Analysis of the World Sugar Economy." Berkeley, Calif.: Giannini Monograph No. 23.

Behrman, J.R. 1977. "International Commodity Stabilization." Working Paper. Washington, D.C.: Overseas Development Council.

Behrman, J.R., and P. Tinakorn. 1978. "The Impact of the UNCTAD Integrated Program on Latin American Export Earnings." Conference on Commodity Markets, Models and Policies in Latin America, Lima, Peru.

Bell, F.W., and others. 1975. "A World Model of Living Marine Resources." In W.C. Labys, ed., *Quantitative Models of Commodity Markets*. Cambridge, Mass.: Ballinger Publishing Co.

Bierber, J.L. 1970. "Diversification Opportunities and Effects of Alternative Policies on Costa Rican Coffee Farms." Ph.D. thesis, University of Florida.

Biondolillo, A.L. 1972. "Social Cost of Production Instability in the Grape Wine Industry: Argentina." Ph.D. thesis, University of Minnesota.

Brandt, S.A. 1967. "Spatial Analysis of the World Coffee Market: The Brazilian Position." Ph.D. thesis, Ohio State.

Brien, R.H. 1967. "Petroleum Refining in Costa Rica: A Study in Industrial Development." Ph.D. thesis, University of Texas.

Brown, C.P. 1975. *Primary Commodity Control*. Kuala Lumpur and London: Oxford University Press.

Brown, L.C. 1974. "An Economic Analysis of the Bolivian Poultry Industry." Ph.D. thesis, University of Maryland.

Burga, G.S. 1971. "Considerations on Development and the Poultry Industry in Peru." Ph.D. thesis, Michigan State.

Burrows, J.; W. Hughes; and J. Vallette. 1972. "An Econometric Analysis of the Silver Industry." Cambridge, Mass.: Charles Rivers Associates.

———. 1978. "Modeling Long Run Adjustments in World Metal Markets." Conference on Commodity Markets, Models and Policies in Latin America, Lima, Peru.

Casperson, Paul Richard. 1974. "Responsive Pricing of Hydroelectricity in a Developing Region: The Case of Minas Gerais, Brazil." Ph.D. thesis, Vanderbilt University.

Cavendar, D. 1976. "The U.S. and the World Zinc Industry: An Econometric Study of Consumption." Working Paper, Iowa State University. Annual Meetings of the American Economic Association, Atlantic City, New Jersey.

Chaipravat, O. 1977. "International Rice Buffer Stock Operations: A Simulation Study." Conference on Stabilizing World Commodity Markets: Analysis, Practice and Policy, Airlie, Virginia.

Chen, J. 1975. "World Cotton Market, 1953–1965: An Econometric Model with Applications to Economic Policy." Rheda, Germany: Institut fur Mathematische Wirtschaft, University of Bielefeld.

Chenery, H.B., and A.M. Strout. 1966. "Foreign Assistance and Economic Development." *American Economic Review* 56, no. 4: 679–733.

Chichilnisky, G. 1977. "Development Patterns and the International Order." *International Affairs* 31, no. 2: 275–304.

Cole, S. 1977. "A Case Study of a Normative Model: The Latin American World Model as a Tool of Analysis in Integrated Planning at a National and Regional Level in Developing Countries." Working Paper, Department of Social Statistics, UNESCO and Science Policy Research Unit, University of Sussex (England).

Cole, W.E. 1965. "The Mexican Steel Industry and its Impact on the Mexican Economy." Ph.D. thesis, University of Texas.

Cutie, T., and A. Jaris. 1975. "Diffusion of Hybrid Corn Technology: The Case of El Salvador." Ph.D. thesis, University of Wisconsin–Madison.

Dammert, A. 1978. "Planning Investments in the Copper Sector in Latin America." Conference on Commodity Markets, Models and Policies in Latin America, Lima, Peru.

Dammert, A., and D. Kendrick. 1976. "A Model of the World Copper Market." Working Paper, University of Texas at Austin. Annual Meetings of the American Economic Association, Atlantic City, September.

Dayal, R. 1975. *Models of Trade and Development: A Theoretical Review.* Monograph No. 13, Center for Economic Research, Zurich: Swiss Federal Institute of Technology.

Deare, S.M. 1973. "Spatial Agricultural Economy: A Theoretical Study with Special Reference to Brazil." Ph.D. thesis, Yale University.

de Vries, J. 1975. "Compensatory Financing: A Quantitative Analysis." Staff Working Paper No. 228. Washington, D.C.: World Bank.

de Vries, J. 1975. "Structure and Prospects of the World Coffee Economy." Bank Staff Working Paper No. 208. Washington, D.C.: World Bank.

Dorr, A. 1975. "International Trade in the Primary Aluminum Industry." Ph.D. thesis, Pennsylvania State University.

Doyle, J. 1976. "World Wheat Economy: Development of Dynamic Analysis of an Imperfect Market." Ph.D. thesis, Kansas State University.

Emery, R. 1967. "The Relation of Exports to Economic Growth," *Kyklos* 20, no. 2: 470–84.

Epps, M.L. 1970. "A Computer Simulation Model of the World Coffee Market." Ph.D. thesis, Duke University.

Ertek, Tumay. 1967. "World Demand for Copper, 1948–63: An Econometric Study." Ph.D. thesis, University of Wisconsin.

Fisher, B.F. 1966. "The Influence of Agrarian Reform on the Mexican Sugar Industry." Ph.D. thesis, Colombia University.

Fisher, F.M.; P.H. Cootner; and M. Baily. 1972. "An Econometric Model of the World Copper Industry." *Bell Journal of Economics and Management Science* 3: 568–609.

Ford, D.J. 1977. "Commodity Market Modeling and the Simulation of Market Intervention: The Case of Coffee." Conference on Stabilizing World Commodity Markets: Analysis, Practice and Policy. Airlie, Virginia.

Gemmill, H.G. 1976. "An Equilibrium Analysis of U.S. Sugar Policy." Working Paper, Wye College, London University.

Goreux, L.M. 1978. "Optimal Rule of Buffer Stock Intervention." Working Paper, Research Department, Washington, D.C.: International Monetary Fund.

——. 1977. "Compensatory Financing: The Cyclical Pattern of Export Shortfalls." *IMF Staff Papers* 24: 613–41.

Goreaux, L., and A. Manne, eds. 1973. *Multilevel Planning: Case Studies in Mexico.* Amsterdam: North-Holland Publishers.

Hakim, O.A. 1972. "The Effects of the U.S. Cotton Policy on the World Market for Extra-Long Staple Cotton." Ph.D. thesis, University of Arizona.

Harris, W.G. 1967. "The Impact of the Petroleum Industry on the Pattern of Venezuelan Economic Development." Ph.D. thesis, University of Oregon.

Hatch, John Keith. 1974. "The Corn Farms of Motupe: A Study of Traditional Farming Practices in Northern Coastal Peru." Ph.D. thesis, University of Wisconsin–Madison.

Hicks, N., et al. 1975. "The Simlink Model of Trade and Growth of the Developing World." Staff Working Paper No. 220. Washington, D.C.: World Bank.

Hirschman, A.O. 1958. *The Strategy of Economic Development.* New Haven: Yale University Press.

Homem de Melo, F.B. 1973. An Analysis of the World Cocoa Economy in 1980." Ph.D. thesis, North Carolina State University at Raleigh.

——. 1974. "An International Cocoa Agreement: Potential Gains to Producing Countries." Instituto de Economia Agricola, Sao Paulo. Mimeographed.

Houck, J.P.; M.E. Ryan; and A. Subotnik. 1972. *Soybeans and their Products: Markets, Models and Policy.* Minneapolis: University of Minnesota Press.

Hughes, H.G. 1971. "Economic Analysis of Sugarcane Production in Brazil." Ph.D. thesis, University of Missouri at Colombia.

Islam, N. 1970. "The Relevance of Development Models to Economic Planning in Developing Countries." *Economic Bulletin for Asia and the Far East.*

Jarvis, L. 1969. "Supply Response in the Cattle Industry: The Argentine Case." Ph.D. thesis, Massachusetts Institute of Technology.

——. 1974. "Cattle as Capital Goods and Ranchers as Portfolio Managers: An Application to the Argentine Cattle Sector." Berkeley: Institute of Business and Economic Research. No. 118, University of California at Berkeley.

Jul, Ana Maria. 1977. "A Macroeconomic Model for Brazil." Ph.D. thesis, University of Pennsylvania.

Kennedy, M. 1974. "An Economic Model of the World Oil Market." *Bell Journal of Economics and Management Science* 5: 540–77.

Kim, H.K.; L.M. Goreux; and D. Kendrick. 1975. "Feedback Control Rule for Cocoa Market Stabilization." In W.C. Labys, ed., *Quantitative Models of Commodity Markets.* Cambridge, Mass.: Ballinger Publishing Co.

Klein, L.R. 1968. "What Kind of Macro-econometric Model for Developing Economies." In A. Zellner, ed., *Readings in Economic Statistics and Econometrics*. Boston: Little, Brown and Co.

——. 1971. "Some Notes on the Introduction of Commodity Models in Project LINK." Link Working Paper. Philadelphia: University of Pennsylvania.

——. 1977. "Potentials of Econometrics for Commodity Stabilization Analysis." Conference for Stabilizing World Commodity Markets: Analysis, Practice and Policy. Airlie, Virginia.

Kofi, T.A. 1972. "International Commodity Agreements and Export Earnings: Simulation of the 1968 Draft International Cocoa Agreement." *Food Research Institute Studies* II.

Kohout, J.C. 1968. "A Price and Allocation Model for the Beef Economy in Argentina." Ph.D. thesis, University of Illinois.

Konandreas, P. 1978. "The World Food Reserve System and Its Implications for Latin America." Conference on Commodity Markets, Models and Policies in Latin America, Lima, Peru.

Kovisars, L. 1975. "World Trade Flows in Copper, an LP-Model." Palo Alto, Calif.: Stanford Research Institute. Unpublished.

——. 1976. "World Production, Consumption and Trade in Zinc-an LP-Model." U. S. Bureau of Mines Contract J-0166003. Palo Alto, Calif.: Stanford Research Institute.

Kruegar, P.K. 1976. "Modeling Future Requirements for Metals and Minerals." In *Proceedings of the XIV Symposium of the Council for the Application of Computers and Mathematics in the Minerals Industries*. University Park, Pa.

Labys, W.C. 1973a. *Dynamic Commodity Models: Specification, Estimation Simulation*. Lexington, Mass.: Heath Lexington Books.

——. 1973b. "Preliminary Results of an Econometric Model of the International Wine Market." Geneva: Graduate Institute of International Studies. Mimeographed.

——. 1975a. *Quantitative Models of Commodity Markets*. Cambridge, Mass.: Ballinger Publishing Co.

——. 1975b. "Commodity Planning Models for East Asia." In *Studies and Documents*. Geneva: Graduate Institute of International Studies.

——. 1976a. "Integrating Primary Commodity Exports in the Macroeconomic Planning Process: Theory and Practice in Southeast Asia." Summary of a research study carried out for the ASEAN Secretariat under the Auspices of the F.A.O. Rome: F.A.O. of the United Nations.

——. 1976b. "International Commodity Markets, Models and Forecasts." *Columbia Journal of World Business* 4: 36–45.

——. 1978. "Commodity Markets and Models: The Range of Experience." In F. G. Adams, ed., *Stabilizing World Commodity Markets: Analysis, Practice and Policy*. Lexington, Mass.: Heath Lexington Books.

——. 1979a. "Analyzing Commodity Price Stabilization Schemes." *Journal of Policy Modeling* (in press).

——. 1979b. "Simulation Analysis of an International Buffer Stock for Jute." *Journal of Development Studies* 15: 154–166.

Labys, W.C., and H. Thomas. 1975. "Speculation, Hedging and Commodity

Price Behavior: An International Comparison." *Applied Economics* 7: 287–301.

Labys, W.C., and T.E. Weaver. 1973. "Towards a Commodity Oriented Development Model." SEADAG Paper 73-11. New York: Southeast Asia Development Advisory Group.

———. 1978. "Interactions Between the Resource Commodity Sector, the Developing Economy and the Environment." Geneva: UNCTAD/UNEP Project 005.

Lattimore, R.G. 1974. "Econometric Study of the Brazilian Beef Sector." Ph.D. thesis, Purdue University.

Lattimore, R., and G.E. Schuh. 1976. "Un Modelo de Politica Para La Industria Brasilena de Ganado Vacuno" ("A Policy Model of the Brazilian Beef Cattle Economy"). *Cuadernos de Economia* 39: 51–75.

Law, A.D. 1975. *International Commodity Agreements*. Lexington, Mass.: Heath Lexington Books.

Ley, R. 1977. "Bolivian Tin and Bolivian Development." Ph.D. thesis, Washington State University.

Lira, Ricardo. 1974. "The Impact of an Export Commodity in a Developing Economy: The Case of Chilean Copper, 1955–1968." Ph.D. thesis, University of Pennsylvania.

Linneman, H. 1966. *An Econometric Study of International Trade Flows.* Amsterdam: North-Holland Publishing Co.

Lord, M. 1978. "Commodity Export Instability and Growth in Latin America." Paper presented at Conference on Commodity Markets, Models and Policies in Latin America, Lima, Peru.

Lydell, H.F. 1975. *Trade and Employment.* Geneva: International Labor Office.

MacBean, A.I. 1966. *Export Instability and Economic Development.* Cambridge, Mass.: Harvard University Press.

Mack, F.G. 1973. "The Impact of Transfer Cost and Trade Policies on International Trade in Beef, 1967–1980." Ph.D. thesis, Texas A & M University.

Mafucci, E. 1974. "Export Earnings Instability—the Argentine Case." Ph.D. thesis, University of Minnesota.

Magueron, G. 1972. "A Quantitative Analysis of the Supply-Demand Patterns in Iron Ore: The Future Possibilities of Brazil." Ph.D. thesis, Columbia University.

Maizels, A., assisted by L.G. Cambell-Boross and P.B.W. Rayment. 1968. *Exports and Economic Growth of Developing Countries.* London: NIESR.

Mamalakis, M. 1971. "Contribution of Copper to Chilean Economic Development." In R.G. Mikesell, ed., *Foreign Investment in the Petroleum and Mineral Industries.* Baltimore: John Hopkins University Press.

Marcus, P.M. 1972. "An Economic Analysis of the World Corn Trade." Ph.D. thesis, Purdue University.

Matetic, J.R. 1971. "An Economic Analysis of the Chilean Fresh Fruit and Vegetable Export Sector." Ph.D. thesis, University of Minnesota.

Mathis, K. 1969. *An Economic Simulation Model of the Cocoa Industry of the*

Dominican Republic. International Programs Info. Rep. 69-2, Department of Agricultural Economics and Sociology, Texas A & M University.

McGarry, J.J. 1968. "The World Beef Industry." Ph.D. thesis, University of Wisconsin.

McGuann, J.M. 1973. "Microeconomic Analysis of Opportunities for Increasing Beef Production: The Pampean Area, Argentina." Ph.D. thesis, Texas A & M University.

Melo, F.H. 1973. "An Analysis of the World Cocoa Economy in 1980." Ph.D. thesis, North Carolina State University at Raleigh.

Mertz, W.N. 1969. "The Feasibility of Nicaraguan Caustic Soda Industry, 1977–80." Ph.D. thesis, University of Houston.

Mueller, C. 1975. "Factors Affecting the Development of the Cattle Industry in Central Brazil." Ph.D. thesis, Vanderbilt University.

Naggar, T.R. 1976. "The role of the iron, copper, lead and zinc petroleum export sectors in the economic development of Brazil, Chile, Mexico and Venezuela: an empirical macroeconomic analysis." Ph.D. thesis, University of Oklahoma.

Nelson, W.E. 1971. "An Economic Analysis of Fertilizer Utilization in Brazil." Ph.D. thesis, Ohio State University.

Nores, G.A. 1972. "Structure of the Argentine Beef Cattle Economy: A Short Run Model, 1960–70." Ph.D. thesis, Purdue University.

Norton, R.D., and L. Bassoco. 1974. "A Quantitative Agricultural Planning Methodology." Bank Staff Working Paper No. 180. Washington, D.C.: World Bank.

Otrera, W.R. 1966. "An Econometric Model for Analyzing Argentine Beef Export Potentials." Ph.D. thesis, Texas A & M University.

Palma-Carillo, P.A. 1976. "A macroeconometric model of Venezuela with oil price impact applications." Ph.D. thesis, University of Pennsylvania.

Panchamukhi, V.R. 1975. "Linkages in Industrialization: A Study of Selected Developing Countries in Asia." *Journal of Development Planning* 9: 121–66.

Paniago, E. 1968. "An Evaluation of Agricultural Price Policies for Selected Food Products: Brazil." Ph.D. thesis, Purdue University.

Parikh, A. 1974. "A Model of World Coffee Economy: 1950–68." *Applied Economics* 6: 23–43.

Parks, L. 1976. "Estimation of Water Production Functions and Farm Demand for Irrigation Water, with Analysis of Alternatives for Increasing the Economic Returns of Water on Chilean Farms." Ph.D. thesis, University of California at Davis.

Pearson, S.R. 1970. *Petroleum and Nigerian Economy*. Palo Alto, Calif.: Stanford University Press.

Pearson, S.R., and J. Cownie. 1975. *Commodity Exports and African Economic Development*. Lexington, Mass.: Heath Lexington Books.

Penna, J.A. 1974. "Optimal Storage and Export Levels of a Tradeable Product and Their Relationship with Annual Price Variability: The Case of Corn in Brazil." Ph.D. thesis, Purdue University.

Pindyck, R. 1976. "Gains to Producers from the Cartelization of Exhaustible Resources." Cambridge, Mass.: Massachusetts Institute of Technology, MITEL76-012WP.

Posada, A. 1974. "A Simulation Analysis of Policies for the Northern Columbia Beef Cattle Industry." Ph.D. thesis, Michigan State University.

Pringle, G.E. 1969. "A Temporal Spatial Analysis of Sugar Production and Marketing in Puerto Rico." Ph.D. thesis, University of Wisconsin.

Pyatt, G., and E. Thorbecke. 1976. *Planning Techniques for a Better Future.* Geneva: International Labor Office.

Quintana, C., and G. Bueno. 1968. "Processes and Location in the Mexican Steel Industry." Vienna: UNIDO, Evaluation of Industrial Projects, No. E. 6711.B23.

Quiros, J.L. 1966. "Engineering and Economic Aspects of the Aluminum Industry with Applications in Panama." Ph.D. thesis, University of Illinois.

Reutlinger, S. 1976. "A Simulation Model for Evaluating Worldwide Buffer Stocks for Wheat." *American Journal of Agricultural Economics* 58: 1–12.

Reynolds, C.W. 1963. "Domestic Consequences of Export Instability," *American Economic Review*, Papers and Proceedings 53: 93–102.

———. 1965. "Development Problems of an Export Economy, the Case of Chile and Copper." In M. Mamalakis and C. W. Reynolds, eds., *Essays on the Chilean Economy.* Homewood, Ill.: R.D. Irwin.

Reynolds, C.W., and L. Spellman. 1975. "Financial Intermediation and Economic Development as Seen Through the Flow of Finds Accounts." Working Paper, Food Research Institute, Stanford University.

Robertson, T. 1968. "Structure, Performance, and Conduct of the Peruvian Fertilizer Industry and a Linear Programming Analysis for Future Plan Sizes and Location." Ph.D. thesis, Iowa State University.

Santos, A. 1976. "International Trade in Iron Ore: An Econometric Analysis of the Determinants of Trade Patterns." Ph.D. thesis, Pennsylvania State University.

Saylor, R.G., and C.F. Trench de Freitas. 1975. "Price, Quality and the Demand for Coffee." Sao Paulo: Instituto de Economia Agricola. Mimeographed.

Schmitz, A. and D. Bawden. 1973. "World Wheat Economy: An Empirical Analysis." Giannini Foundation Monograph No. 32, University of California at Berkeley.

Segura, E.L. 1973. "An Econometric Study of the Fish Meal Industry." Ph.D. dissertation, Columbia University. Published as FAO Fisheries Technical Paper No. 119, FIEF/T119 (En), Rome.

Shaw, J. 1973. "Manganese Model, Parts I and II." Geneva: Miscellaneous Paper, Commodities Division, U.N. Conference on Trade and Development.

Simpson, J.R. 1974. "International Trade in Beef and Economic Development of Selected Latin American Countries." Ph.D. thesis, Texas A & M University.

———. 1978. "Input-Output Modeling and Its Implications for Commodity Planning in Latin America." Conference on Commodity Markets, Models and Policies in Latin America, Lima, Peru.

Simpson, J.R., and J.W. Adams. 1975. "Disaggregation of Input-Output

Models into Product Lines as an Economic Development Policy Tool." *American Journal of Agricultural Economics* 57, no. 4: 584–90.

Singer, H. 1950. "The Distribution of Gains Between Investing and Borrowing Countries." *American Economic Review*, Papers and Preceedings 40: 473–85.

Singh, B. 1971. "An Econometric Study of Raw Materials in International Trade: A Case Study of Hides and Skins." Ph.D. thesis, University of Pennsylvania.

Singh, I.J. 1978. "A Dynamic Multicommodity Model of the Agricultural Sector: A Regional Application in Brazil." Conference on Commodity Markets, Models and Policies in Latin America, Lima, Peru.

Singh, I.J., and C.Y. Ahn. 1973. "The Future of Agriculture in Southern Brazil: Some Policy Projections with a Dynamic Model of the Wheat Region, Rio Grande do Sol (1970–85). Columbus: Ohio State University. Mimeographed.

Smith, G.W. 1975. "An Economic Evaluation of International Buffer Stocks for Copper." Working Paper. Washington, D.C.: U.S. Treasury.

Smith, G.W., and G.R. Schink. 1976. "The International Tin Agreement: A Reassessment." *Economic Journal* 86, no. 344: 715–28.

Smith, J.N. 1968. "A Dynamic Model of the Cattle Industry of Argentina." Ph.D. thesis, University of Maryland.

Smith, R. 1974. "Diversification Alternatives and Inducements in the Columbian Coffee Industry." Ph.D. thesis, University of Texas at Austin.

Spreen, T.A. 1977. "An application of capital theory in a recursive linear programming model of the cattle subsector of Guyana." Ph.D. thesis, Purdue University.

Staloff, S. 1977. "A stock-flow analysis for copper markets." Ph.D. thesis, University of Oregon.

Sugai, Yoshimido. 1974. "A Quota System Policy and Its Impact on the Labor Market in the Sugarcane Industry Analysis Through Dynamic Linear Programming Procedure, Sao Paulo, Brazil." Ph.D. thesis, Iowa State University.

Taplin, G.B. 1973. "A Model of World Trade" in R.J. Ball, ed. *The International Linkage of National Economic Models.* Amsterdam: North Holland Publishing Co.

Tewes, T. 1972. "Sugar: A Short-Term Forecasting Model of the World Market, with a Forecast of the World Market Price for Sugar in 1972–1973." *The Business Economist* 4 (Summer): 89–97.

Thoburn, J.T. 1977. *Primary Commodity Exports and Economic Development.* New York: John Wiley & Sons.

Thompson, R.L., and J.L. Garcia. 1978. "The Export Demand for Maize from Brazil." *Revista de Economia Rural* 16.

Thompson, R.L., and G.E. Schuh. 1978. "Trade Policy and Exports: The Case of Maize in Brazil." Working Paper, Department of Agricultural Economics, Purdue University.

Thorbecke, E., and J.K. Sengupta. 1972. "A Consistency Framework for Employment, Output and Income Projections Applied to Colombia." Washington, D.C.: World Bank.

Thorbecke, E., and A. Stoutjeskijk. 1970. "Employment and Output: A Methodology Applied to Peru and Guatemala." Paris: OECD Working Paper.

Tilton, J. 1966. "The Choice of Trading Partners: An Analysis of International Trade in Aluminum, Bauxite, Copper, Lead, Manganese, Tin, and Zinc." *Yale Economic Essays* 6, no. 2: 416–74.

———. 1978. "Modeling International Trade Flows in Mineral Markets, with Applications to Latin America's Trade Policies." Conference on Commodity Markets, Models and Policies in Latin America, Lima, Peru.

Truett, D.B. 1967. "Sulfur and the Development of a Chemical Fertilizer Industry in Mexico." Ph.D. dissertation, University of Texas.

UNCTAD. 1974 and 1975. "An Integrated Program for Commodities." Paper Series UNCTAD TD/B/C 1/166 to UNCTAD TD/B/C.1/194. Geneva: UNCTAD.

———. 1967. *Trade Expansion and Economic Integration Among Developing Countries.* Geneva: United Nations.

Valdez, M.A. 1972. "The Petroleum Policies of the Venezuelan Government." Ph.D. thesis, New York University Graduate School of Business.

Vernon, R. 1966. "Comprehensive Model Building in the Planning Process: The Case of the Less Developed Economies." *Economic Journal* 76, no. 301: 57–69.

Vilas, A.T. 1975. "A Spatial Equilibrium Analysis of the Rice Economy in Brazil." Ph.D. thesis, Purdue University.

Weymar, F. Helmut. 1968. *The Dynamics of the World Cocoa Market.* Cambridge, Mass.: The MIT Press.

Whitney, J. 1976. "Analysis of Copper Production, Processing and Trade Patterns, 1950–1972." Ph.D. thesis, Pennsylvania State University.

Wickens, M.; J. Greenfield; and G. Marshall. 1971. *A World Coffee Model.* CCP: 71/W.P. 4. Rome: Food and Agricultural Organization of the United Nations.

Williams, R.L. 1973. "Growth, Structure and Performance of the Coffee Industry in Jamaica." Ph.D. thesis, Columbia University.

World Bank. 1975. *Commodity Trade and Price Trends.* Washington, D.C.: World Bank.

Wymer, C.R. 1975. "Estimation of Continuous Time Models with an Application to the World Sugar Market." In W.C. Labys, ed., *Quantitative Models of Commodity Markets.* Cambridge, Mass.: Ballinger Publishing Co.

Yepez, L.F. 1970. "An Evaluation of Venezuelan Sugar Policy." Ph.D. thesis, University of Wisconsin.

Yotopoulos, P., and J. Nugent. 1976. *Economics of Development.* New York: Harper and Row.

Yver, R.E. 1971. "The Investment Behavior and the Supply Response of the Cattle Industry in Argentina." Ph.D. thesis, University of Chicago.

Zinser, J.S. 1967. "Alternative Means of Satisfying Argentine Petroleum Demand." Ph.D. thesis, University of Oregon.

Zulberti, Carlos Alberto. 1974. "The Feasibility of Beef Cattle Feed Lots in Argentina: Methodology of Economic Evaluation." Ph.D. thesis, Cornell University.

3

JAMES R.
SIMPSON

Input-Output Modeling and its Implications for Commodity Planning in Latin America

Input-output (I-O) analysis has become a major analytical tool in the highly complex industrialized economies since Leontief's first publication in 1936. Even though considerable methodological advances in the technique have occurred since then, there have been very few applications to commodity planning or modeling. Nonetheless, I-O modeling does appear to be a helpful technique for use in commodity analysis, and it is likely that empirical uses should be forthcoming in the next decade. The paucity of literature is not surprising for commodity modeling itself is in its infancy, with most work being done in the last five to ten years (Labys 1973 and 1978). Furthermore, while most commodity modeling has direct applicability for the public and private sector, I-O analysis is almost exclusively a public planning tool.

Given that there is a certain amount of misunderstanding, misconception, and lack of knowledge about the potential for input-output analysis in both the agricultural and nonagricultural sectors in Latin America, the objectives of this chapter are to describe several I-O techniques that may be utilized for commodity analysis in Latin America and to explain in detail how the transactions or technical coefficients matrix of existing I-O studies can be disaggregated to produce output and income multipliers for specific commodities. An example of the latter technique with application in Latin America is given for beef.

The concept of I-O analysis goes back over 200 years to Francois Quesnay's *Tableau Economique* of 1758, which described the circular flow and general equilibrium concepts of interindustry relations. More than 100 years passed before the next major advance in the 1870's which was Walras' general equilibrium model describing the interdependence between the production sectors of an economy. A lapse occurred again until 1925, when the Soviets published the first table of interindustry relations describing their economy. The first empirical application of an I-O model in the Anglo-American world was made by Wasily Leontief in 1936 when he published an I-O system of the United States. After this, there were rapid advances made in I-O analysis. In 1941 a 96-sector model of the U.S. economy was published, and by 1944 the first practical application was made (also in the United States). In 1949 a 200-sector model for the 1947 U.S. economy was made available. In 1964 an 81-sector model for the 1958 U.S. economy was published, and was then followed by a 370-sector table of the 1963 U.S. economy (available in 1969). During the 1950s and 1960s there was intense interest in I-O analysis as a technique, and models were constructed for many countries of the world. By the middle 1970s considerable advances had been made in using I-O analysis for rather specialized purposes such as natural resource planning.

POTENTIAL OF INPUT-OUTPUT MODELS FOR ANALYZING THE IMPACT OF PRIMARY COMMODITIES ON THE ECONOMY

I-O techniques can be divided into at least three major categories: the construction of national or world models, regional analysis, and techniques that make use of either one or both of the above such as impact analyses or interregional models. There is substantial potential for using I-O studies at the national level in Latin America to analyze mineral industries such as mining or processing simply because those industries figure so prominently in a country's economy. Examples are copper in Peru or Chile and tin in Bolivia. At the international level, recent work by Leontief (1977) in dividing the world into regions with individualized I-O matrices for sectors such as grain, oilseeds, and livestock, and solving the systems simultaneously, suggests that major advances can be made in linking primary commodities to world trade studies. In fact, it appears that interregional models and applications related to imports, exports, and trade hold some of the greatest potential for model builders concerned with primary commodities.

Regional I-O models (RIO) and techniques have been developed in conjunction with interregional (IRIO) models. Probably the earliest contribution was by Isard (1951), but he was quickly followed by Leontief (1953) who developed an intranational model that shows how regional interaction can be traced through a hierarchy of regions. This effort provided a fundamental link between interregional models and economic impact studies. Further work was done by Moses (1955) on a rather crude interregional model of the United States.

Regional and interregional applications of I-O analysis hold great potential for commodity planning in Latin America and thus deserve considerable attention by model builders interested in this geographic area. These researchers have a wealth of information available to them. For example, Isard and Kuenne (1953) developed a method to measure the economic impact on one region from expanding a major industry in another region. Most recent work, especially in the 1960s, has been on regional rather than interregional models as more immediate results are available. During this time most attention has been given to field surveys for collecting data to calculate technical coefficients by means of sales and purchase flows. Because data collection is expensive, much recent work has been aimed at devising improved national model adjustment techniques to derive regional coefficients.

USES OF INPUT-OUTPUT ANALYSIS AND STUDIES IN LATIN AMERICA FOR MODELING PRIMARY COMMODITIES

Over the past twenty years input-output studies have been constructed by the United Nations Economic Commission for Latin America (ECLA) dealing with numerous Latin American countries such as Argentina, Brazil, Chile, Colombia, Costa Rica, Mexico, Peru, and Uruguay.[1] The studies have been modified and updated at various times, but many policymakers and researchers still question if the relatively costly process of constructing these models is justified by the benefits received in LDCs.

Conceptually, it is probably correct that I-O analysis can be used as extensively in Latin America as in other regions. In reality the practical uses are more restricted because of constraints of budget, manpower, and computer capacity. Nevertheless, a number of realistic potential uses can be suggested:

- With Latin America's concern about economic growth, much more use could be made of impact models. These models, which have been developed by Adams and Holloway (1973) as well as by Stone and Brown (1965) among others, evaluate the impact on expansion (or decline) of one or a few sectors or introduction of new firms or industries. The techniques are fairly well known and frequently used in the industrialized countries. Zygadlo and Niehaus (1978) have used I-O analysis to determine secondary benefits for project analysis studies. This technique is relatively simple and could be used in Latin America commodity modeling.
- More techniques need to be developed that will reduce data collection time in construction of I-O models. Furthermore, there should be research in Latin America on estimating error from different data collection and model construction methods. Morrison and Smith (1974) as well as Stone, Bates, and Bacharach (1963) have provided insights into such analyses.
- As Latin American countries develop their economy, they will correspondingly be able to apply more sophisticated I-O techniques on increasingly varied problems such as environment versus land use. See Davis, et al. (1974) and Kymm (1977).
- One aspect of I-O analysis that has long been recognized but little used in Latin America is its application to various areas of marketing. Probably the greatest value from a marketing standpoint is in appraising the marketing possibilities for those industries that primarily service or supply other industries, instead of industries that sell directly to purchasers of finished goods.
- I-O analysis has important implications because of the insight that an input-output table provides on the way in which the production of a sector that sells to other processing industries is related in the final analysis to demand by consumers, government, investors, and foreign purchasers of finished goods.
- It is very likely that inordinate amounts of time have been spent in Latin America on model construction rather than utilizing the results. In all likelihood, some of the highest benefits can be obtained from researchers in Latin America familiarizing themselves with various applications and actually *using* the accumulated data and model base. Furthermore, the greatest benefits will come from applying existing procedures rather than reinventing the techniques. See Ghosh (1968), Maki (1970), and Rasmussen (1956).
- I-O analysis has particular relevance in Latin America's use of natural resources, a subject of great concern to policymakers. The demand for natural resources and evaluations of their optima⁻ ⁻⁻s can be determined by estimating the demand for final goo

services from which the natural resource demand is derived and by integrating that estimate with the structure of production whereby various inputs are combined to produce a final product. The approach by Bingham and Song Lee (1975), for example, revolves around determining the consumption of natural resources based on data for a single time period; these data are then transformed into a set of direct requirements that have been fitted into the U.S. 83-sector model. The dollar valuation of the transaction flow is replaced by natural flows, and outputs are given in physical terms.

I-O models can also be used to determine future requirements for metals and minerals in a similar manner by converting macroeconomic projections into I-O final demands. In the United States, conversion tables called demand import transformation tables (DITT) serve as the base. The vector of final demands is multiplied by the I-O inverse to generate estimates of industry outputs (Krueger 1976). In this case outputs are in dollar terms. Both of the approaches are variants of impact models that can be quite useful in Latin America for answering questions on the effect of new products or processes or the effects that increased prices will have on production costs and market inflation.

Another potential use for commodity modeling in Latin America is forecasting by projecting technical coefficients matrices. At the regional and interregional level the major uses are for predicting over-the-board changes in final demand, changes in final demand for a sector, or growth of the regional economy. See Miernyk (1975), Allen and Lecomber (1975), Allen and Gossling (1975), Almon et al. (1974), and Brody and Carter (1972). The best forecasting will take place when there is more than one I-O model available. A good reason *why* economists dealing with I-O analysis in Latin America should give considerable attention to forecasting is that their estimates can serve as an additional source of confidence to planners about the benefits from long-term policies.

A major contribution, and one that seemingly has not been explored yet, would be the definition of countries within a common market as regions with the subsequent application of interregional I-O analysis techniques. Appropriate methods are given in Isard (1951), Isard and Langford (1971), McMenamin and Haring (1974), Carter and Brody (1969), Miernyk (1965), and Richardson (1972). As is well known, common markets have not proven to be very successful because of political consideration and poor knowledge about costs and benefits of preferential treatment to products from new industries.

In the past, decisions have been based on trade-related information. Polenske (1970) has shown that employing I-O techniques would add useful information about sectoral impacts on economic growth. The regional models could also be used for projections, as was done by Tiebout (1969). A key point is that additional data requirements would be minimal as most of the data are either in the transactions matrices or macrolevel trade statistics. The major ef- fort would have to be in determining the effect of I-O models having different base years, means of coordination between countries, setting forth procedures to incorporate trade submodels, and improving theoretical weaknesses such as the instability of trade effects. The results obtained would be a realization of effects of shifts in the location of industrial activity and employment, improvements in regional accounts that serve as the basis for multicounty impact studies, the measurement and forecasting of regional export markets, and advances in transportation planning.

DISAGGREGATED INPUT-OUTPUT STUDIES FOR ANALYZING COMMODITY IMPACT IN DEVELOPMENT PLANNING

A method of determining output and income multipliers by opening up either the transactions or technical coefficients matrix in existing input-output studies of developing countries has not been reported in the literature by other researchers. There have been a few studies such as those by Adams (1973) and Miernyk et al (1970) where this technique is used to evaluate *new* industries in developed countries, but the possibility of disaggregating existing industries into product lines does not seem to have been researched either in developed countries or LDCs. To evaluate the use of this technique a study was carried out on beef, one of the most important export commodities in Latin America.

Beef export policy and the development of a viable beef industry have been the focus of technical assistance and national planning in many Latin American countries for over twenty-five years (Breimyer 1962, Brumby 1973, U.S. Department of Agriculture 1970, and United Nations 1970). Even though at least eight input-output studies of Latin American countries have been constructed in the past fifteen years, it is often difficult to assess the impact of the beef export industry from I-O models that treat that industry as a single sector. The basic problem results from the possibility of specializing in exporting different product lines. For example, the Central American countries have traditionally shipped chilled or frozen beef and have done little processing. The South American countries, on the other hand, have exported the entire gamut; live animals, sides of beef, and canned corned beef.

The study focuses on Argentina, Brazil, Paraguay, and Uruguay because of the diversity of their beef export sectors. However, the analysis should have relevance to other Latin American countries. Certainly the methodology has wide application to all types of commodities whether they are agricultural or nonagricultural. The exports studied include live cows, bone-in beef quarters, frozen boneless manufacturing beef, and cooked frozen and canned beef. The analysis is limited to cow beef since the methodological complications of including steer beef are substantial.[2]

Disaggregation of Input-Output Studies

There are two possibilities by which the endogenous portion of the transactions matrix may be expanded. The first is addition of a new industry within the framework of "impact analysis" in order to determine input requirements from other industries and economic effects on the entire area. This is perhaps more frequently done in regional rather than national analysis. The second method is disaggregation of an existing industry or subindustry with the breakdown being as limited or as detailed as necessary. This was the procedure used in the beef study where the meat processing sector (or the food processing sector in some studies) were disaggregated to obtain the multipliers[3] for the four previously mentioned export products. The livestock sector was disaggregated to obtain the multipliers for exports of live cows.

Three different methods are possible for disaggregation of one industry or sector. Given the relevant data, the first method involves computing column totals for the new industry and dividing each transaction by the column total to arrive at the technical coefficients. Multipliers are then calculated, beginning with the expanded technical coefficients matrix.

The second method is utilization of secondary data from the original source for disaggregating the sector under analysis in the transactions matrix. This technique is restricted to situations where data were available when the original matrix was constructed but the model builder was not previously interested in a high degree of disaggregation.

A third procedure, and the one primarily used here, is construction of budgets for the industries by data obtained through samples and inserting the budgets directly in the transactions matrix.[4]

Matrix Disaggregation

The first step in obtaining the product line multipliers was to interview beef packers in the four countries studied. The data obtained were sufficiently detailed to permit the construction of a cost and returns type of economic model for each of the four beef products and live cows on a product weight basis (Table 3–1). A fully integrated packing plant with a 1,400 head capacity was considered "typical" and served as the base.[5] The items in the initial models were then redistributed on an interindustry (sector) basis (Table 3–2). Total gross outlays are assumed to equal total gross output, and except for aggregating the items under "households" and "other," the budgets are ready for the various input-output studies. Since the revised cost and returns models were inserted into four different South American I-O studies, four slightly different models were required.

Two Argentine studies, one for Brazil and one for Uruguay, were chosen as base I-O studies because a general statement relevant to all of the major beef exporting countries was desired. This procedure also provided a reliability test of the disaggregation method. Because the analysis centers on beef, the adjusted budgets on an interindustry basis are based on a ton of product. However, for insertion in the I-O studies, the budgets are considered to be a year's transactions for the whole economy.

The method for expanding (opening up) the transactions matrix and inserting the coefficients for the four processed products can be described graphically and algebraically. The transactions matrix is graphically represented at the top of Figure 3–1 while the disaggregated matrix is shown below it.

Each of the transactions for all four new products were summed for one row and subtracted for the original cell value. This residual is considered as the transactions for all other products in the meat processing industry. The subtracting procedure was carried out in the same manner for all other rows, insuring that the transactions matrix remained completely balanced. That is, the gross output of sector i, x_i, of the original model is given by

$$x_i = \sum_{j=1}^{n} x_{ij} + D_i$$

where x_{ij} = sales from sector i to j and D_i = final demand for sector i's output. Then, assuming that sector n is the sector to be disaggregated, we can write the gross output of sector $i(i = 1, \ldots, n - 1)$ as

$$x_i = \sum_{j=1}^{n-1} x_{ij} + x_{in}^* + \sum_{j=n-1}^{n+4} x_{ij} + D_{ij}$$

where $x_{n+k} = K^{th}$ product line sector and

$$x_{in}^* = x_{in} - \sum_{j=n+1}^{n+4} x_{ij}$$

Table 3–1. Estimated Pretax Costs for Bone-in Beef Quarters, Frozen Boneless Manufacturing Beef, Cooked/Frozen Beef, and Canned Beef, Product Weight and Percentage Basis

| | Direct and Indirect Costs | | | | | | | |
| | Dollars | | | | Percent | | | |
Item	Bone-in Beef Quarters	Frozen Boneless Manufacturing Beef	Cooked/ Frozen Beef	Canned Beef	Bone-in Beef Quarters	Frozen Boneless Manufacturing Beef	Cooked/ Frozen Beef	Canned Beef
Livestock	622.78	865.15	1075.89	966.75	81.09	73.38	70.86	62.27
Fuel and electricity	16.27	24.07	22.27	15.84	2.11	2.04	1.47	1.02
Foods				4.03				.26
Meats				18.86				1.22
Textiles	8.59				1.12			
Ready-made wearing apparel	1.01	5.26	7.59	14.00	.13	.45	.50	.90
Wood		1.00	1.00	2.00		.08	.07	.13
Paper and cartons		19.67	12.23	21.73		1.67	.81	1.40
Printing and publications				2.00				.13
Chemical products				.12				.01
Metals	3.16			6.40	.41			.41
Vehicles and machinery		5.00	7.43	10.00		.42	.49	.65
Other industries		4.05	23.35	3.00		.34	1.54	.20
Commerce	13.57	26.65	41.66	38.37	1.77	2.26	2.74	2.47
Transportation and storage	11.47	17.43	18.26	9.15	1.49	1.48	1.20	.59
Other services	18.49	27.48	34.49	35.03	2.41	2.33	2.77	2.26
Labor	36.75	138.45	199.73	235.91	4.79	11.74	13.16	15.20
Depreciation	23.87	27.28	42.66	64.00	3.11	2.31	2.21	4.12
Defective cans				.50				
Imports	12.00	17.54	31.72	104.80	1.56	1.49	2.09	6.75
Total	767.96	1179.03	1518.28	1552.49	100.00	100.00	100.00	100.00

Source: Banco Central de la Republica Argentina (1964).

Table 3–2. Estimated Cost and Sales Data for Bone-in Beef Quarters, Frozen Boneless Manufacturing Beef, Cooked/Frozen Beef, and Canned Beef, Prepared for Disaggregated 1963 Argentine Input-Output Study, Product Weight Basis

Sector Number	Sector or Item	Bone-in Beef Quarters	Frozen Boneless Manufacturing Beef	Cooked/Frozen Beef	Canned Beef	Live Cow Exports
				----Dollars----		
1	Agriculture	622.78	865.15	1075.89	966.75	302.11
3	Food and beverages				22.89	
4	Textiles	8.59				
5	Ready-made wearing apparel	1.01	5.26	7.59	14.00	
6	Wood		1.00	1.00	2.00	
7	Paper and cartons		19.67	12.23	23.73	
10	Chemical				.12	
11	Petroleum	16.27	24.07	22.27	15.84	
13	Metals	3.16	5.00	7.43	6.40	
14	Machinery		4.05	23.35	10.00	
17	Various				3.00	
20	Commerce	13.57	26.65	41.66	38.37	
21	Transportation and storage	11.47	17.43	18.26	9.15	23.87
23	Services	18.49	27.48	34.49	35.03	2.90
	Subtotal	695.34	995.76	1244.17	1147.28	328.88

Value added					
Households					
Labor	36.75	138.45	199.73	235.91	13.09
Profit	160.31	− 33.73	835.37	177.02	6.47
Subtotal	197.05	104.72	1035.10	412.93	19.56
Other					
Depreciation	23.87	27.28	42.66	64.00	
Customs	4.03	4.03	4.03	14.92	4.03
Defective cans				.50	
Export taxes	565.64	650.72	865.59	634.31	347.53
Subtotal	593.54	682.03	912.28	713.73	351.56
Imports	12.00	17.54	31.72	104.80	
Subtotal	12.00	17.54	31.72	104.80	
Total gross outlays	1497.94	1600.05	3223.27	2378.74	700.00
Gross output (sales)					
Major item	1448.00	1593.40	2922.00	2043.00	700.00
Extract			126.61	177.49	
High price cuts		72.40	72.40	66.61	
Trim to canning		46.26			
Fat		6.47			
Byproduct credit	49.94	69.33	86.52	77.54	
Bone credit		12.19	15.74	14.10	
Total gross output	1497.94	1800.05	3223.27	2378.74	700.00

Source: Banco Central de la Republica Argentina (1964).

		Purchasing sectors	Final demand	Total gross output
Processing sector		$x_{ll} \cdots x_{lj} \cdots x_{ln}$ $x_{il} \cdots x_{ij} \cdots x_{in}$ $x_{nl} \cdots x_{nj} \cdots x_{nn}$	$fd_{ll} \cdots fd_{lj} \cdots fd_{lk}$ $fd_{il} \cdots fd_{ij} \cdots fd_{ik}$ $fd_{nl} \cdots fd_{nj} \cdots fd_{nk}$	X_i
Final payments		$fp_{ll} \cdots fp_{lj} \cdots fp_{ln}$ $fp_{il} \cdots fp_{ij} \cdots fp_{in}$ $fp_{rl} \cdots fp_{rj} \cdots fp_{rn}$	$fe_{ll} \cdots fe_{lj} \cdots fe_{lk}$ $fe_{il} \cdots fe_{ij} \cdots fe_{ik}$ $fe_{rl} \cdots fe_{rj} \cdots fe_{rk}$	
Total gross outlays		X_i		X_{nn}

		Purchasing sectors		Final Demand	Total gross output
		Original	Added		
Processing sectors	Original	$x_{il}^{\cdot}$ $x_{il}^{\cdot}$ $x_{nl}^{\cdot}$	$x_{l(n+1)} \cdots x_{l(n+4)}$ $x_{i(n+1)} \cdots x_{i(n+4)}$ $x_{n(n+1)} \cdots x_{n(n+4)}$	fd	
	Added	$x_{(n+1)l}^{\cdot} \cdots x_{(n+1)n}$ $x_{(n+4)l}^{\cdot} \cdots x_{(n+4)n}$	$x_{(n+1)(n+1)} \cdots x_{(n+1)(n+4)}$ $x_{(n+4)(n+1)} \cdots x_{(n+4)(n+4)}$	$fd_{(n+1)l} \cdots fd_{(n+1)j} \cdots fd_{(n+1)k}$ $fd_{(n+4)l} \cdots fd_{(n+4)j} \cdots fd_{(n+4)k}$	
	Final payments	$fp_{ll}^{\cdot} \quad fp_{ij}^{\cdot} \quad fp_{ln}^{\cdot}$ $fp_{il}^{\cdot}$ $fp_{rl}^{\cdot}$	$fp_{l(n+1)}^{\cdot} \cdots fp_{l(n+4)}^{\cdot}$ $fp_{(n+4)(n+1)} \quad fp_{(n+4)(n+4)}$	$fe_{ll}^{\cdot} \cdots fe_{ll}^{\cdot} \cdots fe_{lk}^{\cdot}$	
Total gross outlays					

FIGURE 3–1.   Original and Disaggregated Transaction Matrix

For the new sectors, gross output can be written as

$$x_{n+k} = \sum_{j=1}^{n-1} x_{ij} + x^* \, in + k + \sum_{j=n+1}^{n+4} x_{ij} + D_{n+k}$$

For sector x_n^* (the residual after the product lines have been taken out) we have

$$x_n^* = \sum_{j=1}^{n+4} x_{ij}^* + D_n^*$$

$$x_{ij}^* = x_{ij} - \sum_{i=n+1}^{n+4} x_{ij}$$

$$D_n^* = D_n - \sum_{i=n+1}^{n+4} D_i$$

The well-known derivation technique for the Type I multiplier shown in Figure 3–2 was then followed to obtain the product line income and output multipliers for live cow exports except that the livestock sector was disaggregated in this case. The Type II multiplier is derived in the same manner except that households are endogenous.

Because of the differences between the time the I-O studies were originally constructed and the product line budgets were prepared, the implicit I-O framework assumption of constant technology with no change in relative prices was carefully scrutinized. The conclusion was that the assumption is not a limiting factor here despite recognition that technological changes over time do affect the pattern of input requirements. The reason for the time period differences not being a constraint is that the purpose of the study is a comparison of *several* multipliers, all of which have been prepared for *one* sector, rather than comparison with original multipliers.

Multipliers

Multipliers show the indirect economic outputs from what are designated backward linkages (Figure 3–3). In other words, they show the inputs (such as labor or machinery) leading to production of an output prior to its entering final demand. Multipliers do not reflect forward linkages (such as storage or retailing) after production is complete. In addition, multipliers do not show changes in an economy's structure such as diversification or externalities caused by production changes. Finally, multipliers, like I-O models, are best utilized for analyzing small changes in final demand. Large changes imply variations in production technology, which violates assumptions about I-O analysis.

```
┌─────────────────────┐
│  To obtain a Type I │
│  output multiplier  │
└─────────────────────┘
           │
           │
   Divide each cell of the
     transaction matrix
    by total gross outlay
          ⇓
  To obtain the technical coefficients
     (direct requirements) matrix
           │
           │
  Then subtract the diagonal coefficients
  from one and change the signs of the
           other elements
           │
           │
       Invert the matrix
          ⇓
  To obtain the (I − A)⁻¹ matrix (interdependence
     coefficients matrix or, as it is also
    known, the indirect requirements matrix)
           │
           │
  Then, sum the column coefficients
          ⇓
      To finally obtain the
        Type I multipliers
```

$$(I - A)^{-1}$$

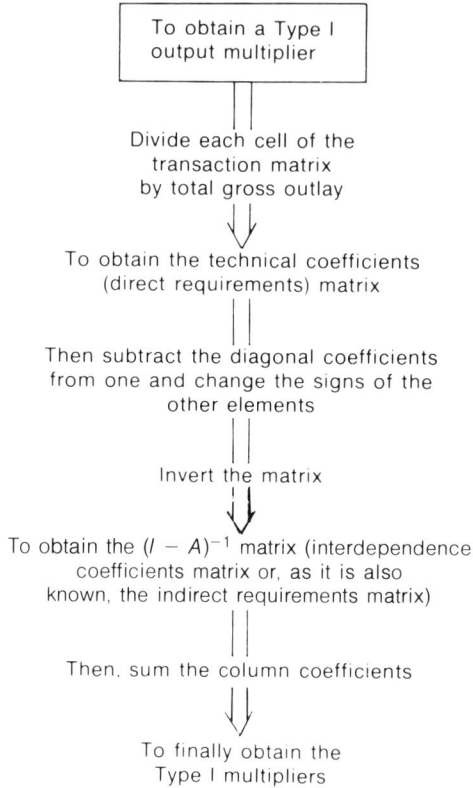

FIGURE 3-2. Steps in Obtaining a Type I Output Multiplier

The technical coefficients presented in Table 3–3 show the direct purchases per dollar of output by the five newly created sectors derived from the I-O structure described in the Argentinian study (1964). The largest purchases were from agriculture in the form of live animals. In order to produce one dollar's worth of frozen manufacturing beef, about six cents was spent on households in the form of wages, salaries, profits, dividends, interest, and similar payments. For one dollar's worth of output from the canned beef sector, on the other hand, forty-one cents had to be spent in agriculture and seventeen cents on households. The second largest category, "other," was mostly taxes levied on exports.

The Type I and II output multipliers from the four different South American I-O studies are presented in Table 3–4 for the four processed beef products as well as live cow exports. As expected, the highest multipliers are for products undergoing the greatest processing.

Backward Linkages   Forward Linkages

| Owners of productive resources • land • labor • capital | ← | Input supplying industries | ← | Primary impact activity agriculture | → | Transportation processing, and merchandising system for food and fiber | → | Consumers |

Induced By   Stemming From

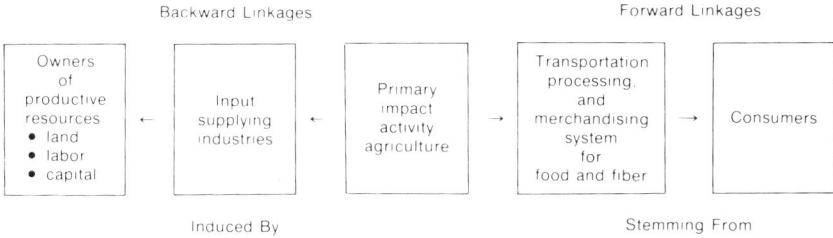

FIGURE 3–3. Secondary Market Impact Classification

Cooked frozen beef has the largest Type II output multiplier while canned beef is close behind. Exporting live cows, for example, only generates $3.33 worth of direct, indirect and induced economic activity in Argentina for every dollar's worth of sales while cooked frozen beef yields $4.87.

As a means of investigating the general applicability of the multipliers, a sensitivity test was made by inserting the budgets in the Grubb (1973) I-O study for the state of Texas, hypothesizing that this would represent an extreme situation. Texas exports large amounts of bone-in beef, but it is part of a developed interdependent economy. The multipliers turned out 25 percent lower than the Argentina studies, probably because of the leakage from imports of cattle and materials from other states. Cooked and canned beef differed less from the manufacturing beef reference point while quarters varied more; however, the *ordering* of the multipliers was essentially the same.[7]

CONCLUSIONS AND DISCUSSION

After reviewing hypothetical I-O model applications, a technique was presented in this chapter that demonstrates how statistical information from personal interviews with processors can be combined with existing disaggregation techniques to develop I-O models based on product lines. An application was made to the beef export industry of Latin America, but the technique is relevant for any type of commodity, ranging from copper to coffee.

One ramification of the study is the recognition that it may be possible to prepare and insert budgets for industrywide feasibility studies for one country in the input-output study for another country to obtain comparative multipliers. In other words, if an investigator, say in the Dominican Republic for which there is no I-O study, wanted to determine whether oranges from the citrus industry should be exported raw, as canned juice, as frozen concentrate, or packaged as powder, the investigator could develop the budgets and insert them in

Table 3–3. Direct Purchases per Dollar of Output; Live Cow Exports, Processing of Bone-in Beef Quarters, Frozen Boneless Manufacturing Beef, Cooked/Frozen Beef and Canned Beef, Disaggregated 1963 I-O Study

Sector Number	Sector	Live Cow Exports	Bone-in Beef Quarters	Frozen Boneless Manufacturing Beef	Cooked/Frozen Beef	Canned Beef
1	Agriculture	0.43157	0.41578	0.48067	0.33379	0.40643
2	Food					0.00963
3	Textiles		0.00574			
4	Clothes		0.00067	0.00294	0.00236	0.00589
5	Wood			0.00056	0.00031	0.00084
6	Paper and Printing			0.01094	0.00378	0.00996
7	Petroleum		0.01082	0.01339	0.00692	0.00664
8	Metals					0.00269
9	Machinery		0.00207	0.00278	0.00230	0.00420
10	Electric machinery			0.00222	0.00723	0.00126
11	Commerce		0.00908	0.01478	0.01294	0.01614
12	Transportation	0.03414	0.00768	0.00967	0.00568	0.00387
13	Service	0.00414	0.01235	0.01528	0.01070	0.01472
	Household	0.02786	0.13158	0.05817	0.32113	0.17360
	Other		0.39622	0.37889	0.28303	0.30006
	Imports	0.50229	0.00801	0.00972	0.00983	0.04406
	Total	1.00000	1.00000	1.00000	1.00000	1.00000

Source: Banco Central de la Republica Argentina (1964).

Table 3–4. Output and Income Multipliers for Export of Live Cows, Bone-in Beef Quarters, Frozen Boneless Manufacturing Beef, Cooked/Frozen Beef and Canned Beef from Five Different Disaggregated Input-Output Studies

| Input-Output Studies | Type of Beef Export Product | | | | | | | | | |
| | Live Cows | | Bone-in Quarters | | Frozen Boneless Manufacturing | | Cooked/ Frozen | | Canned | |
	Type I	Type II	Type I	Type II	Type I	Type II	Type I	Type II	Type I	Type II
Output Multiplier										
1963 Argentina	1.73	3.33	1.72	4.04	1.86	4.00	1.60	4.87	1.76	4.41
1970 Argentina			1.76	4.04	1.90	4.02	1.63	4.84	1.79	4.40
1959 Brazil	1.62	3.19	1.62	3.76	1.75	3.67	1.52	4.75	1.66	4.17
1961 Uruguay	1.66	3.02	1.65	3.47	1.78	3.44	1.54	4.18	1.68	3.79
1967 Texas			1.81	3.07	1.96	3.15	1.67	3.37	1.83	3.24
Income Multiplier										
1963 Argentina	9.66	20.38	2.78	6.25	5.82	13.10	1.61	3.62	2.41	5.43
1970 Argentina			2.81	6.06	5.90	12.74	1.62	3.49	2.43	5.25
1959 Brazil	8.08	21.83	2.47	6.44	4.90	12.79	1.49	3.90	2.14	5.60
1961 Uruguay	8.98	20.18	2.62	5.51	5.44	11.44	1.56	3.28	2.30	4.84
1967 Texas			3.08	5.18	6.57	11.07	1.70	2.86	2.60	4.39

Sources: Banco Central de la Republica Argentina (1973); Republica Argentina (1973); Universidad de la Republica Uruguay (1969); Ellis (1969); and Grubb (1973).

an I-O matrix for another country. Wilkins (1978) also points this out. Naturally, considerable judgment would be necessary in selecting a country with similar conditions, but the five I-O analyses in which data for cow beef exports were studied show that the multipliers were fairly stable between countries. Furthermore, the multipliers for each product were stable when inserted in I-O studies for different periods for the same country.

More research in other industries is needed employing the disaggregation method to determine problems not uncovered here. In addition, as McKusick and Zygadlo (1978) have observed, extreme care must be used in applying I-O multipliers in isolation from the parent models as interregional flows (import-export balances) and other leakages out of the region can bias the multiplier approach. But they also suggest conducting more tests to compare broad geographical or sectoral multipliers to more specific regional multipliers. Certainly, a good point of departure is application of I-O analysis to the common market approach suggested earlier in the chapter.

The disaggregation technique presented in this chapter offers commodity model builders a shortcut technique to projecting the impact of a new industry if it can be assumed that the new industry will act in a similar fashion to an existing one. The technique is also an efficient tool for answering the question, which is the best subindustry, x or y? While other techniques only deal with new industries or subindustries, the disaggregation method offers the researcher an ideal way of dealing with existing situations. Finally, it provides a means of comparing and evaluating the effect on the economy from a projected new subindustry (such as a palm oil project) to an existing subindustry such as the manufacture of oil from soybeans.

Overall, the disaggregation of I-O studies used in the LDCs seems to have considerable usefulness for planning. The scope and application depends, of course, on the imagination and innovativeness of both theoretical and applied commodity model builders.

NOTES

1. A complete discussion of I-O models in Latin America was prepared in 1973 by ECLA in Santiago, Chile. Preliminary findings are reported in United Nations (1973). For more detail see the reference to Barna (1963).

2. The problem is that steers, although comprising the majority of all the above beef exports, are almost always broken down into numerous wholesale cuts that depend on market conditions and customers' orders at the time of slaughter. In contradistinction an entire cow is frequently directed to one of

the four product forms listed. Thus restricting the analysis to cow beef is a vehicle for simplicity in preparation of the budgets.

3. For a detailed discussion on multiplier derivation see Hirsch (1959); Leontief (1953); Simpson and Adams (1975).

4. Rather than inserting the budgets in the transactions matrix, each item can be divided by the total to obtain the technical coefficients matrix. This procedure has been used by Adams (1973); in this study it is done for the 1970 Argentina study in which the technical coefficients matrix was updated from the 1963 study by a dynamic procedure.

5. For more information about South American packing plants see Simpson and Farris (1975).

6. The two Argentine studies are listed in the bibliography under Banco Central de la Republica Argentina (1964) and Republica Argentina (1973); the Brazil study is found in Ellis (1969); the Uruguay study is under Universidad de la Republica (1969).

7. The effects of changes in final demand on output and income, as well as application of the model to planning in Uruguay, are presented in Simpson and Adams (1975).

BIBLIOGRAPHY

Adams, John. 1973. "The Economic Impact of Selected New or Expanding Industries on the Economy of the Lower Rio Grande Region of Texas." Department of Agricultural Economy, Texas A & M University. Unpublished.

Adams, John W., and Milton L. Holloway. 1973. "The Economic Impact of Selected New or Expanding Industries on the Economy of the Lower Rio Grande Region of Texas." Texas Agricultural Experiment Station and Office of Information Services. College Station: Texas A & M University.

———. n.d. "An A Priori Estimate of the Economic Impact of Selected Industrial Changes on a Regional Economy," Technical Article 11024 of the Texas Agricultural Experiment Station. College Station: Texas A & M University.

Allen, R.I.G., and W.F. Gossling, eds. 1975. *Problems of Estimating and Projecting Input-Output Coefficients.* London: Input-Output Publishing Company.

Allen, R.I.G., and J.R.C. Lecomber. 1975. "Some Tests on a Generalized Version of RAS." In R.I.G. Allen and W.F. Gossling, eds., *Problems of Estimating and Projecting Input-Output Coefficients.* London: Input-Output Publishing Company.

Almon, Clopper, Jr.; Margaret B. Buckler; Lawrence M. Horowitz; and Thomas C. Reimbold. 1974. *Interindustry Forecasts of the American Economy,* Lexington, Mass.: Heath Lexington Books.

Banco Central de la Republica Argentina. 1964. *Transacciones Intersectoriales de la Economia Argentina.* Buenos Aires, April.

Barna, Tibor, ed. 1963. *Structural Interdependence and Economic Development.* New York: St. Martins Press.

Bingham, Tayler H., and Bun Song Lee. 1975. "Estimates of the Inter-relationships Between Consumer Expenditures and National Resource Consumption." Research Triangle Institute, Research Triangle Park, North Carolina. Unpublished.

Breimyer, Harold F., et al. 1962. "Agricultural Development and Economic Growth." Report to the United States and Argentina government. Buenos Aires. Unpublished.

Brody, A., and A.P. Carter, eds. 1972. *Input-Output Techniques*. New York: North Holland/American Elsevier.

Brumby, P.J. 1973. "International Lending for Livestock Development." *World Animal Review* 5.

Carter, A.P., and A. Brody, eds. 1969. *Applications of Input-Output Analysis*. Amsterdam: North Holland Publishing Company.

Davis, R.M., et al. 1974. "Development of an Economic-Environmental Trade-off Model for Industrial Land-Use Planning." Paper presented at the Southern Regional Science Association meeting, Washington, D.C., April 4–5.

Ellis, Howard, ed. 1969. *The Economy of Brazil*. Berkeley: University of California Press.

Ghosh, A. 1968. *Planning, Programming and Input Output Models: Selected Papers on Indian Planning*. Cambridge: Cambridge University Press.

Grubb, Herbert W. 1973. *The Structure of the Texas Economy*. Vols. I and II. Austin, Texas: Office of the Governor, March.

Hirsch, Werner. 1959. "Interindustry Relations of a Metropolitan Area." *The Review of Economics and Statistics* 41 (November): 360–69.

Isard, Walter. 1951. "Interregional and Regional Input-Output Analysis: A Model of a Space Economy." *The Review of Economics and Statistics* 35, no. 4: 318–28.

Isard, Walter, and R.E. Kuenne. 1953. "The Impact Upon the Greater New York–Philadelphia Urban Industrial Region." *Review of Economics and Statistics* 35: 289–301.

Isard, Walter, and Thomas W. Langford. 1971. *Regional Input-Output Study*. Cambridge, Mass.: MIT Press.

Krueger, Paul K. 1976. "Modeling Future Requirements for Metals and Minerals." Washington, D.C.: Federal Preparedness Agency. Unpublished.

Kymm, Kern O. 1977. "Interindustry Energy Demand and Aggregation of Input-Output Tables," *The Review of Economics and Statistics* 61, no. 3 (August): 317–74.

Labys, Walter C. 1973. *Dynamic Commodity Models: Specification, Estimation and Simulation*. Lexington, Mass.: Heath Lexington Books.

———. 1978. "Commodity Markets and Models: The Range of Experience." In F.G. Adams and S. Klein, eds. *Stabilizing World Commodity Markets: Analyses, Practice and Policy*. Lexington, Mass.: Heath Lexington Books.

Leontief, W. 1953. "Interregional Theory." In Leontief, et al., *Studies in the Structure of the American Economy*, pp. 53–90. New York: OUP.

———. 1966. *Input-Output Economics*. New York: Oxford University Press.

——. 1977. *The Future of the World Economy*. Oxford: Oxford University Press.

Leontief, W., and A. Strout. 1963. "Multiregional Input-Output Analysis." In T. Barna, ed., *Structural Interdependence and Economic Development*, pp. 119–49. London: MacMillan.

Maki, Wilbur R. 1970. "Small Area Applications of Input-Output." Minneapolis: University of Minnesota, Department of Agricultural Economy. Staff Paper, December.

McKusick, Robert, and Linda Zygadlo. 1978. "Conclusions and Recommendations." In *Regional Development and Plan Evaluation: The Use of Input-Output Analysis*. ESCS Agriculture Handbook 530, Washington, D.C.: U.S. Department of Agriculture, May.

McMenamin, David G., and Joseph E. Haring. 1974. "An Appraisal of Nonsurvey Techniques for Estimating Regional Input-Output Models." *Journal of Regional Science* 14 (August): 191–205.

Miernyk, William H. 1965. *The Elements of Input-Output Analysis*. New York: Random House.

——. 1969. "Sampling Techniques in Making Regional Industry Forecasts." In A.P. Carter and A. Brody, eds., *Applications of Input-Output Analysis*, pp. 305–21. Amsterdam: North-Holland.

——. 1975. "The Projection of Technical Coefficients for Medium-Term Forecasting." In W.F. Gossling (ed.), *Medium Term Dynamic Forecasting*. London: Input-Output Publishing Co.: 29–41.

Miernyk, W.H., and others. 1970. *Simulating Regional Economic Development*. Lexington, Mass.: Heath Lexington Books.

Morrison, W.I., and P. Smith. 1974. "Nonsurvey Input-Output Techniques at the Small Area Level: An Evaluation." *Journal of Regional Science* 14 (April): 1–3.

Moses, L. 1955. "The Stability of Interregional Trading Patterns and Input-Output Analysis." *American Economic Review* 45: 803–32.

Mulkey, David, and James Hite. 1974. "A Two-Stage Heuristic Model for Intermediate-Run Sectorial Petroleum Allocation in a Multi-Regional Setting." *Review of Regional Studies* 4 (Winter): 1–18.

Polenske, Karen R. 1970. "Empirical Implementation of a Multi-Regional Input-Output Gravity Trade Model." In *Contributions to Input-Output Analysis*, A.P. Carter and A. Brody, eds. Amsterdam: North-Holland Publishing Co.

Rasmussen, P.N. 1956. *Studies in Inter-Sectoral Relations*. Amsterdam: North-Holland Publishing Co.

Republica Argentina, Secretaria de Planeamiento y Accion de Gobierno Subsecretaria de Desarrollo. 1973. *Modelo Economico Sectorial Dinamico*. Buenos Aires, May.

Richardson, Harry W. 1972. *Input-Output and Regional Economics*. New York: John Wiley & Sons.

Shulman, A.A. 1972. "DITT Data Estimates and Input-Output Review." IST-103 MCL. Washington, D.C.

Simpson, James R. 1975. "Proyecciones de Produccion y Consumo de Carne Vacuna en America Latina." *La Hacienda* 70 no. 1 (Enero): 25–28.

Simpson, James R., and John W. Adams. 1975. "Disaggregation of Input-Output Models Into Product Lines as an Economic Development Policy Tool." *Am. J. Agr. Econ.* 57, no. 4 (November): 584–90.

Simpson, James R., and Donald E. Farris. 1975. "The Benefits for Economic Development from Selected South American Beef Exports." *World Animal Review* 13: 9–15.

Stone, Richard, and Alan Brown. 1965. "Behavioral and Technical Change in Economic Models." In E.A.G. Robinson, ed., *Problems in Economic Development*, pp. 428–443. London: Macmillan & Company Ltd.

Stone, Richard; John Bates; and Michael Bacharach. 1963. *Input-Output Relationships, 1954–1966*. Cambridge, Mass.: MIT Press.

Tiebout, Charles M. 1969. "An Empirical Regional Input-Output Projection Model: The State of Washington 1980." *Review of Economics and Statistics* 51: 334–40.

United Nations, Economic Commission for Latin America. 1970. *Development Problems in Latin America*. Austin: University of Texas Press.

——. 1973. Economic Commission for Latin America, "El Sector Externo en las Experiencias de Insumo-Producto de America Latina." Paper presented at the Seminario Internacional Sobre Estadisticas de las Relaciones Economicas Internacionales, Santiago, August.

Universidad de la Republica, Instituto de Economia. 1969. *Uruguay: Estadisticas Basicas*. Montevideo.

U.S. Department of Agriculture. 1970. *Argentina Agriculture: Trends in Production and World Competition*. ERS-Foreign 216, Washington, D.C., July.

Wilkins, John. 1978. "General Application of I-O Analysis and its Multipliers." In *Regional Development and Plan Evaluation: The Use of Input-Output Analysis*. ESCS Agriculture Handbook 530. Washington, D.C.: U.S. Department of Agriculture, May.

Zygadlo, Lynda, and Robert Niehaus. 1978. "Regional Development and Plan Evaluation." In *Regional Development and Plan Evaluation: The Use of Input-Output Analysis*. ESCS Agriculture Handbook 530. Washington, D.C.: U.S. Department of Agriculture, May.

4

ALFREDO
DAMMERT

Planning Investments in the Copper Sector in Latin America

The purpose of this chapter is to investigate investment policy in the copper industry in Latin America within a worldwide framework. The copper sector is of high relevance for Latin America for two main reasons:

1. Copper can be counted among its most important nonferrous metals.[1]
2. Peru and Chile are among the most important Third World copper exporters.

The method used is a cost-minimizing multiperiod linear mixed integer programming model of the type described by Kendrick and Stoutjesdijk (1975), which takes into account economies of scale in the investment activities. The model has been extended to consider the notion of declining ore grades. Additional versions of the model consider the impact of tariffs on semimanufactures as well as shipment constraints.

The processes of copper production and fabrication are illustrated in Figure 4–1. These processes range from mining to semimanufacturing

The author feels indebted to David Kendrick of the University of Texas for his encouragement and guidance and to Ardy Stoutjesdijk for providing the support of the World Bank. Thanks also to Alex Meeraus of the World Bank for his invaluable help with the initial version of the model.

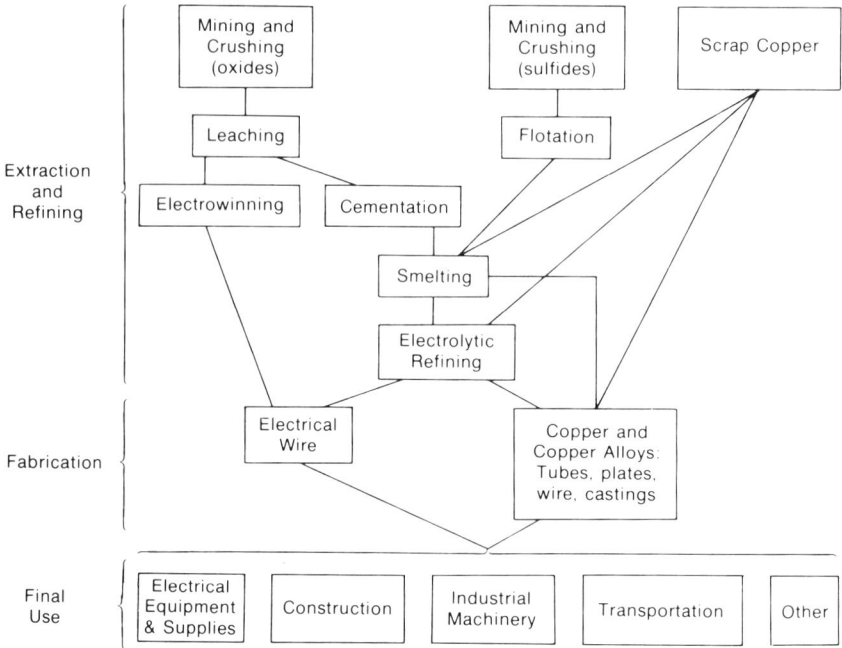

Source: Martijena (1966).

FIGURE 4-1.   Process of Copper Refining and Fabrication

and are included in the model. Thirteen producing areas and thirteen market areas are considered. Two time periods are covered: 1975 through 1984 and 1985 through 1994. The solution to the model provides information on investment for timing and location as well as shipments of blister copper, refined copper, and copper semimanufactures. Production levels for each activity are also given by the model but are not presented in this chapter.

Although the model is solved on a worldwide basis, this chapter focuses on its implications for Latin America. A more detailed analysis of the model is presented in Dammert (1977).

DESCRIPTION OF THE MODEL

The model is solved as a mixed integer linear program set to minimize total discounted cost of investment, operation, and transportation over a time horizon, subject to material balance constraints, capacity constraints, investment constraints, and market requirements.[2] This section presents the equations that form the structure of the model. The variables for each equation are described in order of appearance. The plants and markets for the model appear in Table 4–1, 4–2, and 4–5.

The Objective Function

$$\text{Min } \xi = \sum_{t\in T} \delta_t \, (\phi_{kt} + \phi_{rt} + \phi_{st} + \phi_{kgt} + \phi_{rgt} + \phi_{sgt}) \qquad (4\text{-}1)$$

Total
Cost

where

$$\phi_{kt} = \sum_{\tau=1}^{t}\sum_{i,m} \sigma_m \, (\alpha_m \, h_{mit} + \beta_m s_{mit}) \qquad (4\text{-}1a)$$

proportional part size dependent
of investment cost part
      of investment
      cost

$$\phi_{rt} = \sum_{C\in C_r}\sum_{i\in I} (p_{dict} \, d_{cit}) \qquad (4\text{-}1b)$$

cost of raw materials

$$d_{cit} = \sum_{p\in p_i} a_{cpit} \, z_{pit}$$

$$\phi_{st} = \sum_{c\in C_f} \left(\sum_{i\in I}\sum_{j\in J} \mu_{cijt} x_{cijt} \right) \qquad (4\text{-}1c)$$

transport cost
of final product

$$+ \sum_{c\in C_{ms}}\sum_{i\in I_p}\sum_{i\in I_s} (\mu_{cii't} \, x_{cii't})$$

transport cost of
intermediate products

The variables ϕ_{kgt}, ϕ_{rgt} and ϕ_{sgt} are similar to ϕ_{kt}, and ϕ_{rt}, and ϕ_{st} but for the processing of semis.
 The description of the variables follows:

ξ = the total discounted cost of production and transportation of copper from mining to distribution of copper semi-manufactures to markets

ϕ_{kt} = total capital cost from mining to refining for year t

ϕ_{rt} = total recurrent cost for mining to refining in year t

ϕ_{st} = total transport cost for mining to refining in year t

ϕ_{kst} = total capital cost for semimanufactures for year t

ϕ_{rst} = total recurrent cost for semimanufactures for year t

ϕ_{sst} = total transportation cost (including tariffs) for semimanufactures for year t

x_{cijt} = shipments of product c from producing region i to market j at time t

$x_{cii't}$ = shipments of product c from plant i to be used as an intermediate product at plant i' at time t

z_{pit} = process level (production level) for production process p at plant i and time t expressed in units of copper content

h_{mit} = continuous investment decision for productive unit m at plant i during time t

s_{mit} = $\{\tilde{h}_{mit} - h_{mit}$ for $\tilde{h}_{mit} \geq h_{mit}\}$

$\quad\quad$ 0 $\quad\quad\quad\quad\quad$ otherwise

$\quad\quad$ = difference in capacity between the minimum size plant h_{mit} where economies of scale are no longer operative and the plant size h_{mit} being constructed. s_{mit} becomes 0 when actual plant to be built is larger than $\tilde{h}_{mit}$

The parameters for Equations 4–1a through 4–1c are:

σ_m = capital recovery factor for productive unit m

σ_m = $\dfrac{p\,(1 + p)^{zm}}{(1 + p)^{zm} - 1}$

z_m = life of productive unit m

α_{mi} = proportional part of investment cost

β_m = part of investment cost that depends on plant size

$\tilde{h}_m$ = limits of economies of scale for productive unit m

$\bar{h}_m$ = upper bound on capacity expansion in a single period in productive unit m

δ_t = discount factor that transforms costs from time period t to present value according to

$$\delta_t = \overset{\theta}{\Sigma}\,(1 + \rho)^{-\theta(t-1)-\gamma}$$

γ = 1

θ = number of time intervals per time period

ρ = discount rate

p_{cpit} = recurrent costs to produce commodity c, that is, the domestic cost of raw materials and labor, net of the revenue of by-products

Part II

Modeling Latin America's Commodity Markets

purposes. The description of the variables that appear in Equation 4–8 is as follows:

$x_{cii't}$ = shipments of product c from plant i to be used as an intermediate product at plant i' at time t

z_{pit} = process level for production process p at plant i and time t expressed in units of copper content

and the parameter

$r_{c'i't}$ = market requirements for refined copper for uses other than semimanufactures of wire, tubes and rods, and sheet, plate, and strip

In addition, the following equations of market requirements for semis are included:

$$\sum_{j \in J} x_{cjj't} \geq r_{cj't} \qquad \begin{matrix} c \in C_f \\ j' \in J \\ t \in T \end{matrix} \qquad (4–9)$$

$$\begin{bmatrix} \text{shipments of } c \\ \text{from } j \text{ to } j' \end{bmatrix} \geq \begin{bmatrix} \text{market} \\ \text{requirement} \end{bmatrix}$$

where $x_{cjj't}$ = shipments of product c (wire, tubes or sheet) from producing region j to market j' at time t

Constraints on Processing Different Ore Grades

$$z_{pit} \leq g_{cpit} \qquad p \in OM, OM2 \qquad (4–10)$$

This constraint places an upper limit on the annual exploitation of high-grade ores and of second-grade ores where

$$g_{cpit} = \text{annual availability of ore grade } c$$

$$\sum_{t \in T} 10 z_{pit} \leq v_{pi} \qquad \begin{matrix} p \in OM, OM2, OM3 \\ i \in I \end{matrix} \qquad (4–11)$$

Equation 4–11 places an upper limit on total availability of each ore grade. The coefficient 10 relates the activities z_{pit} expressed in annual values to the time periods that represent 10 years each where:

v_{pi} = total reserves of ore grade in processing area i

The equation is included in the model in order to consider the limitation on reserves over the time horizon being covered. Equations 4–10 and 4–11 represent alternative specifications. However, for the lower ore grades only Equation 4–11 is used since actual reserves of such grade are less well covered because of their present subeconomic status, and therefore they may be underestimated.

Shipment Constraints on the Third and Fourth Versions

$$x_{cjj't} - t_{cjj't} \qquad c \epsilon C_f \qquad (4\text{--}12)$$
$$j' \epsilon J$$
$$t \epsilon T$$

Nonnegativity Constraints
For all variables.

Owing to the size of the model and the difficulties of obtaining more detailed data, only the main production processes were considered. These processes are: (1) open pit mining and concentration of high-, medium-, and low-quality ore, (2) underground mining and concentration, (3) smelting, refining, and wire semimanufacturing, (4) tubes and rods semimanufacturing, and (5) sheets, plate, and strip semimanufacturing. Scrap processing was considered at the smelting, refining, and semimanufacturing stages. As mentioned earlier two time periods were considered, 1975 through 1984 and 1985 through 1994. Thus the planning horizon covered is twenty years.

The main characteristics of the model are the economies of scale in the investment activities that give rise to the need for a zero-one variables, that is, the mixed integer part of the model and the declining ore grades of the available reserves. Different versions of the model were considered. The first version was the least cost solution without tariffs. The second version included tariffs on semimanufactures in order to consider the actual situation. Finally, a third and fourth version included both tariffs in semimanufactures and lower bounds on shipment activities in order to determine the effect that decisions by less industrialized copper-producing countries would have of selling a certain amount of their copper in the form of semimanufactures. The third and fourth versions differ between each other only in the number of plants considered in some regions. This is important because it shows the difference in costs when a group of countries agree upon building a single plant to serve the region instead of building one plant in each country.

DATA UTILIZED

Forecasts of the demand for semimanufactures were obtained from econometric estimates constructed for such purpose. Details of the methodology of estimation are given in Dammert (1977). The results are presented in Table 4–1. The investment costs associated with mines and concentrators, smelters, and refineries are given in Table 4–2. The data for mines and concentrators is for the higher ore grades. Table 4–3 presents the investment costs for copper semimanufacturing plants.

The operating costs for mines to refineries were estimated from

Table 4–1. Market Demand for Semimanufactures
(Thousands of Metric Tons)

Countries	Wire	Tubes and Rods	Sheet Strip and Plate	Other		Total
				From Refined Copper	From Scrap	
1980						
United States	2367	571	694	154	295	4081
Mexico	89	21	12	9	—	131
Eastern South America	224	53	30	22	—	329
Western South America	58	14	8	5	—	85
Western Europe	2272	1305	580	362	316	5835
Soviet Union and Eastern Europe	1145	528	330	198	—	2201
Central Africa	30	13	14	3	—	60
South Africa	46	20	21	5	—	92
Asia	176	60	43	5	—	284
Japan and S. Korea	1207	428	253	17	42	1947
China and N. Korea	327	111	79	11	—	528
Australia	80	19	23	16	—	138
Canada	164	40	48	14	17	283
1990						
United States	3225	779	945	229	383	5561
Mexico	169	40	22	17	—	248
Eastern South America	423	100	56	43	—	622
Western South America	109	26	14	11	—	160
Western Europe	3210	1844	819	545	411	6869
Soviet Union and Eastern Europe	1832	846	528	317	—	3523
Central Africa	57	25	26	6	—	114
South Africa	87	38	40	9	—	174
Asia	334	113	81	10	—	538
Japan and S. Korea	1968	698	413	41	55	3175
China and N. Korea	619	210	150	20	—	999
Australia	96	23	28	19	—	166
Canada	208	50	61	18	22	359

Table 4–2. Investment Costs (Millions of U.S. Dollars of 1974 per Thousand Metric Tons)

Productive Unit	Mines and Concentrators			Smelters			Refineries		
	Fixed Cost[a]	Variable Cost[a]	Maximum Size For Economies of Scale	Fixed Cost	Variable Cost	Maximum Size For Economies of Scale	Fixed Cost	Variable Cost	Maximum Size For Economies of Scale
Region									
Peru	20	2.8	100	25	1.083	150	2.8	.501	150
Chile	20	2.8	100	25	1.083	150	2.8	.501	150
Zambia	60	2.9	380	25	1.083	150	2.8	.501	150
Zaire	60	2.9	380	25	1.083	150	2.8	.501	150
Mexico	20	2.8	100	25	1.083	150	2.8	.501	150
South Africa	20	2.8	100	25	1.083	150	2.8	.501	150
U.S. West	20	2.53	75	20	.916	150	2.0	.287	150
Canada	20	2.53	75	20	.916	150	2.0	.287	150
Soviet Union and Eastern Europe	20	2.53	75	20	.916	150	2.0	.287	150
Australia	20	2.53	75	20	.916	150	2.0	.287	150
Western Europe	14	3.74	50	20	.916	150	2.0	.287	150
Japan	14	3.74	50	20	.916	150	2.0	.287	150
U.S. East	14	3.74	50	20	.916	150	2.0	.287	150

Source: Computed from Bennett et al. (1973), and from *Engineering and Mining Journal* (1976).

[a]Investment Cost = fixed cost plus variable cost × capacity up to maximum size for economies of scale. Beyond the range for economies of scale it is computed as average cost × capacity.

Table 4–3. Investment Costs for Copper Semimanufacturing Plants
(Millions of U.S. Dollars of 1974 per Thousand Metric Tons)

Plants	*Variable Cost[c]*	*Fixed Cost[c]*	*Size after which no Economies of Scale*
Plants for Electrical Wire			
— Industrial Regions[a]	.86	1.69	20
— Less Industrialized Regions[b]	.92	1.80	20
Plants for Tubes and Rods			
— Industrial Regions[a]	0.47	2.82	30
— Less Industrialized Regions[b]	.50	3.0	30
Plants for Sheet, Plate and Strip			
— Industrial Regions[a]	0.67	4.32	30
— Less Industrialized Regions[b]	.72	4.60	30

Source: Martijena (1966).

[a]United States, Western Europe, Soviet Union and Eastern Europe, Japan-Korea, Australia and New Zealand, Canada.

[b]Mexico, Eastern South America, Western South America, Central Africa, South Africa, Asia, China.

[c]See footnote to Table 4–2.

individual country reports and from unpublished sources. For semimanufactures, these costs were estimated using as a basis cost data from Martijena (1966) and adapted for differences in wages across regions. Tables 4–4 and 4–5 summarize operating costs for mines to refineries and for semimanufactures, respectively.

An important feature of the model is that it includes the concept of declining ore grades. Thus constraints on reserves for each region and

Table 4–4. Operating Costs
(U.S. Dollars of 1974 per Metric Ton of Copper Content)

Countries	*Open Pit Mines and Concentrators*	*Smelting*	*General for Mining To Smelting*	*Refining*	*Total*
Peru[a]	385.2	141.8	92.8	68.0	687.8
Chile	398.2	174.6	279.4	99.5	951.7
Zambia	365.9	101.6	132.0	31.5	631.0
Zaire	286.2	121.0	136.4	38.0	581.6
U.S. West[b]	425.2	107.9	44.0	74.9	652.0

Sources: Bennett et al. (1973) and from talks with World Bank officials.

[a]Used also for Mexico, South Africa.

[b]Estimates used for all industrial countries but scaled for copper grades.

Table 4–5.   Recurrent or Operating Costs, Excluding Copper
(Thousands of U.S. Dollars per Metric Ton, 1974)

Countries	*Wire*	*Tubes and Rods*	*Sheet, Place, and Strip*
United States	0.875	0.924	1.223
Mexico	0.564	0.822	1.065
Eastern South America	0.564	0.822	1.065
Western South America	0.564	0.822	1.065
Europe	0.641	0.848	1.105
Soviet Union and Eastern Europe	0.563	0.822	1.065
Central Africa	0.517	0.807	1.042
South Africa	0.517	0.807	1.042
Asia (excluding Japan, Korea, China and North Korea	0.478	0.794	1.022
Japan and South Korea	0.721	0.825	1.147
China and North Korea	0.478	0.794	1.022
Australia and New Zealand	0.579	0.827	1.073
Canada	0.848	0.915	1.210

Source: Estimated from Martijena (1966).

ore grade were considered. The total availability on reserves is presented in Table 4–6.

The availability of scrap to be processed at smelters, refineries, and tubes, sheet, and other semimanufactures was projected from data for 1973 from Metalgesellschaft's *Metal Statistics*. Actual plant capacity estimates were necessary in order to determine investments necessary for capacity expansion. These data are not presented in this chapter.

Table 4–6.   Reserve Availability (Thousands of Metric Tons)

Countries	*Higher Ore Grade*	*Medium Ore Grade*	*Low Ore Grade*
Peru	23,500	3,000	6,000
Chile—Open Pit Underground	45,900	6,000	14,000
	9,100	—	—
Zambia	26,000	4,000	6,000
Zaire	18,000	3,000	4,000
Mexico	20,000	2,000	5,000
South Africa	6,000	1,000	2,000
United States—Open Pit Underground	64,600	9,000	19,200
	7,200	—	—
Canada	30,000	4,000	6,000
Soviet Union—Open Pit Underground	27,300	6,000	11,000
	10,700	—	—
Australia	13,000	1,000	4,000
Western Europe	17,000	5,000	—
Japan	25,000	5,000	—
United States East	3,200	800	—

Source: Computed from Banks (1974).

For transportation, the model considers shipments of blister copper (produced at smelters) from less industrialized (Peru, Chile, Zambia, Zaire, Mexico, and South Africa) to industrialized areas (western United States, Canada, Soviet Union, Western Europe, Japan, and eastern United States) and of refined copper and copper semimanufactures between all regions. The modes of transportation included in the model are by ocean and by railroad. The costs were estimated as directly proportional to the shipping distance, but they differ for ocean and rail transportation and for the type of product. Ocean transport was considered at U.S. $0.005 per metric ton nautical mile for blister and refined copper and at U.S. $0.010 per metric ton nautical mile for semimanufactures. Railroad transportation was estimated at U.S. $0.05 per metric ton scale mile and U.S. $0.10 per metric ton scale mile for blister or refined copper and semimanufactures, respectively.

Tariffs on imports of semimanufactures were considered in version two, version three, and version four where they were included in transportation costs. Table 4–7 shows the data utilized for tariffs.

RESULTS

Versions One and Two
Table 4–8 presents the results of the main cost categories for both versions. These results are accompanied by Table 4–9, which shows

Table 4–7.   Tariffs on Copper Semimanufactures

Countries	Tariff (Percent of Price)	Tariff/Metric ton (Thousand of 1974 US$)
United States	4.5%	.076
Mexico[a]	15	.255
Eastern South America[a]	15	.255
Western South America[a]	15	.255
Western Europe	8	.136
Soviet Union and Eastern Europe[a]	15	.255
Central Africa[a]	15	.255
South Africa[a]	15	.255
Asia (excluding Japan, South Korea, China and North Korea)[a]	15	.255
Japan and South Korea	15	.255
China[a]	15	.255
Australia and New Zealand[a]	15	.255
Canada	7.5	.128

Source: Banks (1974).

[a]For regions that do not have uniform tariffs for all member countries or for centrally planned economies a uniform rate of 15% on price was used. This rate is low compared to those in practice (see Morrison, 1976), but due to lack of more detailed information, it was considered adequate for the model since it protected local industry.

Table 4–8. Results of Versions 1 and 2 Cost Categories
(Millions of U.S. Dollars of 1974)

Period Costs	*Version 1* *(without tariffs)*	*Version 2* *(with tariffs)*
Objective Function =	207140.0	211315.1
Time Period 1		
Investment cost	842.8	843.1
Recurrent cost	7082.5	7083.1
Transport cost	207.4	199.2
Investment cost semis	573.9	444.4
Recurrent cost semis	9759.5	10088.1
Transport cost semis	128.9	349.6
Total Cost	20197.3	20601.2
Time Period 2		
Investment cost	3831.2	3831.2
Recurrent cost	12864.1	12864.1
Transport cost	331.4	318.3
Investment cost semis	1268.2	1125.1
Recurrent cost semis	14502.8	15126.3
Transport cost semis	170.6	417.5
Total Cost	35051.4	35766.0

Source: Based on the author's computations.

the investment activities resulting from each version. In Latin America, investments in mines are scheduled for Peru and Mexico for the first time period and for Peru and Chile for the second time period. Main competing investments in other parts of the world are the western part of the United States for the first time period and Zambia, Zaire, Canada, the Soviet Union, and Eastern Europe for the second time period. Smelters in Latin America are scheduled for Peru, Chile, and Mexico only for the first time period. No new refineries are included in the solution for Latin America because of higher infrastructure costs than in industrialized regions.

The models without tariffs and with tariffs differ for Latin America mainly in the size of semimanufacturing plants to be built. Western South America and eastern South America produce mainly for their regional markets. One wire plant seems optimal for western South America for the first time period for the case with tariffs, but three wire plants have optimal feasibility for the second time period. However, only one plant for tubes and one for sheet are included in the solution for 1990 in western South America. Thus economies of scale seem important for this region.

Eastern South America seems to benefit from tariffs, especially for

Table 4–9.   Investment Activities for Versions 1 and 2
(Thousands of Metric Tons)

| | 1980 | | 1990 | |
Countries	Version 1 (without tariffs)	Version 2 (with tariffs)	Version 1 (without tariffs)	Version 2 (with tariffs)
Peru				
Open Pit Mines	400	400	306	306
Smelters	604	604		
Chile				
Open Pit Mines			1400	1400
Smelters	1323	1323		
Western South America				
Wire Plant 1	—	5.9	16.9	20
Wire Plant 2	—	—	20	11
Wire Plant 3	—	—	20	20
Total	—	5.9	56.9	51
Tubes Plant 1	—	—	—	11.2
Tubes Plant 2	—	—	11.2	—
Tubes Plant 3	—	—	—	—
Total	—	—	11.2	11.2
Sheet Plant 1	—	—	—	—
Sheet Plant 2	—	—	9.2	—
Sheet Plant 3	—	—	—	6.5
Total	—	—	9.2	6.5
Zambia				
Open Pit Mines	—	—	313.2	313.2
Smelters	—	—	240.1	240.1
Zaire				
Open Pit Mines	—	—	1263.4	1263.4
Smelters	—	—	601.1	601.1
Central Africa				
Wire Plant 1	—	17	20	20
Wire Plant 2	—	—	364.3	7
Total	—	17	384.3	27
Tube Plant 1	7.5	7.5	—	—
Tube Plant 2	7.5	—	20	12
Total	15	7.5	20	12
Sheet Plant 1	—	8.1	—	—
Sheet Plant 2	—	—	20.1	12
Total	—	8.1	20.1	12
South Africa				
Open Pit Mines	—	—	11.0	11
Wire	506	746	—	—
Tubes	—	—	—	8
Sheet	24.5	1	2.4	19
Mexico				
Open Pit Mines	571	571	—	—
Smelters	487	487	—	—
Wire	2099	1773	1417	1039
Tubes	—	3.5	—	19
Sheet	—	3.8	—	10

Table 4-9. continued

Countries	1980 Version 1 (without tariffs)	1980 Version 2 (with tariffs)	1990 Version 1 (without tariffs)	1990 Version 2 (with tariffs)
Eastern South America				
Wire	–	81	—	199
Tubes	19	19	47	47
Sheet	—	11	30	26
U.S. West				
Open Pit Mines	728.9	728.9	—	—
Refineries	615.8	615.8	—	—
U.S. East				
Refineries	—	—	392.4	1434.3
United States				
Wire	—	—	—	—
Tubes	192.9	192.9	213.1	213.1
Sheet	175.8	174.9	239.6	240.6
Canada				
Open Pit Mines	75	75	1808.2	1808.2
Smelters	251	251	804.8	804.8
Refineries	269	269	1586.4	1353.2
Wire	—	—	—	—
Tubes	—	—	5	5
Sheet	—	—	—	—
Western Europe				
Smelters	—	—	52.3	52.3
Wire	—	279	—	938
Tubes	13	6.8	339.2	544.9
Sheet	—	—	108.9	216.2
Soviet Union & Eastern Europe				
Open Pit Mines	—	—	2930	2930
Smelters	—	—	948	948
Refineries	—	—	986	1177
Wire	153	153	1241	687
Tubes	70	70	540	318
Sheet	—	44	360	198
Japan & South Korea				
Open Pit Mines	—	—	386	386
Wire	—	—	—	746
Tube	25.6	25.6	137.9	238
Sheet	—	—	74.3	157
China				
Wire	1317	110	1053	292
Tube	—	19.4	190	117
Sheet	—	26.5	140	71
Other Asia				
Wire	405	109	—	158
Tube	—	37.4	90.4	53
Sheet	30	39.7	47.7	38

Source: Based on the author's computations.

wire plants. Investments in wire fabricating plants increase by about 50 percent since tariffs cut imports of such products from South Africa.

Semimanufactures in both western and eastern South America are mainly for the local markets because the U.S. and Canadian markets are served by Mexico, which has a similar cost structure but lower transportation costs. Main investments in semimanufactures in Mexico are in wire plants. It can be seen from Table 4–9 that investments in wire semimanufactures decrease with tariffs by about 15 percent for 1980 and by about 30 percent for 1990. Although not shown here, the reason for this lower level of investment is that South Africa, owing to tariff protection in Western Europe and eastern South America, diverts its shipments of wire to the United States and Canada, thus reducing shipments of Mexican wire to those regions.

Shipment Constraints in the Case with Tariffs (Versions Three and Four)

The versions with shipment constraints were simulated in order to explore the possibilities for western South America and Central Africa, which are important copper exporting regions, to capture a small fraction of foreign markets for semimanufactures. In order to consider a feasible strategy, it was assumed that South America and Central Africa would capture 6 percent of the Asian market (excluding Japan and China) and 3 percent of the rest of the world's market. This section reports only the results for western South America.

Two versions with shipment constraints were considered. Both versions included the same shipment constraints but differed as to the number of semimanufacturing plants to be built. The reason for having two versions was to evaluate the impact of building large plants versus that of building smaller plants. Version three considered three plants for each line of semimanufactures and for each time period. Version four considered for the first time period three plants for wire but only one plant for tubes and one plant for sheet.

The difference in investment costs between the third and the fourth version seemed significant. The total investment cost for three plants for tube semimanufactures with total capacity of 37.4 thousand metric tons for 1980 is 27.7 million U.S. dollars compared to 22.4 million U.S. dollars if only one plant is built as in the fourth version. Similarly, for sheet semimanufactures, the total investment cost for three plants with total capacity of 25.9 thousand metric tons is 32.1 million U.S. dollars compared to 23.1 million U.S. dollars for one equivalent plant. Thus, building one plant for tube semimanufactures costs 19 percent less and for sheet semimanufactures 28 percent less than building three plants for each product, which would add the same manufacturing capacity.

CONCLUSION

This chapter considers a model for determining investments in copper mining, smelting, refining, and semimanufacturing. Although the discussion has focused on Latin America, it has been necessary to take into consideration worldwide supply and demand because of the international character of the copper market.

It can be claimed that the model handles in an intuitively appropriate way the impact of different factors on the copper market. For example, variation in ore grades has a decisive influence on investments in copper mining. At the other end of the process, labor costs in semimanufactures as well as transportation costs seem to determine the location of these activities. In considering economies of scale, the main effects appear to be at the regional level when determining the number of plants per region.

NOTES

1. *Oxford Economic Atlas of the World* (1972: 44).
2. The computer program employed was the APEX III mixed integer programming system (Control Data Corporation).

BIBLIOGRAPHY

Banks, Ferdinand E. 1974. *The World Copper Market: An Economic Analysis.* Cambridge, Mass.: Ballinger Publishing Co.

Bennett, Harold; Lyman Moore; Lawrence Welborn; and Joseph Toland. 1973. *An Economic Appraisal of the Supply of Copper from Primary Domestic Sources.* Bureau of Mines Information Circular. Washington, D.C.: U.S. Department of the Interior.

Control Data Corporation. 1976. *APEX III Reference Manual.* Minneapolis.

Dammert, Alfredo J. 1977. "A World Copper Model for Project Design." Ph.D. Dissertation, University of Texas at Austin.

Engineering and Mining Journal. 1976. *E/MJ Survey of Mine and Plant Expansion.* New York: McGraw-Hill, January.

Fisher, Franklin; Paul Cootner; and Martin Bailey. 1972. "An Econometric Model of the World Copper Industry." *Bell Journal of Economics and Management Science* 3, no. 2 (Autumn): 568–609.

Kendrick, David. 1967. *Planning Investments in the Process Industries.* Cambridge, Mass.: MIT Press.

Kendrick, David, and Ardy Stoutjesdijk. 1975. *The Planning of Industrial Investment Programs: A Methodology.* Washington, D.C.: I.B.R.D., Development Research Center.

Martijena, E. 1966. *Influencia de las Economias de Escala en las Industrias de Transformacion del Cobre y sus Allaciones.* Santiago: C.E.P.A.L.

Metallgesellschaft Aktiengesellschaft. Annual. *Metal Statistics*. Frankfurt am Main.

Morrison, Thomas K. 1976. *Manufactured Exports from Developing Countries*. New York: Praeger.

Oxford Economic Atlas of the World. 1972. Oxford University Press, London.

United Nations Statistical Office. 1964–1972. *World Trade Annual and Supplements*. New York: Walker and Company.

Woods, Donald R. 1975. *Financial Decision Making in the Process Industry*. Englewood Cliffs, N.J.: Prentice-Hall.

5

FREDERICK R.
DEMLER and
JOHN E.
TILTON

Modeling
International Trade
Flows in Mineral
Markets

The trade pattern for refined tin, blister copper, bauxite, or any other mineral commodity can be described by a matrix, such as that shown below. Its elements, T_{ij}, indicate the quantity of the commodity shipped from country i to country j during the period under consideration. Total exports of the ith country (T_i^X) can be calculated from this matrix simply by summing the ith row $(\Sigma_{j=1}^m T_{ij})$, and the total imports of the jth country (T_j^M) by summing the jth column $(\Sigma_{i=1}^n T_{ij})$. Total world trade in the commodity (T) is the sum of all elements $(\Sigma_{i=1}^n \Sigma_{j=1}^m T_{ij})$.

T_{11}	T_{12}	· ·	· T_{1j}	· ·	· T_{1m}	T_1^X
T_{21}	T_{22}	· ·	T_{2j}	· ·	T_{2m}	T_2^X
·	·		·		·	·
·	·		·		·	·
·	·		·		·	·
T_{i1}	T_{i2}	· ·	· T_{ij}	· ·	· T_{im}	T_i^X
·	·		·		·	·
·	·		·		·	·
T_{n1}	T_{n2}	· ·	· T_{nj}	· ·	· T_{nm}	T_n^X
T_1^M	T_2^M		T_j^M		T_m^M	T

This paper is based on research that the Department of Mineral Economics at The Pennsylvania State University is conducting on metal trade patterns under a grant from Resources for the Future, Inc. The authors are a graduate student and professor of mineral economics, respectively. They are grateful to Andre L. Dorr, Barry A. Hillman, and Simon D. Strauss for the information they provided on tin and zinc trade, and to Christopher Rogers for his comments on an earlier version of this study. The research on tin and zinc trade patterns described in subsequent sections was conducted by Demler.

85

The trade patterns described by the above matrix are important. A country's choice of trading partners may facilitate or impede its access to markets if the country is an exporter or to available raw material supplies if it is an importer. Despite this fact, traditional trade literature has paid little attention to trade patterns. Classical, neoclassical, factor endowment, and the more recent theories of trade that take into account the creation and the diffusion of new technology as well as other dynamic variables all concentrate on explaining comparative advantage, that is, why countries are net importers or exporters of various commodities. The question of trade patterns is often bypassed by assuming that the world is composed of only two countries or two regions. Where this is not true, transportation costs and other factors shaping the flow of trade are generally ignored in order to simplify the analysis.

Outside the mainstream of the international trade literature, location theorists have for many years emphasized the importance of transportation costs and stressed the influence that such costs have on both trade patterns and the overall level of exports and imports. Their studies, however, have usually ignored the influence that political blocs, international ownership ties, product differentiation, and other factors besides transportation costs have on trade patterns. Just why this is so is far from clear, for even a cursory look at the structure of trade for many commodities suggests that such factors are important.

Location studies such as the more traditional trade literature generally presume that trade flows are flexible and thus can be easily altered to accommodate new sources of supply, new sources of demand, changes in transportation costs, and shifts in comparative advantage in production. But if other factors, such as political blocs and ownership ties are important, this may not be a valid assumption.

This chapter describes research conducted over the last several years on trade patterns in a number of mineral industries. The next section examines a simple econometric model that has been used to identify the major factors shaping trade flows and to assess the relative importance of these factors. The third section summarizes the principal findings of previous studies that have applied this model to analyze trade patterns in aluminum, bauxite, copper, iron ore, and nickel. The fourth and fifth sections report on the latest application of the model to explain world trade in tin and zinc. The sixth and final section examines the implications of the findings for the resource and trade policies of mineral producing and exporting countries in Latin America and elsewhere.

THE MODEL

In the early 1960s, Tinbergen (1962: appendix VI) and Linnemann (1966) working in the Netherlands and Poyhonen (1963) and Pulliainen (1963) working in Finland developed a model, now known as the structure of trade model, to analyze aggregate trade flows between countries. Their efforts involved the compilation of trade matrices, similar to that described earlier, that encompassed total trade between countries rather than only trade in a single commodity. They then explained trade flows on the basis of export-supply factors in exporting countries, import-demand factors in importing countries, and the resistance to trade between exporting and importing countries as determined by distance and other considerations.

The model used here to analyze trade in mineral commodities is based on these early efforts to explain aggregate trade flows.[1] In its simplest form, it consists of a single relationship whose parameters are estimated by classical least squares regression analysis. The dependent variable (T_{ij}) is the quantity of a mineral commodity shipped between various pairs of importing and exporting countries as reflected in the trade matrix for the commodity. This variable is assumed to be a linear function of: (1) the potential of country i to export the mineral commodity (XP_i), (2) the potential of country j to import the mineral commodity (MP_j), and (3) the resistance to trade between country i and country j (R_{ij}). In equation form this relationship can be expressed:

$$T_{ij} = a_0 + a_1 XP_i + a_2 MP_j + a_3 R_{ij} + e_{ij} \qquad (5-1)$$

where the a's are parameters and e_{ij} is the disturbance term.

The potential of country i to export the mineral commodity is presumed to depend on the country's capacity to produce the commodity (P_i) minus some fraction (b_1) of its capacity to use the commodity (U_i). That is:

$$XP_i = P_i - b_1 U_i \qquad \text{where } 0 \leqslant b_1 \leqslant 1 \qquad (5-2)$$

If government regulations, ownership ties, or other factors dictate that domestic needs for the mineral commodity be satisfied before exports are permitted, b_1 is equal to one. At the other extreme, if domestic consumers have no preferential access to domestic production, the export potential of a country is equal to its production capacity, and b_1

is equal to zero. If some but not total preference is shown domestic consumers, b_1 will be positive but less than one. The value of b_1 can be determined on the basis of a priori information or it can be estimated by the model itself.

Since the jth country imports the mineral commodity, its capacity to use the commodity (U_j) is likely to exceed its capacity to produce the commodity (P_j). In this case, its potential to import can be estimated by the expression

$$MP_j = U_j - b_2 P_j \qquad \text{where } 0 \leqslant b_2 \leqslant 1 \tag{5-3}$$

The parameter b_2 should equal one if domestic consumers for one reason or another buy from foreign producers only after domestic production is exhausted. Alternatively, if domestic producers must compete equally with foreign producers for the domestic market, b_2 is zero. If some but not total preference is given to domestic producers, b_2 will be positive but less than one. Like b_1, this parameter can be determined by a priori information or it can be estimated by the model.

A number of factors may increase or decrease the resistance to trade between countries. In this regard, the distance between two countries (D_{ij}) has already been mentioned. Since transportation costs tend to rise with distance, this variable should inhibit trade. Alternatively, membership in the same political bloc (B_{ij}), such as the British Commonwealth, the French Community, or the European Economic Community, would be expected to stimulate trade between the two countries. Similarly, when multinational corporations based in the importing country own production facilities in the exporting country, ownership ties (O_{ij}) may promote trade.

There is also some evidence that, if two countries are neighbors (N_{ij}) in the sense of sharing a common border, their trade tends to be larger than expected even after taking into account the short distance between them. Among the possible reasons for this is the fact that businessmen are more likely to be familiar with the language, customs, business traditions, and consequently the commercial opportunities available in neighboring countries than in more distant states.

Another factor that may stimulate trade between two countries is product differentiation (S_{ij}). Mineral ores and concentrates, for example, may contain difficult impurities or valuable by-products that only certain smelters can remove. An interesting example is found in copper concentrate trade. The Philippines, which ships most of its output to Japan for smelting, has for years sent a significant quantity of concentrates to the United States despite high transportation costs. This unusual trade flow arose and has continued simply because Tacoma,

Washington, has one of the few smelters in the world that can treat the high arsenic copper ores found in the Philippines. Similarly, there are differences in the nature and composition of bauxite ores. Alumina refineries are designed to handle a particular type of bauxite and can be modified only at some expense to handle other types of ores.

Finally, in some applications of the trade model long-term contracts (L_{ij}) covering the sale of the mineral commodity from country i to country j are considered. Whether long-term contracts should be included in the model depends on the nature of the questions being addressed. If one is primarily interested in determining the extent to which trade flows are flexible, and thus can be quickly and easily altered to accommodate new sources of supply or demand, the effects of long-term contracts ought to be taken into account. Alternatively, if the primary objective is to identify the fundamental factors shaping trade and to appraise their relative importance, long-term contracts should not be included, for they are for the most part merely the result or consequence of more basic determinants of trade patterns.

The preceding identifies all of the factors that have been explicitly incorporated into the trade model to date. In new applications, other variables may be important, and the model can easily be modified to take account of the effects of these variables as well.

If one includes all of the above variables and assumes that the influences of these variables are independent and additive, resistance to trade (R_{ij}) between any two trading partners can be measured.

$$R_{ij} = c_1\,D_{ij} + c_2\,B_{ij} + c_3\,O_{ij} + c_4\,N_{ij} \qquad (5\text{--}4)$$
$$+ c_5\,S_{ij} + c_6\,L_{ij}$$

Substituting Equations 5–2, 5–3, and 5–4 into Equation 5–1 gives the following relationship, which can be estimated.

$$T_{ij} = d_0 + d_1(P_i - b_1\,U_i) + d_2(U_j - b_2\,P_j) + d_3\,D_{ij} \qquad (5\text{--}5)$$
$$+ d_4\,B_{ij} + d_5\,O_{ij} + d_6\,N_{ij} + d_7\,S_{ij} + d_8\,L_{ij} + e_{ij}$$

In this equation dummy variables must be used for B_{ij}, N_{ij}, and S_{ij}, which take the value of one when countries i and j belong to the same political bloc, are neighbors, or have special ties due to product differentiation, and which take the value of zero otherwise.[2] However, the effect on trade of these variables is likely to vary depending on the maximum trade possible (M_{ij}) between the two countries. One would expect, for example, that common membership in the British Commonwealth should stimulate imports into Britain from a large exporting country more than from a small exporting country.

For this reason, it is more appropriate to use slope dummy variables, rather than level dummy variables, as shown in the following modification of Equation 5–5

$$T_{ij} = d_0 + d_1(P_i - b_1\,U_i) + d_2(U_j - b_2\,P_j) \qquad (5\text{--}6)$$
$$+\, d_3\,D_{ij} + d_4\,B_{ij}\,M_{ij} + d_5\,O_{ij} + d_6\,N_{ij}\,M_{ij}$$
$$+\, d_7\,S_{ij}\,M_{ij} + d_8\,L_{ij} + e_{ij}$$

Here the maximum possible trade (M_{ij}) between country i and country j can be estimated by the export potential of country i or the import potential of country j, whichever is smaller. That is,

$$M_{ij} = XP_i, \text{ if } XP_i \leqslant MP_j$$
$$= MP_j, \text{ if } XP_i \geqslant MP_j$$

Equation 5–6 measures only the direct effects of the various independent variables on trade flows although these variables may also have important indirect effects. For example, the incidence of ownership ties between two countries may be influenced by the distance that separates them. This appears to have been the case in bauxite, at least in the 1950's when North American producers built bauxite facilities in a number of Caribbean and South American countries while the major European producers invested in mines in Europe and Africa. In this case, distance in addition to its direct effect on trade also appears to have influenced trade indirectly through ownership ties.

The basic model given in Equation 5–6 can be modified in two ways to assess the indirect effects of independent variables. First, in the case just cited, the equation could be rerun without the ownership tie variable. The new coefficients obtained for distance and any other independent variable thought to influence ownership ties could then be compared with those obtained when the ownership tie variable is included in the model. Second, the model can be enlarged in a recursive manner. A second equation could be introduced to explain the incidence of ownership ties between country i and country j as a function of the distance between the two countries and other factors. Similarly, equations could be included in the model to explain other independent variables, such as the exporting country's production capacity, the importing country's capacity to use the mineral product, and long-term contracts.

The trade model described in this section does have certain limitations that should be noted. In particular, it assumes that the relationship between trade flows and the various determinants of these flows is linear. If this is not the case, the model suffers from specification error. Much of the work noted earlier on aggregate trade flows assumes a multiplicative rather than linear relationship. In some respects a multiplicative relationship is appealing, because if either the export potential of country i or the import potential of country j is zero, trade between the two countries should be zero as the multiplicative relationship would dictate. However, the latter also requires that trade between two countries be zero when resistance to trade is zero, which is not what one would expect. Moreover, when the structure of trade model is applied to individual commodities, trade flows between some pairs of importing and exporting countries can be zero, and they usually are. Since the logarithm of zero is undefined, when this is the case, the parameters of a multiplicative relationship cannot be estimated by a linear transformation of this relationship. This complicates the estimation procedure. Thus, in the absence of strong a priori reasons favoring the multiplicative relationship, the linear relationship was chosen for practical considerations. In making this decision, however, the analysis presumes that such a relationship is a close approximation to the true relationship over the range of variable values considered.

A second shortcoming is that the model can produce results that are internally inconsistent in the sense that the expected trade flows predicted by the model when summed may exceed the export or import potential of certain countries. In addition, expected trade flows may in some cases be negative. Such inconsistencies are particularly disconcerting if the model is to be used to project individual trade flows. They are less of a problem when the objective is to appraise the importance of various factors influencing trade patterns.

It should also be noted that the model is in a sense a reduced form model. Ideally, in analyzing trade flows one would like a model that encompasses separate supply and demand models for each country and then integrates these models by taking into account shipping costs, political blocs, ownership ties, neighboring country effects, and other relevant considerations. The difficulty with this approach, however, is that it requires accurate information on production costs and prices by country for the commodity being analyzed. This information is always difficult and frequently impossible to obtain. In the simpler model used here this information is not needed for the effects of production costs and prices on trade patterns are taken into account by the export potential and import potential variables. As a result, this model is far easier to apply.

APPLICATIONS

In recent years, the model described in the previous section, or a variation of it, has been used to investigate international trade in aluminum (Dorr, 1975; Tilton and Dorr, 1975), copper (Whitney, 1976), iron ore (Santos, 1976), and nickel (Hubbard, 1975). These studies examine trade at fixed time intervals over the postwar period, and with the exception of the study on iron ore, at various stages of processing.[3] A comparison of these findings provides some insights into the important factors shaping international trade patterns and how these factors vary from one mineral commodity to another, by stage of processing, and over time.

Table 5–1 identifies the independent variables considered by these studies for various mineral commodities for the years 1955 and 1972. It also denotes the variables found to be significant determinants of trade patterns with an 'S' and those found to be insignificant with an 'T'. The omission of a variable from a model, indicated by a blank in the table, generally implies that it is irrelevant to the analysis. For example, for some commodities none of the major importers and exporters are neighbors or belong to the same political bloc.

All of these studies find that ownership ties, and the multinational resource companies that are largely responsible for international ownership ties, greatly influence trade flows at least at one stage of production. However, there has been some decline over time in the importance of ownership ties for certain mineral commodities, particularly refined copper. The reasons for this are not hard to identify. First, in copper and iron ore as well, a number of important facilities have been nationalized over the last decade. There have also been instances of nationalization in the aluminum and nickel industries, but such incidents have been fewer and less important. Second, the nature of financing new mineral ventures has evolved in a way that has loosened the ties of ownership on trade. In the early postwar period, multinational resource companies typically owned completely the foreign operations they developed and managed. In the 1960s this began to change as many firms turned increasingly to project financing. Joint ventures became more prevalent, and debt capital was used more heavily. Long-term contracts were arranged to assure a market for the output of new projects, and at times the collection rights to these contracts were pledged or sold to raise funds. Third, Japan, a country that has relied more on long-term contracts and less on ownership ties than the United States and Western European countries to assure access to raw material supplies, has become increasingly important in mineral trade. Despite these developments, however, ownership ties remain a

Table 5-1. Results of Recent Studies Concerning the Determinants of Trade Patterns

Commodity	Export Potential		Import Potential		Distance		Ownership Ties		Political Blocs		Neighboring Countries		Long-Term Contracts	
	1955	1972	1955	1972	1955	1972	1955	1972	1955	1972	1955	1972	1955	1972
Bauxite	I[a]	I[a]	I[a]	I[a]	I[a]	I	I[a]	S	S					S
Alumina[b]	I[a]	I[a]	I	I	I	I[a]	S	S						S
Aluminum	S	S	I[a]	S	I	S	I	I	S[c]	S[c]	S	S		
Copper Concentrate[d]	I	I	I	I	S	S	I	I			I	I		
Blister Copper[d]	S	S	S	S	I[a]	I	S	S	S[e]	S[e]				
Refined Copper	I	S	S	S	I	I	S	I	S[f]	S[g]	S	S		
Iron Ore[h]	S	S	I[a]	S	I[i]	S	S	S			S	S		S
Refined Nickel	I[a]	I[a]				S			S[j]	S[j]	S[k]	S[k]		

Sources: Dorr (1975); Hubbard (1975); Santos (1976); and Whitney (1976).

"S" indicates that the variable is statistically significant at the 95 percent probability level (using a one-tailed t-test), "I" indicates that it is insignificant. A blank means that the variable was not included in the model. In most such cases, the variable was not a relevant factor affecting trade patterns for that commodity.

[a]This is a significant variable in the modified model that includes only export potential, import potential, and distance, which suggests that this variable may have an indirect influence on trade patterns by affecting ownership ties and other independent variables not included in the modified model.

[b]The information shown for alumina under 1955 is for 1960. Very little trade in alumina took place before 1960.

[c]The variable for the British Commonwealth is significant, whereas that for the European Economic Community is not.

[d]The information shown for copper concentrate and blister under 1955 is for 1960. Models for copper concentrates and blister were not estimated for 1955.

[e]The variable for Belgium and Zaire is significant, whereas those for the British Commonwealth and the European Economic Community are not.

[f]The variable for the British Commonwealth is significant, whereas that for Belgium and Zaire is not.

[g]The variables for the British Commonwealth and the ties between Belgium and Zaire are significant, whereas the European Economic Community is not.

[h]The information shown for iron ore under 1972 is actually for 1973.

[i]This variable is, however, significant at the 90 percent probability level.

[j]The variables for the British Commonwealth and the French Community are both significant for 1972. They are insignificant in 1955 at the customary 95 percent probability level, but are significant at the 90 percent probability level.

[k]In the refined nickel model the neighboring country effect was restricted to trade between the United States and Canada.

potent force shaping the structure of mineral trade. Indeed, in bauxite and alumina trade this variable is by far the dominant factor affecting trade flows, and there is little to suggest that its importance is waning over time.

Multinational resource companies are generally vertically integrated from mining through refining. Many of these companies are also active in fabrication, but at this stage of production they compete with many independent and nonintegrated producers. Since the sales of refined metal to the latter are not likely to be dictated by ownership ties, one would expect to find the influence of ownership ties on trade of less importance at the refined stage than at earlier stages of production. While this is the case for aluminum and nickel, copper is an exception. The copper concentrate that enters international trade is primarily produced by nonintegrated producers and thus is little affected by ownership ties.

The importance of ownership ties also varies with the mineral commodity. In aluminum and steel, where most of the value added in production comes in processing rather than in mining, the major firms in the industrialized countries have established subsidiaries abroad to insure an adequate supply of ore for their domestic processing plants. Consequently, ownership ties are a particularly important determinant of trade flows in these industries at early stages of processing. In the two other industries where mining accounts for a much larger share of the total value added, ownership ties are instrumental in shaping trade flows for unprocessed nickel and blister copper, but not, as just noted, for copper concentrates.

Political blocs have also been identified as important determinants of the structure of mineral trade. Unlike ownership ties, however, they have little or no influence on trade in ores and concentrate. Instead, their impact is largely on trade in refined products. The reason for this, presumably, is the fact that most mineral importing countries impose few, if any, barriers to trade on ores and concentrates. This is not the case for refined products.

Interestingly, the political blocs found to be important are all based on former colonial empires, such as the British Commonwealth, the French Community, and Belgium's ties with Zaire, the former Belgium Congo. In contrast, no significant increase in mineral trade has been detected among member states of the European Economic Community. Since the colonial empires on which the significant political blocs were built have been dismantled over the last twenty years, one would expect the influence of these blocs on trade to have diminished. The studies that have been done, however, find very little evidence of this.

In all of the refined mineral products examined, political blocs were important in the early postwar period and remain important today. Apparently, once strong commercial ties are established in mineral markets, they tend to perpetuate themselves for many years.

Only the studies analyzing iron ore, bauxite, and alumina trade explicitly include long-term contracts in their trade models. In all three of these cases, long-term contracts were of negligible importance during the 1950s. However, during the 1960s long-term contracts became more common, and thus by the 1970s such arrangements constituted a significant determinant of trade patterns. To some extent this development occurred because of the growth of Japan's imports of mineral commodities, particularly unprocessed minerals. As already noted, this country has opted to satisfy its raw material requirements through long-term contracts rather than develop its own subsidiaries abroad. In addition, as project financing and other developments have reduced the role of ownership ties elsewhere, long-term contracts have grown in importance as a means of assuring producers a market and consumers an adequate supply of mineral resources.

Sharing a common border has also been found to stimulate trade significantly among neighboring countries, particularly in refined metals, but in iron ore as well. Since fabricators tend to be smaller and more numerous than firms engaged in smelting and refining, they are more likely to concentrate on domestic markets and those in neighboring countries for their raw material supplies. For this reason, presumably, the neighboring country effect is a significant factor in aluminum, refined copper, and refined nickel trade, whereas it apparently has little influence on trade patterns in bauxite, alumina, copper concentrate, and blister copper. Moreover, despite the great improvements in international communications that have occurred over the postwar period, there is little indication that the effect of this variable on trade in refined commodities is abating.

Little can be said yet about the importance of special ties arising from product differentiation, for the studies that have been completed to date have not included this variable in their trade equation. In some instances, such as those noted earlier concerning the high arsenic, copper concentrate mined in the Philippines and the various types of bauxite, these studies have tried to assess the importance of such special ties qualitatively. However, the first attempt to introduce this factor explicitly into the trade equation is described in the next section.

The last variable that the previous section identifies as an influence on the resistance to trade between countries is distance. One would expect distance to have a greater impact on the trade patterns of ores and concentrates than of refined metals since transport costs constitute a larger percentage of the total value of the former. The copper study provides some support for this hypothesis, but the aluminum study does not. Moreover, while distance is a significant factor influencing trade flows in iron ore, the same is also true for refined nickel. For similar reasons, distance should be a more important determinant of trade patterns of mineral commodities with a relatively low value. On this basis, one would expect to find distance more influential in copper and aluminum trade than nickel trade, but this is not the case. The impact of distance can also be seen as declining, because of the sharp fall in transportation costs. This cost decrease is a consequence of increases in vessal size and technological advances in vessals as well as in supporting infrastructure and overland transportation. But here again the evidence is far from clear and consistent.

Part of the problem lies in the fact that distance, although a statistically significant factor in many instances, is simply not a major determinant of mineral trade patterns compared to ownership ties and other factors. The same is also true, perhaps more surprisingly, for export and import potential. All of the studies employing the trade model of the previous section estimate a modified version of Equation 5–6 that includes only the export potential, import potential, and distance variables. The results are compared with those obtained when ownership ties, political blocs, the neighboring country effect, and long-term contracts are included in Equation 5–6. In few cases does the modified model account for or explain more than 30 percent of the variation in trade flows among the major importing and exporting countries, even though this specification of the model considers both the direct and indirect effects of these three variables on trade flows. In contrast, the full equation often explains over 80 percent of the variation in trade flows, and only for copper concentrate trade does this figure fall below 60 percent.

Thus, the studies that have been conducted on mineral trade patterns to date consistently find that these patterns cannot be adequately explained simply on the basis of export potential, import potential, and distance alone. The other factors that shape trade flows may vary from one mineral commodity to another, by stage of processing, and over time, but as a group they have a major impact on the direction of trade of all the mineral commodities examined. Moreover, these factors— ownership ties, political blocs, neighboring country effects, and long-term contracts—all introduce a degree of stability and rigidity in mineral trade patterns, and so may make it more difficult for new importers or new exporters to break into the market.

INTERNATIONAL TRADE IN TIN

Tin is an unusual metallic commodity in several respects. Though underground mining is important in certain areas, such as Bolivia, most tin is recovered from alluvial deposits. For this and other reasons, tin-producing firms are far more numerous and generally much smaller than the firms found in other metal industries. Consequently, the multinational resource companies are much less important in this industry, and the incidence of international ownership ties is less widespread.

These aspects of the tin industry raise the possibility that a different set of factors govern trade patterns in this industry. To determine if this is the case, the trade model described above has recently been employed to analyze trade flows in tin. The results of this investigation, which have not been reported elsewhere, are discussed in this section. Since tin enters international trade in the form of concentrates and refined metal, the pattern of trade is examined at each of these stages of production.

Tin Concentrate Trade

Trade matrices indicating the average annual quantity of tin concentrate trade over three-year periods centered on 1955, 1965, and 1975 are shown in Table 5–2. These matrices identify the trade flows between the major exporting and importing countries outside the Communist bloc. Trade among the Communist countries is excluded since it presumably is shaped by a different set of forces. Trade flows between minor exporting and importing states, which in Table 5–2 are aggregated under the category of "other," are also excluded from the analysis since their contribution to tin trade is small.

In the tin concentrate model, trade between the major exporting and importing countries (T_{ij}) as shown in Table 5–2 is assumed to depend on the following variables:

1. The export potential of country i (XP_i). Because it is difficult to obtain reliable information on the mine capacities of tin-exporting countries, this variable is estimated by the largest annual quantity of tin concentrate exports from country i over the preceding five years measured in thousands of metric tons of contained tin.[4]

2. The import potential of country j (MP_j). For similar reasons, this variable is estimated by the largest annual volume of tin concentrate imports into country j over the preceding five years measured in thousands of metric tons of contained tin.[5]

3. The ocean distance between country i and country j (D_{ij}) in

Table 5–2. Trade in Tin Concentrates (Thousands of Metric Tons of Contained Metal)

1955

	United Kingdom	United States	Malaysia	Benelux	Netherlands	Germany	Other[a]
Indonesia	16.50	5.53			26.75	0.53	0.68
Bolivia	0.40	10.10					
Zaire		0.60					0.30
Thailand		1.80	9.92	10.50			0.40
Nigeria	8.50						
Other[a]	0.91	0.15	0.81			0.03	2.01

1965

	United Kingdom	United States	Malaysia	Benelux	Netherlands	Germany	Other[a]
Indonesia	16.57	6.29	15.10		17.20		
Bolivia	0.16				0.63	1.56	
Zaire				3.10	0.47		
Australia	0.53		0.55		0.40		0.57
Other[a]	1.54	0.07	0.59	1.43	4.30		0.14

1975

	United Kingdom	United States	Malaysia	Benelux	Spain	Germany	Other[a]
Indonesia	7.27	7.00	7.70		0.50		
Bolivia				0.15	1.46	2.20	1.36
Zaire				2.79	1.00		
Rwanda				1.12			
Australia	0.72		3.57		0.94		0.13
Burma			2.40	0.16	0.03		0.21
Republic of South Africa	0.72			0.03	0.28		
Other[a]	0.95	0.40	0.60		0.60		3.00

Sources: International Tin Council (various years); *Metal Statistics* (various years).

[a]Figures reported for "other" countries are estimates.

thousands of nautical miles, as reported by the U.S. Naval Oceanographic Office (1965).

4. A dummy variable (S_{ij}) to take account of the unusual nature of Bolivian ore. Compared with tin mined in the rest of the world, which comes mostly from alluvial deposits and so is relatively clean, Bolivian ore is difficult to refine. This is both because it contains impurities that require complex metallurgical processes to remove and because it contains valuable by-products that must be separated from the ore in a way that permits their economic recovery. Outside of Bolivia, only a few refineries that can process this country's ore exist. These facilities are found in the United States, the United Kingdom, and the Netherlands. To capture this constraint on Bolivian tin concentrate trade, S_{ij} takes the value of one if country i is Bolivia and if country j possesses a tin refinery capable of processing Bolivian concentrates. Otherwise, it is zero.

Since the stimulating effect of this variable on trade when it is equal to one will depend on the maximum amount of trade (M_{ij}) possible between countries i and j, S_{ij} is multiplied by M_{ij}. The latter is assumed to equal XP_i or MP_j, whichever is smaller.

5. A dummy variable for the neighboring country effect (N_{ij}), which assumes the value of one if country i and country j share a common border and zero otherwise. This variable is also multiplied by the maximum amount of trade (M_{ij}) possible between two countries.

6. Three dummy variables for political blocs. The first $(B1_{ij})$ takes the value of one for trade flows between Benelux and Zaire; the second $(B2_{ij})$ for trade flows between the United Kingdom and members, or former members, of the British Commonwealth; and the third $(B3_{ij})$ for trade flows between the Netherlands and Indonesia. These variables are all multiplied by the maximum amount of trade possible (M_{ij}) between the exporting and importing countries.

7. A dummy variable for ownership ties (O_{ij}) that takes the value of one when an appreciable portion (30 percent or more) of the tin mine capacity in country i is owned by interests in country j.[6] Again, this variable is multiplied by the maximum amount of trade (M_{ij}) possible between two countries.

The coefficients for the tin concentrate equation are shown in Table 5–3 for both the full model and a modified model that includes as independent variables only the export potential of country i, the import potential of country j, and distance between countries. This table also indicates the coefficient of determination (R^2) and the number of observations (n) for each equation.

The modified model is estimated for two reasons. First, by comparing the coefficients of the export potential, import potential, and dis-

Table 5–3. Results of the Tin Concentrate Model

	Constant	D_{ij}	XP_i	MP_j	$S_{ij}M_{ij}$	$N_{ij}M_{ij}$	$B1_{ij}M_{ij}$	$B2_{ij}M_{ij}$	$B3_{ij}M_{ij}$	$O_{ij}M_{ij}$	R^2	n
1975	1.370[a]	−0.216[a]	0.059[a]	0.076	0.559[a]	0.625[a]	0.568[a]	0.169	⋯	0.017	0.91	42
	(0.454)	(0.049)	(0.019)	(0.026)	(0.057)	(0.081)	(0.162)	(0.507)		(0.495)		
	2.176[a]	−0.408[a]	0.157[a]	0.039							0.52	42
	(0.912)	(0.095)	(0.035)	(0.053)								
1965	2.701	−0.305	0.019	−0.033	0.318[a]	0.653[a]	⋯	0.234	0.212	0.425	0.78	24
	(2.627)	(0.291)	(0.056)	(0.091)	(0.112)	(0.225)		(1.56)	(0.684)	(0.658)		
	1.453	−0.616[a]	0.153[a]	0.191[a]							0.38	24
	(3.235)	(0.337)	(0.066)	(0.107)								
1955	2.511	−0.343	0.016	−0.013	0.308[a]	0.083	0.476	0.136	0.670[a]	0.252	0.79	30
	(1.678)	(0.213)	(0.053)	(0.054)	(0.074)	(0.252)	(0.291)	(0.256)	(0.212)	(0.187)		
	−0.801	−0.421	0.155[a]	0.163[a]							0.17	30
	(2.652)	(0.320)	(0.082)	(0.080)								

Source: Based on the authors' computations.
[a]Significant at the 95 percent probability level, one-tailed test.

tance variables obtained for this model with those for the full model, one can assess the magnitude of the indirect effects that these variables have on the structure of tin concentrate trade through ownership ties, political blocs, and other independent variables found only in the full model. Second, by subtracting the coefficient of determination (R^2) for the full equation from that for the modified equation, one can appraise the marginal contribution of the neighboring country effect, political blocs, ownership ties, and the differentiated nature of Bolivian concentrates in explaining the trade flows shown in Table 5–2.

The results found in Table 5–3 indicate that the percentage of variation in trade flows that can be accounted for by export potential, import potential, and distance alone has increased from 17 percent in 1955 to 52 percent in 1975. Over the same period, the additional explanation of trade flows obtained by taking into account the differentiated nature of Bolivian ore, the neighboring country effect, political blocs, and ownership ties has fallen from 62 to 39 percent. Even though the combined effect of these latter variables has declined over the last twenty years, they still retain a substantial influence over the pattern of tin concentrate trade.

Looking at the coefficients for the individual variables affecting resistance to trade between countries, one finds that all of these coefficients have the expected sign, though some are not significantly different from zero at the 95 percent probability level. This is the case, for example, for the coefficients of the ownership tie variable and the political bloc variable for the British Commonwealth. The variable reflecting political ties between the Netherlands and Indonesia is significant only in 1955, and that for Benelux and Zaire only in 1975. In contrast, the differentiated nature of Bolivian ore is significant over the entire period, and the neighboring country effect from 1965 on. The coefficient for distance tends to fall in absolute value over the period, suggesting that the inhibiting effect of this variable on trade may be declining; however, the coefficient is significant only in 1975.

When these findings are compared with those of earlier studies on bauxite, copper concentrate, unprocessed nickel, and iron ore, political blocs appear more important and ownership ties less important in shaping trade in tin concentrate than is the case for the other mineral commodities, with the one exception of copper concentrates where ownership ties are unimportant. In addition, except for iron ore, the earlier studies do not find the neighboring country effect to be an important determinant of trade flows. Since firms producing tin concentrate tend to be smaller than their counterparts in other metal industries, it would not be surprising if they sold most of their output in nearby markets. Moreover, this variable, which helps explain the relatively large exports of Thai and Indonesian tin concentrates to Malaysia, may also be picking up the effects of product differentiation because the tin mined in Thailand and Indonesia, like that in Malaysia, comes from alluvial deposits and hence can be easily processed in the Malaysian refineries. This coupled with the importance of the variable reflecting the unusual nature of Bolivian tin suggests that the effects of product differentiation are more important for trade in tin concentrates than for most other mineral commodities.

Refined Tin Trade

Trade matrices showing the average annual quantity of refined tin trade over three-year periods centered on 1955, 1965, and 1975 are found in Table 5–4. These matrices, like those in Table 5–2 for tin concentrates, identify the trade flows between the major exporting and importing countries outside the Communist bloc.

The refined tin model assumes that trade between these countries (T_{ij}) as shown in Table 5–4 depends on many of the same variables found in the tin concentrate model:

1. The export potential of country i (XP_i), as indicated by that country's largest annual volume of refined tin exports over the preceding five years measured in thousands of metric tons.[7]

2. The import potential of country j (MP_j), as indicated by that country's largest annual volume of refined tin imports over the preceding five years again measured in thousands of metric tons.[8]

3. The ocean distance between country i and country j (D_{ij}) in thousands of nautical miles, as reported by the U.S. Naval Oceanographic Office (1965).

4. The dummy variable for the neighboring country effect (N_{ij}), multiplied by the maximum amount of refined tin trade possible (M_{ij}) between country i and country j. Again, M_{ij} is assumed to be equal to XP_i or MP_j, whichever is smaller.

5. The three dummy variables for political blocs. The first ($B1_{ij}$) covers the special ties between Benelux and Zaire; the second ($B2_{ij}$) the special ties between the United Kingdom and other members, or former members, of the British Commonwealth; and the third ($B3_{ij}$) the special ties between the Netherlands and Indonesia. All of these variables are multiplied by the maximum amount of trade possible (M_{ij}) between countries.

6. The dummy variable for ownership ties (O_{ij}), which takes the value of one when an appreciable portion (30 percent or more) of the refinery capacity in country i is controlled by interests in country j, and the value of zero otherwise.[9] This variable, like the other dummy variables, is multiplied by the maximum amount of trade possible (M_{ij}) between countries.

In addition to the preceding variables, which are all included in the tin concentrate model, the refined tin model contains:

7. A dummy variable $(B4_{ij})$ that takes the value of one when country i and country j are both members of the European Economic Community, and zero otherwise. This variable is also multiplied by the maximum amount of trade possible (M_{ij}) between countries.

8. A dummy variable (P_{ij}) to reflect the strong apparent preference of tin users in the United States for Malaysian tin. This variable takes the value of one when country j is Malaysia and country i the United States, and it is zero in all other instances. It too is multiplied by the maximum amount of trade possible (M_{ij}) between countries.

In competing for Malaysian tin, which has a reputation for high quality, the United States does not appear to have any particular advantage over other importing countries. It simply is willing to pay the price necessary in the competitive Straits tin market to acquire a large share of the output of Malaysian tin. Consequently, the special trading tie that the American preference for Malaysian tin has created between the two countries does not appear to have made it more difficult for other buyers or sellers to enter this market. Other countries that so desire can go into the market and bid Malaysian tin away from the United States if they are willing to pay the price. For this reason, three sets of results for the refined tin model are shown in Table 5–5. The first is for the full model; the second is for a modified model that excludes only the dummy variable (P_{ij}) reflecting the preference of the United States for Malaysian tin; and the third is for a modified model that excludes all the independent variables except the export potential of country i, the import potential of country j, and the distance between countries.

The results indicate that export potential, import potential, and distance alone can explain between 40 and 46 percent of the variation in trade flows of refined tin, which is a higher percentage than found for aluminum, refined copper, and refined nickel. Table 5–4 also indicates clearly the importance of the American preference for Malaysian tin. This variable by itself increases the ability of the model to explain trade in refined tin by 53 percent in 1955, 42 percent in 1965, and 31 percent in 1975. In sharp contrast to the findings for other refined metals, however, ownership ties, political blocs, and the neighboring country effect collectively have little effect on the structure of refined tin trade. In no instance does the addition of these variables appreciably improve the ability of the model to explain trade flows. Moreover, rarely are the coefficients for these variables significant, and in many instances they have the wrong sign.

These findings suggest that the international market for refined tin, unlike the market for tin concentrate and the other refined and

Table 5–4. Trade in Refined Tin (Thousands of Metric Tons)

1955

	United States	Japan	United Kingdom	France	Germany	Italy	Netherlands	Benelux	Other[a]
Malaysia	42.87	4.81	3.36	2.82	0.54	2.35	2.06	0.22	11.80
United Kingdom	4.56			0.05	0.13	0.87	0.43	1.68	2.70
Netherlands	7.27	0.04	0.17	5.00	2.95	0.03		0.02	4.00
Belgium	6.10		0.46	1.15	0.69	0.03	0.19		1.33
Indonesia	0.75	0.60		0.09	3.63				0.28
Zaire	0.38							2.06	0.09
United States			0.19		0.03				0.65
Other[a]	0.40	0.05	0.02	0.01		0.60	0.03	0.01	3.40

1965

	United States	Japan	United Kingdom	France	Germany	Italy	Netherlands	Benelux	Other[a]
Malaysia	28.26	14.70	2.68	3.13	1.68	3.98	2.37	0.89	11.70
United Kingdom	1.16			0.90	1.12		0.44		1.20
Netherlands	0.53		0.61	2.20	7.24	1.11		0.17	1.80
Benelux	0.10		0.15	1.84	1.15	0.03	0.74	0.89	0.07
Thailand	5.90		0.15	1.51	1.10	0.10	0.60		0.40

	United States	Japan	United Kingdom	France	Germany	Italy	Netherlands	Benelux	Other[a]
Nigeria	1.41		7.50	0.23	0.80		1.28		0.45
United States			0.03		0.08		0.20	0.11	
Bolivia	0.53				0.10				
Indonesia	0.16	0.04		0.65	0.15	0.01		0.01	
Other[a]	0.09	0.02	0.06	0.09	1.40	0.10	0.05	0.60	1.20

1975

	United States	Japan	United Kingdom	France	Germany	Italy	Netherlands	Benelux	Other[a]
Malaysia	25.06	15.80	1.45	4.73	2.44	4.69	0.72	1.46	11.60
United Kingdom	0.86			0.93	1.32	0.08	1.01	0.15	0.62
Thailand	6.77	5.68			3.71	0.50	0.64		
Indonesia	4.53			1.80	4.03	0.75	1.78		0.40
Bolivia	1.10			0.35	0.50				2.00
United States							1.80		
Nigeria	0.20		0.09	0.17	0.07		0.53		0.80
Brazil	1.04		2.50		0.69		0.025		
Australia	0.26	0.07	1.05						0.30
Netherlands	0.07		1.20		0.30	0.22		0.21	2.50
Benelux				0.73	0.65	0.07	0.24		1.20
Other[a]	3.70			1.09	0.41		0.95	0.67	2.50

Sources: International Tin Council (various years); *Metal Statistics* (various years).

[a]Figures for "other" countries are estimates.

Table 5-5. Results of the Refined Tin Model

	Constant	D_{ij}	XP_i	MP_j	$N_{ij}M_{ij}$	$B1_{ij}M_{ij}$	$B2_{ij}M_{ij}$	$B3_{ij}M_{ij}$	$B4_{ij}M_{ij}$	$O_{ij}M_{ij}$	$P_{ij}M_{ij}$	R^2	n
1975	0.222 (0.586)	-0.121 (0.075)	0.063* (0.010)	0.042* (0.015)	-0.102 (0.283)		-0.913 (0.288)	-0.053 (0.199)	-0.046 (0.145)	-0.021 (0.200)	0.399* (0.041)	0.77	84
	-0.742 (0.867)	-0.107 (0.112)	0.096* (0.014)	0.083* (0.022)	-0.066 (0.425)		-0.213 (0.433)	-0.051 (0.299)	0.035 (0.218)	-0.046 (0.300)		0.46	84
	-0.716 (0.609)	-0.118 (0.086)	0.093* (0.013)	0.085* (0.021)								0.46	84
1965	0.322 (0.504)	-0.137* (0.070)	0.053* (0.010)	0.018 (0.016)			-0.108 (0.202)	0.565 (1.339)	0.185 (0.080)	0.426* (0.149)	0.497* (0.040)	0.84	68
	-0.929 (0.938)	-0.127 (0.132)	0.094* (0.018)	0.080* (0.029)			-0.573 (0.384)	1.135 (2.539)	0.156 (0.151)	0.234 (0.281)		0.42	68
	-0.605 (0.833)	-0.163 (0.117)	0.096* (0.017)	0.085* (0.028)								0.40	68
1955	-0.294 (0.340)	-0.120* (0.055)	0.031* (0.007)	0.051* (0.009)		0.521 (0.332)	0.237 (0.281)	0.132 (0.449)		[a]	0.521* (0.021)	0.95	52
	-1.564 (1.239)	-0.089 (0.206)	0.094* (0.027)	0.144* (0.033)		0.790 (1.242)	-0.576 (1.046)	0.469 (1.680)		[a]		0.43	52
	-1.430 (1.201)	-0.081 (0.197)	0.089* (0.025)	0.143* (0.032)								0.42	52

Source: Based on the authors' computations.

* Significant at the 95 percent probability level, one-tailed test.

[a] In 1955 perfect multicollinearity existed between $O_{ij}M_{ij}$ and the sum of $B1_{ij}M_{ij}$ and $B2_{ij}M_{ij}$. For this reason, $O_{ij}M_{ij}$ was excluded from the model. The variables $B1_{ij}M_{ij}$ and $B2_{ij}M_{ij}$ thus reflect the influence of ownership ties as well as political blocs on trade.

unrefined metals examined, may approximate the type of free market often assumed in the traditional trade literature. Here, apparently, political blocs, ownership ties, product differentiation, and the neighboring country effect do not strongly mold the structure of trade or create rigidities in trade flows that inhibit new producers and new consumers trying to enter the market. The preference of the United States for Malaysian tin does affect the pattern of trade, but the manner in which this preference is exercised, through the competitive Straits tin market, suggests that it can constrain the flow of tin trade only so long as the United States is willing to outbid other importing countries for this source of supply.

INTERNATIONAL TRADE IN ZINC

Zinc is an important metal. In recent years its volume of output has been exceeded only by iron and steel, aluminum, and copper. It is also widely traded. Over fifty countries produce zinc concentrate, and over thirty possess smelter capacity for refining zinc. Asarco, Texasgulf Sulfur, Rio Tinto, Mitsui, and other multinational firms play an important role in the production and trade of zinc. The significance of such international ownership ties and other variables in shaping zinc trade patterns is assessed in this section with a model similar to that used for tin. Since zinc enters international trade in both concentrate and refined metal forms, separate models are specified for each of these stages of production.

Zinc Concentrate Trade

Trade matrices showing the average annual trade over three-year periods centered on 1965 and 1975 are shown in Table 5–6.[10] These matrices, like those for tin, identify the trade flows between the major exporting and importing countries outside the Communist bloc. Trade involving the minor exporting or importing states is reported under the category of "other." Major exporting countries include Canada, Peru, Australia, Sweden, and Mexico. The major importing countries are Japan, Benelux, Germany, France, and the United States.

In the zinc concentrate model, trade between the major exporting and importing countries (T_{ij}) shown in Table 5–6 is assumed to depend on the following variables:

1. The export potential of country i (XP_i). Mine capacities for zinc-exporting countries are difficult to obtain, so therefore this variable is estimated by the largest annual quantity of zinc concentrate exports from country i during the preceding five years measured in thousands of metric tons of contained zinc.[11]

Table 5-6. Trade in Zinc Concentrates (Thousands of Metric Tons Contained Metal)

					1975					
	Japan	Benelux	Germany	France	Netherland	United States	United Kingdom	Norway	Italy	Others[a]
Canada	335.3	352.0	255.1	102.3	69.1	99.8	13.4	3.2	71.2	102.1
Peru	300.5	9.8	22.3	111.4	20.9	5.9	56.1		48.3	16.1
Australia	205.7	31.2	7.7	9.3	122.1	3.6	29.7	7.8		24.1
Sweden		42.6	69.2	33.4	6.3			52.1		19.6
Mexico	24.1	25.2	39.7	3.8	7.5	10.7			15.1	6.5
Republic of South Africa		4.4	66.3							21.2
Iran	19.5	4.7	5.3	7.1	1.0		7.2			12.7
Greenland		6.0	22.3		6.1	0.3			13.1	6.5
Ireland		20.9	39.1	42.5	2.9	0.3	13.2		9.1	12.1
Bolivia	23.1	0.1	5.4	8.4		0.6				3.2
United States	17.1	18.5	15.1	0.1	3.9		3.7	3.3	5.3	4.5
Netherlands		32.1					2.9			1.2
Others[a]	125.1	67.6	48.4	44.2	47.1	21.1	1.6	6.4	31.4	140.1

1965

	Japan	Benelux	Germany	France	Netherlands	United States	United Kingdom	Norway	Others[a]
Canada	32.6	231.6	34.6	58.2	9.1	221.4	9.3	9.0	85.1
Peru	186.6	3.8	10.7	42.6	2.6	65.1		1.3	18.6
Australia	35.3	12.1	4.6	1.6	0.8	3.1	184.0	14.0	21.7
Sweden		41.3	38.6	15.1	.9		0.5	47.3	9.4
Mexico	39.2	3.4		3.8		100.6			32.5
Republic of South Africa	2.8	7.1		1.3		9.1	16.0		5.6
Iran	5.0	9.3	6.4	11.1	13.6		18.0		5.2
France		71.6	12.1	13.2	0.9				7.6
Morocco		1.3		70.5		3.8			7.9
Zaire		76.6	6.4	13.1	12.6		4.0		15.1
Germany		9.1		5.2		7.2	5.0		7.2
Italy		5.6	3.6	11.1	0.6				20.1
Algeria		3.0		34.6		1.7		0.7	2.1
Others[a]	72.1	23.7	27.4	66.9	5.4	19.5	23.4	16.0	130.2

Sources: *Metal Statistics* (various years); U.S. Bureau of Mines (various years); Great Britain, Overseas Geological Surveys (various years).
[a]Figures reported for "other" countries are estimates.

2. The import potential of country j (MP_j). For similar reasons, this variable is estimated by the largest annual volume of zinc concentrate imports into country j over the preceding five years measured in thousands of metric tons of contained zinc.[12]

3. The ocean distance between country i and country j (D_{ij}) in thousands of nautical miles, as reported by the U.S. Naval Oceanographic Office (1965).

4. A dummy variable (S_{ij}) to take account of the unusual nature of the lead-zinc bulk concentrates produced by certain mines in Canada and Australia. The imperial furnace is the only smelter suitable for treating such ores. Importing countries with imperial smelters include the United Kingdom, France, Germany, Italy, and Japan. To capture this constraint on zinc concentrate trade, S_{ij} takes the value of one if country i is Canada or Australia and if country j possesses an imperial smelter. Otherwise, it is zero. This variable is then multiplied by the maximum amount of zinc concentrate trade possible (M_{ij}) between country i and country j, where M_{ij} is assumed to equal XP_i or MP_j, whichever is smaller.

5. A dummy variable for the neighboring country effect (N_{ij}) that takes the value of one if country i and country j share a common border, and zero otherwise. This variable is also multiplied by the maximum amount of trade (M_{ij}) possible between the two countries.

6. Four dummy variables for political blocs. The first $(B1_{ij})$ takes the value of one for trade flows between Benelux and Zaire; the second $(B2_{ij})$ for trade flows between the United Kingdom and members or former members of the British Commonwealth; the third $(B3_{ij})$ for trade flows between France and the French Community (Morocco and Algeria); and the fourth $(B4_{ij})$ for trade flows between members of the European Economic Community. All these variables are multiplied by the maximum amount of trade possible (M_{ij}) between countries.

7. A dummy variable for ownership ties (O_{ij}) that takes the value of one when an appreciable portion (25 percent or more) of the zinc mine capacity in country i is owned by interests in country j.[13] Again, this variable is multiplied by the maximum amount of trade possible (M_{ij}) between countries.

The coefficients for the zinc concentrate model are shown in Table 5–7 for both the full model and a modified model that includes as independent variables only export potential, import potential, and distance. This table also shows the coefficient of determination (R^2) and the number of observations (n) for each equation.

The results indicate that the percentage variation of trade flows accounted for by export potential, import potential, and distance only increased from 27 percent in 1965 to 51 percent in 1975. The differ-

Table 5–7. Results of the Zinc Concentrate Model

	Constant	D_{ij}	XP_i	MP_j	$S_{ij}M_{ij}$	$N_{ij}M_{ij}$	$B1_{ij}M_{ij}$	$B2_{ij}M_{ij}$	$B3_{ij}M_{ij}$	$B4_{ij}M_{ij}$	$O_{ij}M_{ij}$	R^2	n
1975	−7.486 (9.445)	−4.629* (1.440)	0.106* (0.019)	0.057* (0.013)	0.137* (0.035)	−0.113 (0.176)		−0.326 (0.191)		−0.311 (0.508)	0.290* (0.605)	0.63	106
	−22.989* (9.408)	−4.423* (1.479)	0.158* (0.017)	0.028* (0.013)								0.51	106
1965	−10.912 (7.897)	−1.0692 (0.909)	0.080* (0.024)	0.049* (0.018)	0.001 (0.047)	0.136* (0.080)	0.186 (0.251)	0.113 (0.081)	0.338 (0.306)	−0.094 (0.277)	0.325* (0.051)	0.63	103
	−19.300* (9.824)	−1.452 (1.128)	0.145* (0.027)	0.073* (0.023)								0.27	103

Source: Based on the authors' computations.

*Significant at the 95 percent probability level, one-tailed test.

entiated nature of zinc ores, neighboring country effect, political blocs, and ownership ties explained an additional 36 percent in 1965, but only an additional 12 percent in 1975 of trade flow variation. The combined effect of all the independent variables has remained constant at 63 percent over the ten-year period.

The results for individual variables show that the coefficients for export potential and import potential have the right signs and are significantly different from zero. The distance variable also has the correct sign, but it is significant only in the 1975 trade equation.

In both periods the coefficient for ownership ties is positive and highly significant. The coefficient of the differentiated nature of zinc concentrates is positive in both years, though only significant in 1975. In contrast, the results provide little evidence that political blocs greatly influence the flow of zinc concentrate trade. The coefficients for these variables are not significant, and in some cases they have the wrong sign. The final variable considered by the model is the neighboring country effect. Its coefficient is positive, as expected, and significantly different from zero in 1965, but it turns negative and insignificant in 1975.

The results suggest that ownership ties, the differentiated nature of ores (in 1975), and the neighboring country effect (in 1965) are important forces shaping the flow of trade in zinc concentrates. These findings are consistent with many of the earlier studies on metal trade patterns that found that ownership ties have a substantial impact on trade patterns for ores and concentrates.

According to the coefficients of determination, the full model explains nearly two-thirds of the variation in trade flows for both time periods examined. What remains unexplained is due to variables not explicitly taken into account in the model. One such factor is the extensive use of long-term contracts between certain trading countries. Substantial quantities of zinc concentrates, for example, are shipped from Canada and Australia to Japan under such contracts, and the same is true for Canadian concentrates destined for Belgium. Since the model does not include a variable for long-term contracts, it anticipates far less trade between these three sets of trading partners than actually takes place.

Another factor whose influence is not fully captured by the model is the differentiated nature of zinc ores. In addition to the preference to use the Imperial furnace for processing lead-zinc bulk concentrates (which the model does consider), there are certain processing facilities that require high-quality ores. In particular, the electrolytic smelter must use higher quality ores than other smelters. Because data on the quality of ore coming from different mines is unavailable, this aspect of the differentiated nature of zinc ores cannot be explicitly taken into account by the model.

Refined Zinc Trade

Trade matrices for refined zinc trade are shown in Table 5–8 that indicate the average annual volume of trade between the major exporting and importing countries outside the Communist bloc over three-year periods centered on 1955, 1965, and 1975. The United States, the United Kingdom, Germany, France, and Sweden are among the most important importing countries, whereas Canada, Benelux, Australia, Mexico, and Peru are among the most important exporting countries.

The model used to analyze trade patterns for refined zinc contains the following independent variables:

1. The export potential of country i (XP_i), estimated by the largest annual volume of refined zinc exports from country i over the preceding five years measured in thousands of metric tons.[14]

2. The import potential of country j (MP_j) estimated by the largest annual volume of refined zinc imports into country j over the preceding five years measured in thousands of metric tons.[14]

3. The ocean distance between country i and country j (D_{ij}) in thousands of nautical miles, as reported by the U.S. Naval Oceanographic Office (1965).

4. A dummy variable for the neighboring country effect (N_{ij}) multiplied by the maximum amount of refined zinc trade possible (M_{ij}) between importing country j and exporting country i, where M_{ij} is again assumed equal to the smaller of XP_i or MP_j.

5. Three dummy variables for political blocs. The first $(B1_{ij})$ represents the special ties between Belgium and Zaire; the second $(B2_{ij})$ the special ties between the United Kingdom and members or former members of the British Commonwealth; and the third $(B3_{ij})$ the special ties between members of the European Economic Community. These variables are multiplied by (M_{ij}), the maximum amount of trade possible between countries.

6. An ownership tie variable (O_{ij}) that equals the amount of smelter capacity in country i controlled (at least 50 percent ownership) by firms in country j.

In addition to the full model, which includes all of the preceding variables, a modified model containing only the first three variables was estimated. The results are shown in Table 5–9, and they indicate that export potential, import potential, and distance have had a declining influence on trade, accounting for 40 percent of the variation in trade patterns in 1955, 36 percent in 1965, and 33 percent in 1975. The coefficients for the export potential and import potential variables

Table 5–8.   Trade in Refined Zinc (Thousands of Metric Tons)

1975

	United States	United Kingdom	Germany	France	Sweden	Netherland	Italy	Brazil	Benelux	Other[a]
Canada	234.5	42.6	3.4	0.6	0.1	0.4	0.2	2.0	1.6	10.1
Benelux	23.2	13.2	71.0	32.2	1.1	11.0	11.3	5.0		31.1
Australia	28.6	12.1	0.3			0.5		0.1	2.3	2.8
Mexico	31.2	8.4	1.6	3.5	0.6	0.6	3.0	7.1	9.3	14.4
Peru	21.2	0.2	0.6	0.2		0.4	3.2	11.6	1.9	12.0
Zaire	19.4		1.0	0.2	0.2				5.6	1.9
Germany	25.1	9.3		10.1	0.1	17.2	12.2	0.7	1.7	5.6
Netherlands	7.2	52.0	17.2	9.3	1.2		0.4	0.1	6.4	4.1
Finland	18.7	32.3	3.4	0.7	13.2	0.2	1.6			2.9
Japan	20.0	0.9	0.8		0.1	0.1	0.5	1.0	1.4	5.9
Other[a]	55.4	23.1	21.1	8.6	18.0	4.4	9.6	7.1	9.2	129.7

1965

	United States	United Kingdom	Germany	France	Sweden	India	Italy	Brazil	Other[a]
Canada	84.3	95.5	5.5	0.8		14.1	5.0	1.1	17.1
Benelux	11.1	7.5	57.8	9.6	2.4	0.3	5.9	2.8	30.2
Australia	8.6	23.3	2.1		0.2	0.3	4.4	13.3	36.5
Mexico	14.3	0.5			1.1		0.1	6.1	6.9
Peru	14.6	6.8	3.6	0.4	0.6	0.3	2.0	13.3	12.1
Zaire	10.2	4.6	10.7				1.6		8.1
Germany	6.1	1.5		1.0	0.1	0.3	8.1	0.4	2.1
Netherlands	0.1	0.8	15.4	6.3	0.3	0.1	0.7	0.4	4.0
Other[a]	14.1	39.3	24.1	7.1	15.2	15.6	2.0	9.1	62.1

	United States	United Kingdom	Germany	France	Sweden	India	Other[a]
Canada	101.4	74.3	0.2	0.1		3.3	6.5
Benelux	18.3	14.6	29.1	26.2	7.2	1.1	4.1
Australia	4.3	11.2				16.7	2.1
Mexico	13.7	14.5	0.2	0.2	2.5	0.7	12.1
Peru	7.0	1.7	0.6				4.5
Zaire	14.3	8.2					3.1
Germany	6.7	3.8		5.1	0.2		9.1
Norway	0.4	1.1	9.1	10.1	9.4		2.2
United States		14.6	6.4	0.1	5.6	0.1	4.1
Other[a]	15.1	5.4	16.1	1.5	2.1	3.5	30.1

Sources: *Metal Statistics* (various years); *Mineral Yearbooks* (various years); Great Britain, Overseas Geological Surveys (various years).

[a]Figures reported for "other" countries are estimates.

Table 5-9. Results of the Refined Zinc Model

	Constant	D_{ij}	XP_i	MP_j	$N_{ij}M_{ij}$	$B1_{ij}M_{ij}$	$B2_{ij}M_{ij}$	$B3_{ij}M_{ij}$	O_{ij}	R^2	n
1975	-4.385 (3.420)	-0.046 (0.385)	0.028* (0.016)	0.039* (0.008)	0.488* (0.051)	0.050 (0.372)	0.077* (0.046)	0.007 (0.045)	0.198* (0.111)	.85	87
	-2.757 (6.267)	-1.430* (0.697)	0.091* (0.031)	0.072* (0.014)						0.33	87
1965	-2.386 (1.585)	0.186 (0.196)	0.022* (0.007)	0.029* (0.008)	0.412* (0.023)		0.389* (0.020)	0.072* (0.037)	0.001 (0.021)	0.95	63
	-4.775 (4.864)	-0.658 (0.619)	0.098* (0.024)	0.090* (0.025)						0.36	63
1955	-1.517 (2.460)	-0.037 (0.296)	0.025* (0.015)	0.042* (0.013)	0.437* (0.030)		0.388* (0.037)		a	0.91	52
	-4.241 (6.076)	-0.768 (0.724)	0.127* (0.034)	0.098* (0.031)						0.40	52

Source: Based on the authors' computations.

*Significant at the 95 percent probability level, one-tailed test.

aThe ownership tie variable was excluded from the 1955 full model because its inclusion produced implausible results.

have the correct sign and are significant at the 95 percent probability level in both models. The coefficient for the distance variable also has the correct sign (except in the 1965 full model), but it is significant only in 1975.

The results for the full model reveal that the other independent variables can explain an additional 51 to 59 percent of the variation in trade patterns. The neighboring country effect and the British Commonwealth political bloc are particularly important determinants of refined zinc trade. The coefficients for these variables have the correct sign and are significant for all of the years examined. Ownership ties, the special ties between Zaire and Belgium, and the European Economic Community appear to have less influence on refined zinc trade. With the exception of ownership ties in 1975 and the European Economic Community in 1965, these variables are insignificant.

Overall the results for zinc correspond more closely to the findings of earlier studies of metal trade patterns than those for tin. Ownership ties are particularly important in shaping trade flows of concentrates, whereas at the refined metal stage certain political blocs and the neighboring country effect are far more significant. The latter variables appear to introduce rigidities in the patterns for refined zinc trade that one does not find for refined tin. However, at the concentrate level, zinc and tin are similar in one respect; that is, trade in both of these commodities is significantly influenced by the differentiated nature of their ores.

IMPLICATIONS FOR LATIN AMERICA'S TRADE AND RESOURCE POLICIES

Mining and mineral processing are important sources of foreign exchange and government revenues for a number of Latin American countries. For this and other reasons, public involvement in the mineral sector has been growing over time. In this regard the last twenty-five years have witnessed two particularly important developments in Latin America as well as elsewhere. The first is the increasing incidence of public ownership in the mineral sector. Far less frequently are projects completely owned and controlled by the multinational resource companies today than was the case in the 1950s. Indeed, many countries now insist that the government hold a major interest in domestic mining ventures, and in some countries governments have assumed total control. The second major development involves the aspirations and efforts of many Latin American countries to increase the amount of mineral processing done domestically.

While such efforts may enhance the benefits producing countries realize from their mineral wealth, they may create problems as well. Countries that reduce or completely sever international ownership ties may lose the preferential access to certain markets that the multinational resource companies can provide. Countries that upgrade their domestic processing operations so that they export refined rather than unrefined mineral commodities may find a large portion of the market they are trying to enter foreclosed by political blocs, ownership ties, and other considerations unless they are willing to accept less for their products than other countries.

The models described in this chapter and the studies of mineral trade patterns based on this model suggest that ownership ties, political blocs, product differentiation, the neighboring country effect, and long-term contracts are often as important, or perhaps even more important, in shaping trade flows than the variables (export potential, import potential, and distance) usually considered in analyzing trade problems. While there are exceptions to this finding, as refined tin trade illustrates, they appear to be few.

This does not necessarily mean that governments should stop pursuing efforts to increase national control over domestic mining operations or to promote downstream processing, but it does suggest the need to consider carefully the impact that such actions may have on a country's access to markets. This, in turn, requires an understanding of the nature of trade patterns and the various factors that faciliate or constrain trade flows. The model described in this chapter is designed specifically for this purpose and can be useful in this endeavor.

NOTES

1. Structure of trade models have rarely been used to analyze trade in individual commodities. Tilton (1966) and Margueron (1966) are the only previous attempts of which we are aware to apply this type of model to individual mineral commodities.

2. Dummy variables may also be used for O_{ij} and L_{ij} if the available data for these two variables do not allow precise quantification.

3. In nickel, a model of trade was estimated only for the refined metal. Trade flows in semiprocessed nickel, which includes ore, matte, concentrates, and nickel oxide, are few in number and easily assessed qualitatively.

4. The sources for this information are the same as those for Table 5–2.

5. The sources for this information are the same as those for Table 5–2.

6. Information on ownership ties was obtained from Engineering and Mining Journal (1975); *World Mines Register 76/77* (1976); U.S. Bureau of Mines (annual); U.S. Department of Commerce (1953); Schanz (1954); Tilton (1966); and discussions with corporate officials.

7. The sources for this information are those cited in Table 5–4.

8. The sources for this information are those cited in Table 5–4.

9. The sources for ownership ties are the same as those noted earlier for tin concentrates.

10. Data are not available to construct a trade matrix for 1955.

11. The sources of this information are given in Table 5–6.

12. The sources of this information are given in Table 5–6.

13. Information on ownership ties was obtained from Engineering and Mining Journal (1975); *World Mines Register 76/77* (1976); U.S. Bureau of Mines (annual); Tilton (1966); and discussions with corporate and government officials.

14. The sources for this information are given in Table 5–8.

BIBLIOGRAPHY

Dorr, Andre L. 1975. "International Trade in the Primary Aluminum Industry." Ph.D. dissertation, Pennsylvania State University.

Engineering and Mining Journal. 1975. *International Directory of Mining and Mineral Processing Operations.* New York: McGraw-Hill.

Great Britain, Overseas Geological Surveys, Mineral Resources Division. Annual. *Statistical Summary of the Mineral Industry: World Production, Exports and Imports.* London: Her Majesty's Stationery Office.

Hubbard, David A. 1975. "Nickel in International Trade," M.S. thesis, Pennsylvania State University.

International Tin Council. Annual. *Statistical Year Book.* London: International Tin Council.

Linnemann, Hans. 1966. *An Econometric Study of International Trade Flows.* Amsterdam: North Holland Publishing Co.

Margueron, Claudio. 1966. "A Quantitative Analysis of the Supply-Demand Patterns in Iron Ore: The Future Possibilities of Brazil." Ph.D. dissertation, Columbia University.

Metal Statistics. Annual. Frankfurt am Main: Metallgesellschaft Aktiengesellschaft.

Poyhonen, Pentti. 1963. "A Tentative Model for the Volume of Trade Between Countries." *Weltwirtschaftlickes Archiv* XC: 93–100.

Pulliainen, Kyosti. 1963. "A World Trade Study: An Econometric Model of the Pattern of the Commodity Flows in International Trade in 1948–1960." *Ekonomiska Samfundets Tidskrift* 2:78–91.

Santos, Teodoro M. 1976. "International Trade in Iron Ore: An Econometric Analysis of the Determinants of Trade Patterns and Comparative Advantage." Ph.D. dissertation, Pennsylvania State University.

Schanz, John J., Jr. 1954. "The United States and a Post War Tin Control Agreement." Ph.D. dissertation, Pennsylvania State University.

Tilton, John E. 1966. "The Choice of Trading Partners: An Analysis of International Trade in Aluminum, Bauxite, Copper, Lead, Manganese, Tin, and Zinc." Ph.D. dissertation, Yale University. This dissertation minus appendixes was published under the same title in *Yale Economic Essays* (Fall): 416–74.

Tilton, John E., and Andre L. Dorr. 1975. "An Econometric Model of Metal Trade Patterns." In William A. Vogely, ed., *Mineral Materials Modeling: A State-of-the-Art Review*. Washington, D.C.: Resources for the Future.

Tinbergen, Jan. 1962. *Shaping the World Economy*. New York: Twentieth Century Fund.

U.S. Bureau of Mines. Annual. *Minerals Yearbook*. Washington, D.C.: U.S.G.P.O.

U.S. Department of Commerce, National Production Authority. 1953. *Materials Survey: Tin*. Washington, D.C.: U.S.G.P.O.

U.S. Naval Oceanographic Office. 1965. *Distances Between Ports*. Washington, D.C.: U.S.G.P.O.

Whitney, John W. 1976. "An Analysis of Copper Production, Processing, and Trade Patterns, 1950–1972." Ph.D. dissertation, Pennsylvania State University.

World Mines Register 76/77. New York: 1976. Miller Freeman Publications.

6

GORDON
GEMMILL

An Equilibrium Policy Model of the World Sugar Economy

This chapter reports on the specification, estimation, and use of a spatial equilibrium model of the world sugar economy. The research differs from previous work on such models in two ways. First, special attention has been given to econometrically estimating individual supply relations for each of the major countries of the world, since it was hypothesized that supply-response was the major influence in determining market behavior. Second, the model has been designed specifically to test the effects of alternative trade policies. Thus, tariffs, quotas, variable levies, and export taxes were included as policy instruments that could be applied by any chosen country and the repercussions observed in terms of price and quantity in that country and elsewhere. The work really extended an earlier model of Bates (1965), increasing the disaggregation from thirty-two to seventy-five regions and incorporating many policy instruments that he did not include. This approach may be contrasted with the aggregate econometric models of Tewes (1972) and of Adams and Behrman (1976), which illuminate more of the temporal aspects of the market but are less informative about the spatial effects of alternative policies.

Stated formally, the objectives of the research were:

1. To estimate sugar supply and demand functions for the major producing and consuming regions of the world.
2. To construct a model, using these functions, with which to ascertain the effects of alternative national and international sugar policies.

Originally it had been intended to solve the model for a series of years, but problems of computation arose. Consequently the results relate to the equilibrium that would have occurred in 1974 if producers had been able to adjust completely to their desired levels of output. This will be called a "long-run" equilibrium although, as will become apparent, some cane sugar producing countries are in fact still "trapped" in this equilibrium by the fixity of assets committed in previous periods.

This chapter is necessarily brief and only the main features of the model and results are given. A fuller presentation may be seen elsewhere (Gemmill, 1976). Although the research was primarily directed to U.S. policy, the implications for the Central and South American countries, which together produced 31 percent of the world's sugar in 1974, will be emphasized throughout.

The remainder of this introductory section outlines the features of the sugar market relevant to the model. The following section gives the structural relations of the model and very briefly reviews the supply and demand estimates that were incorporated. The third section is concerned with the results from the model and their welfare implications (in terms of producers' and consumers' surplus and government revenue). The fourth section concentrates on policy implications for Latin American countries. In the final section concluding comments are offered.

Features of the Sugar Market Relevant to the Model

In building a model, one seeks out the minimum degree of disaggregation necessary to satisfy the objective of the research. Why was it necessary to identify seventy-five regions in this model instead of disaggregating it into only two regions, say the developed and developing regions? The first response to this question is that sugar production and consumption are not concentrated in a few countries but are widely distributed worldwide. Table 6–1 gives five-year averages for production, consumption, and trade. It shows that Western Europe, Eastern Europe, Central America, South America, and Asia were all about equal producers of sugar in 1972–1976. The really large producers were the European Economic Community (EEC), Soviet Union, Brazil, Cuba, and the United States, in that order. Regarding consumption, the rank order is the Soviet Union, European Economic Community, United States, Brazil, China, and Japan. Trade in sugar flows from the surplus regions of Central America, South America, and Oceania to North America, Asia, and Europe.

Wide distribution alone does not justify a disaggregated model. The

Table 6–1. Average Production, Exports, Imports, and
Consumption of Centrifugal Sugar (tonnes, raw value) in
Major Countries of the World, 1972–1976

Countries	*Five-Year Average, 1972–76*[a]			
	Production	*Exports*	*Imports*	*Consumption*
Western Europe	13,031,370	1,680,864	3,571,665	14,692,107
EEC	10,189,220	1,506,671	2,184,403	10,716,217
Other W. Europe	2,842,150	1,174,193	1,387,262	3,975,890
Eastern Europe	13,646,518	726,234	3,840,643	16,525,244
G.D.R.	592,280	118,926	246,263	718,100
Poland	1,776,797	271,693	31,433	1,573,875
U.S.S.R.	8,907,200	73,236	2,681,511	11,300,800
Other E. Europe	2,370,241	262,380	881,436	2,932,469
North America	4,722,389	120,814	5,536,159	11,034,256
Canada	125,013	52,133	980,318	1,050,639
United States	4,597,376	67,681	4,555,841	9,983,617
Central America	11,938,787	7,817,232	35,072	4,021,962
Cuba	5,714,876	5,187,109	0	497,605
Dominican Republic	1,207,572	1,047,994	0	164,163
Jamaica	367,864	270,153	2,306	100,441
Mexico	2,733,753	377,522	0	2,390,117
Other C. America	1,914,722	934,456	32,766	869,656
South America	11,661,357	3,574,768	261,252	8,324,094
Argentina	1,474,609	353,722	0	1,038,625
Brazil	6,710,730	2,179,495	0	4,609,807
Colombia	886,545	154,409	0	736,244
Peru	936,564	411,191	0	518,537
Venezuela	522,540	39,967	50,857	512,290
Other S. America	1,130,369	435,984	210,395	908,591
Asia	15,546,977	3,315,088	6,330,616	18,241,008
China	3,670,000	96,854	552,759	4,070,000
China-Taiwan	805,253	482,921	0	295,621
India	4,452,815	562,456	0	3,880,580
Japan	561,783	37,906	2,622,149	3,171,399
Philippines	2,500,704	1,374,487	0	836,805
Thailand	1,099,926	614,918	0	492,302
Other Asia	2,456,496	145,546	3,155,708	5,494,301
Africa	5,357,013	2,114,404	1,841,723	4,953,612
Mauritius	690,578	634,530	23	36,787
South Africa	2,023,173	891,169	23,898	1,145,551
Other Africa	2,643,262	588,705	1,817,802	3,771,274
Oceania	4,234,755	2,441,750	198,972	1,023,452
Australia	2,942,952	2,172,727	0	759,353
Fiji	302,377	268,783	152	28,321
Hawaii	989,426	0[b]	0	34,578
Other Oceania	0	0	198,820	201,200
World Total	80,139,164	21,791,154	21,616,104	78,815,756

Source: raw data from International Sugar Organization (1977).

[a]Horizontal totals do not sum, due to the omission of changes in stocks.

[b]All exports to mainland U.S.A.

second reason for such disaggregation is the political nature of trade in sugar. Almost all exporting nations control the size of the sugar sector by quotas on individual mills or farmers. Almost all importing nations have quotas or tariffs on the entry of sugar that protect their own domestic sugar industries. The research attempts to show the effects of changes in the policies of different nations which should be separately identified in the model. It is not sufficient to identify only a few nations in this context because the trade in sugar has been characterized by international arrangements that tie together different groups of countries. Table 6–2 gives a breakdown of the sugar trade in 1973 under different arrangements: roughly 50 percent in the free market, 20 percent under the U.S. Sugar Act, 14 percent under special Cuba-Communist nation arrangement, and 8 percent under the Commonwealth Sugar Agreement. To find out who might gain and who might lose from a rearrangement of policy and trade means that interested countries have to be identified in the model but grouped for special trade arrangements.

The politicization of trade in sugar may have arisen as a response to fluctuations in its traded price. Sugar is among the most volatilely priced commodities by any measure (House of Lords, 1977). On the other hand, only about 25 percent of the sugar produced is traded, and the unstable international price is partly the consequence of policies designed to give domestic price stability. The seventy-five regions of the model are listed in Table 6–3. Each region has its own demand function and many have their own supply function. The type of supply function estimated for a particular region is also given in Table 6–3.

THE MODEL, POLICIES, AND SUPPLY-DEMAND ESTIMATES

The Model

The model is one of spatial equilibrium. It assumes that the difference in the price of sugar between any two countries is equal to the transportation cost per unit plus the price effect of any trade restrictions that exist between the two. Figure 6–1 demonstrates the equilibrium that would arise in a two-country world in which transportation costs are zero but where there is a fixed tariff of $FTAR_j$ in country j. The tariff lowers the exporter's price to P_i^T and raises the importer's price to P_j^T from the free market equilibrium of P_j^E. Trade is reduced by the tariff from a free market equilibrium of q_E to q_T. The tariff raises a revenue of $\pi\epsilon\lambda\rho$ of which $\sigma\mu\lambda\rho$ is extracted from the exporting nation's producers and $\pi\epsilon\mu\sigma$ from the importing nation's consumers.

The structure of the model is as follows. Let there be m producing

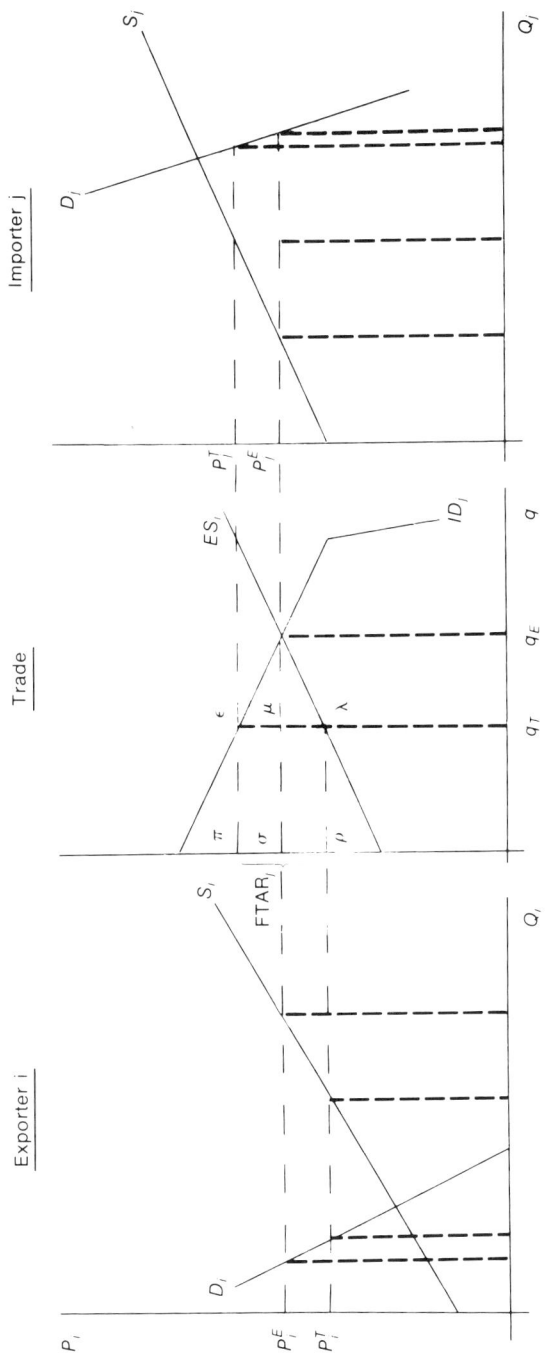

FIGURE 6–1. Two-Country Equilibrium with Tariff *FTAR_j*

125

and n consuming regions, subscript i always denoting a producing region and subscript j a consuming region.

Let $Q_j^p =$ the quantity of raw sugar demanded in the jth region;
$Q_i^s =$ the quantity of raw sugar supplied by the ith region;
$P_j =$ the wholesale price of raw sugar in the jth region;
$q_{ij} =$ shipment of raw sugar from region i to region j;
$G_{ij} =$ cost of shipment, including trade barriers, from region i to region j.

The interrelations between these variables are described in equations 6–1 to 6–8:

Demand relations for each consuming region:

$$Q_j^p = Q_j^p \ (P_j), j = 1, 2, \ldots, n \tag{6–1}$$

Supply relations for each producing region:[1]

$$Q_i^s = Q_i^s \ (P_i), i = 1, 2, \ldots, m \tag{6–2}$$

Total quantity demanded in equilibrium equals the sum of all shipments:

$$Q_j^p = \sum_i q_{ij}, j = 1, 2, \ldots, n \tag{6–3}$$

Total quantity supplied in equilibrium equals the sum of all shipments:

$$Q_i^s = \sum_j q_{ij}, i = 1, 2, \ldots, m \tag{6–4}$$

Shipments are non-negative:

$$q_{ij} \geqslant 0 \quad i = 1, 2, \ldots, m \tag{6–5}$$
$$j = 1, 2, \ldots, n$$

At equilibrium the prices in any two regions cannot differ by more than transfer cost per unit:

$$P_j - G_{ij} - P_i \leqslant 0, \quad i = 1, 2, \ldots, m \tag{6–6}$$
$$j = 1, 2, \ldots, n$$

At equilibrium the sum of transfer expenditures is exactly balanced

Table 6–2. International Trade in Sugar by Type of Market in 1973

Type of Market	Exporter	Importer	Per 000 Metric Tons	Percent of World Exports	Price in Cents Per Pound
Under U.S. Sugar Act	Philippines	U.S.A.	1,319		
	Dominican Republic		676		
	Brazil		591		(Duty-paid
	Mexico		577		in New York)
	Others		1,672		
Total			4,835	21.8	10.29
Under Commonwealth Sugar Agreement (Negotiated Price Quota)	W. Indies & Guyana	U.K.	736		(f.o.b. in
	Mauritius		386		Caribbean)
	Australia		340		
	Others		308		
Total			1,770	8.0	5.36[a]
Under Bilateral Cuban Agreements	Cuba	U.S.S.R.	1,661		
		China	302		(f.o.b. in
		E. Germany	259		Cuba)
		Bulgaria	213		
		Others	561		
Total			2,996	13.5	6.0–11.0

Free Market Exports	Brazil	2,530		
	Cuba	1,774		
	Australia	1,497		
	EEC	1,468		
	South Africa	824		
	China-Taiwan	428		
	Poland	422		
	Dominican Republic	396		
	Argentina	396		
	Others	1,930		(f.o.b. in Caribbean)
Total		11,665	52.7	9.61
Free Market Imports	Japan	2,395		
	U.S.S.R.	1,016		
	Canada	952		
	Iraq	474		
	Yugoslavia	368		
	Malaysia	331		
	Indonesia	307		
	Iran	302		
	Others	5,658		(f.o.b. in Caribbean)
Total		11,803	53.2	9.61
Gross Exports in all markets		22,145	100.0	
Net Exports in all markets		19,208		
Domestically consumed		55,950		
World Production		78,095		

Source: International Sugar Organization (1977).

aPlus a bonus of 1.18 cents per pound for West Indies and Guyana and 0.75 cents per pound to other "less developed" suppliers.

Table 6–3. Regions and Types of Supply Functions in the Model

Continent	Region	Type of Supply Function				
		Log-Linear	Asymmetric	Time Only	Point	None
Europe	Austria	✓				
	Belgium				✓	
	Czechoslovakia	✓				
	Denmark					✓
	Finland			✓		
	France	✓				
	Germany (West)	✓				
	Germany (East)	✓				
	Greece	✓				
	Iceland					✓
	Ireland	✓				
	Italy	✓				
	Netherlands	✓				
	Norway	✓				
	Poland	✓				
	Portugal					✓
	Spain			✓		
	Sweden			✓		
	Switzerland				✓	
	Turkey	✓				
	U.S.S.R. (West)	✓				
	U.S.S.R. (East)	✓				
	U.K.	✓				
Eastern Europe:	Albania, Bulgaria, Hungary, Romania, Yugoslavia			✓		
North America	Canada (West)	✓				
	Canada (East)	✓				
	U.S.A. (West)				✓	
	U.S.A. (South)	✓				
	U.S.A. (East and North)	✓				

129

Central America

Barbados
Cuba
Dominican Republic
Guatemala
Jamaica
Mexico
Nicaragua
Puerto Rico

Central America:[a]

Trinidad and Tobago
Bahamas, Belize, Bermuda,
Costa Rica, Ecuador,
El Salvador, Malta,
Honduras, Netherlands
Antilles, Panama, Surinam,
Virgin Isles

South America

Argentina
Bolivia and Chile
Brazil
Colombia
Guyana
Paraguay and Uruguay
Peru
Venezuela

Asia

China
China—Taiwan
Hong Kong
India
Indonesia
Iran
Japan
Korea (North and South)
Pakistan and Bangladesh
Philippines
Saudi-Arabia
Singapore
Sri Lanka
Thailand

Table 6–3. (continued)

Continent	Region	Type of Supply Function				
		Log-Linear	Asymmetric	Time Only	Point	None
Near East:	Iraq, Israel, Jordan, Lebannon, Syria			✓		
Far East:	Afghanistan, Burma, Malaysia, Nepal, Vietnam			✓		
Africa	Mauritius		✓			
	South Africa		✓			
North Africa:	Algeria, Egypt, Libya, Morocco, Tunisia			✓		
West Africa:	Cameroun, C.A.R., Chad, Dahomey, Equatorial Guinea, Gambia, Ghana, Guinea, Ivory Coast, Liberia, Mali, Niger, Nigeria, Senegal, Sierra Leone, Spanish Sahara, Togo, Upper Volta			✓		
North-East Africa:	Ethiopia, Sudan, Somalia			✓		
East Africa:	Burundi, Kenya, Rwanda, Tanzania, Uganda, Botswana, Malawi			✓		
South-Central Africa:	Mozambique, Rhodesia, Swaziland, Zambia			✓		
South-West-Central Africa:	Angola, Congo, Nambia, Zaire			✓		
Oceania	Australia	✓				
	Fiji		✓			
	Hawaii		✓			
	New Zealand					✓
TOTALS	75	17	28	18	4	8

[a]Ecuador and Surinam strictly part of South America; also including French possessions.

131

by the sum of price differences times quantities shipped for all regions:

$$\sum_i \sum_j \{(P_j - G_{ij} - P_i)\ q_{ij} = 0,\ i = 1, 2, \ldots, m \qquad (6\text{--}7)$$
$$j = 1, 2, \ldots, n$$

Equations (6–3) to (6–5) are nothing more than the well-known transportation model, given the particular unit costs of transportation, G_{ij}. The addition of the demand and supply equations, (6–1) and (6–2), adds to the complexity of solution but not greatly to the conception. Equation (6–7) represents a check on equilibrium involving both equalities (6–5) and inequalities (6–6) (see Zusman et al., 1969).

Although it may be shown under certain conditions that any quota may be represented by an equivalent tariff, it is simpler in this context to treat quotas separately since they are used in such a widespread manner by importing countries. Hence there is an additional identity

$$0 \leqslant QUOT_{ij} \leqslant q_{ij}, \qquad i = 1, 2, \ldots, m \qquad (6\text{--}8)$$
$$j = 1, 2, \ldots, n$$

where $QUOT_{ij}$ is the quota given by importing region j to exporting region i.[2]

The Model and Trade Policies

Thus far the composition of G_{ij}, the transfer cost, has not been discussed. The transfer cost between regions i and j comprises: (1) the cost of transportation per unit T_{ij}; (2) tariff costs, the latter including specific or fixed tariffs, $FTAR_j$, variable or ad valorem tariffs, $VTAR_j$, and variable levies, $VLEV_j$; and (3) export taxes, $ETAX_i$. The identity for transfer cost G_{ij} combines these components as follows.

$$G_{ij} = T_{ij} + FTAR_j + VTAR_j + VLEV_j + ETAX_i \qquad (6\text{--}9)$$
$$i = 1, 2, \ldots, m$$
$$i \neq j$$
$$j = 1, 2, \ldots, n$$
$$j \neq i$$

The ad valorem tariff is itself a function of price

$$VTAR_j = P_j/(1 + V_j), j = 1, 2, \ldots, n, j \neq i \qquad (6\text{--}10)$$

where V_j = the ad valorem tariff rate in percentage terms.

Similarly, the variable levy, such as that of the European Economic Community, depends on the threshold (minimum import) price at destination and supply price at origin as given by

$$VLEV_j = PTH_j - T_{ij} - P_i, \qquad \begin{aligned} i &= 1, 2, \ldots, m \; i \neq j \\ j &= 1, 2, \ldots, n \; j \neq i \end{aligned} \quad (6\text{--}11)$$

$$VLEV_j \geq 0$$

where PTH_j = the predetermined threshold price in region j, below which imports may not occur.

Information concerning tariffs was obtained from the *International Customs Journal*. Information on the cost of transportation was provided by Thomas Bates of San Francisco State University. Bates developed a complex cost function that was approximated informally, allowing for inflation to 1974, by

$$t_{ij} = 0.03 \; (D_{ij})^{0.5} \qquad (6\text{--}12)$$

where t_{ij} = the cost in 1974 cents per pound per nautical mile
and D_{ij} = the distance between i and j in nautical miles

The per unit transportation cost is the product of these two variables.

$$T_{ij} = t_{ij} D_{ij}. \qquad (6\text{--}12a)$$

A matrix of distances was drawn up using the U.S. naval publication, "Distances Between Ports" (U.S. Naval Oceanographic Office, 1964). Distances within Europe, the Soviet Union, the United States, and Canada were included on an overland basis where appropriate. Overland costs were assumed to be the same as those by sea. As an example of the shipping costs implied by Equation (12a), the Cuba-New York route (1,199 nautical miles) is estimated to cost 1.04 cents per pound, whereas the Australia-New York route (9,692 nautical miles) costs 2.95 cents per pound. The distances in the matrix assumed the Suez Canal to be closed. This was a reasonable assumption in simulating 1974 equilibria but would slightly distort prices (particularly in the Near East) in projections.

Such spatial equilibrium models were introduced by Samuelson (1952) and solved by Takayama and Judge (1964) using quadratic programming. Considered as a maximization problem, the objective is to maximize the global sum of producers' and consumers' surplus

BEGIN

INITIALISE
transport costs;
trade barriers;
supply/demand
functions;
initial values for
quantities;

(8)

DEDUCT
enforced
quota
trade-
flows

(3)
(4)
(5)

LINEAR PROGRAM
determines min-
imum cost di-
rection of a
given quantity
of trade or
production

(6)*

CHECK
if equilib-
rium reached

YES

ADD-IN
enforced
quota
trade-
flows

RESULTS
quantities supplied
and demanded by
each region; price
in each region;
direction of trade;
total transpor-
tation costs;
tariff and tax
revenues;

NO

(1)
(2)
(6)**

REACTIVE PROGRAM (RP)
adjusts quantity supplied/
demanded, one country at a
time, until that country is
in price-equilibrium with
all others, using a Newtonian process

ADJUST
supply and de-
mand functions
if second deri-
vatives = 0

YES

20
RP
itera-
tions?

NO

(9)

(10)
(11)

ADJUST
transfer costs
for ad valorem
tariffs and
variable levies
as ruling prices
change

END

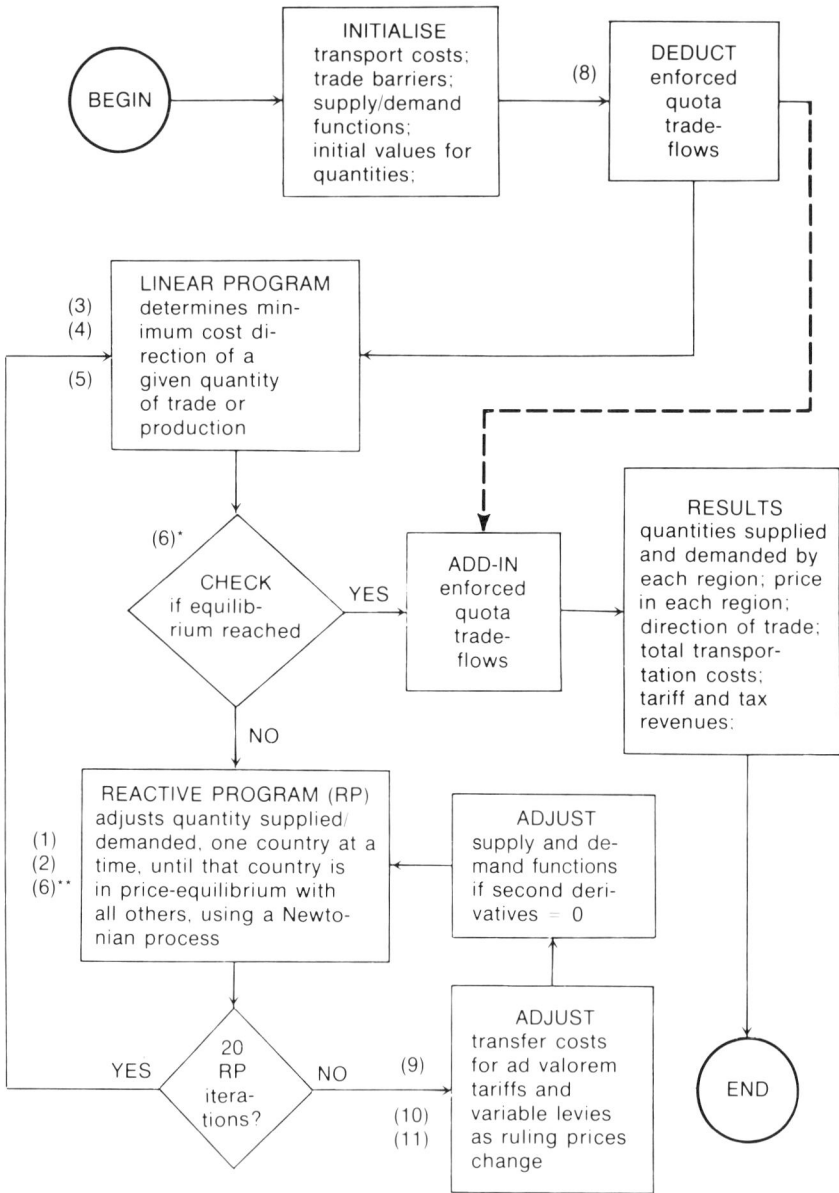

Numbers in parentheses are equation numbers.
*(6) for all countries simultaneously, which with (5) satisfies (7).
**(6) for one country at a time, i.e., $i = 1, 2, \ldots m$ and $j = 1$ or 2 or $\ldots n$.

FIGURE 6–2. Flow Diagrams for Solution of Sugar Model

after the deduction of transfer costs. Samuelson called this net social payoff (*NSP*) and it may be written:

$$NSP = \sum_{j}^{n} \int_{0}^{Q_{j}^{D}} P_{j}\,(Q_{j})dQ_{j} - \sum_{i}^{m} \int_{0}^{Q_{i}^{S}} P_{i}\,(Q_{i})\,dQ_{i} - \sum_{i}\sum_{j} q_{ij}G_{ij} \qquad (6\text{--}13)$$

Tramel and Seale (1963) developed approximate solutions by a method called reactive programming, and a modification of that approach, starting from an algorithm by King and Ho (1972), was used in the present work. Figure 6–2 gives an approximate idea of how the model is solved. Following initialization of the variables, quota flows are deducted. A linear program then allocates quantities to different markets, minimizing transfer costs. A check is then made for price equilibrium, and if it does not exist, the reactive program adjusts quantities supplied and demanded using a Newtonian process. After each iteration, transfer costs are adjusted, and as ad valorem tariffs and variable levies change, prices change. After every twentieth iteration of the reactive program, the linear program is again used. When equilibrium is reached to the desired tolerance, quota flows are added in again and the results provided.

Summary of Supply and Demand Estimates

A model is only as credible as the functions that comprise it. Considerations of space prevent a full presentation of the supply and demand equations, which may be seen elsewhere (Gemmill, 1976). Equations for U.S. and European beet sugar supply were of a double logarithmic form. U.S. cane sugar supplies were projected under an assumption of profit-maximizing adjustment, using an analysis based on cross-section and time-series data. The own-price elasticities for each of the beet sugar producing countries and for U.S. cane sugar are presented in Table 6–4. As a general characterization of responsiveness, weighted average price elasticities are given in the subtotal rows. These indicate an EEC elasticity of 1.05, an elasticity for Eastern Europe of 0.26, and an overall U.S. elasticity of 1.77.

Altogether twenty-eight major cane sugar producing countries were recognized in the model. Separate cane area and yield equations were estimated, but the latter proved unimportant and are not presented here. The functions concerned with cane investment in terms of land area were of the form:

$$(HA_{t}/PP_{t}^{*}) = \beta_{0}\gamma + \beta_{1}\gamma\,(PP_{t}^{*}/PMX_{t}) \qquad (6\text{--}14)$$

$$+ (1 - \gamma)\,(HA_{t-1}/PP_{t-1}^{*})$$

(continued on page 138)

Table 6–4. Supply Elasticities For Beet Sugar and U.S. Cane-Sugar

Country	Production in Thousand Tonnes Raw Value 1974	Elasticity With Respect to			Percent Annual Change Due to Other Factors
		Own Price[b]	Input Price	Alternative Product Price	
Belgium	604	0.30	-0.30	—	3.85
Denmark	416	1.30	-1.65	—	0.93
France	2,945	1.64	-2.09[c]	—	0.53
West Germany	2,436	0.87	-0.10[c]	-0.61 (wheat)	2.60
Ireland	146	—	—	—	0.25
Italy	1,008	0.57	-0.55	-0.03 (apples)	1.56
Netherlands	777	1.14	-3.87[c]	-0.29 (potatoes)	4.33
United Kingdom	617	0.44[d]	-0.27[c]	—	2.00
Sub-Total (EEC)[a]	9,305	1.05	—	—	1.88
Austria	403	—	—	—	—
Finland	82	—	—	—	—
Greece	187	—	—	—	6.84
Portugal	9	—	—	—	—
Spain	667	—	—	—	4.75
Sweden	301	—	—	—	—
Switzerland	72	—	—	—	—
Turkey	834	—	—	—	3.43
Sub-Total (Other Western Europe)	2,555	—	—	—	2.43

	(1,000 tonnes)				
Czechoslovakia	750	—	0.01	—	—
East Germany	570	—	0.32	—	—
Poland	1,600	—	0.28[c]	—	0.37[e]
U.S.S.R.	8,256	—	0.32	—	2.27
Rest of Eastern Europe	1,699	—	—	—	—
Sub-Total (Eastern Europe)	13,145	—	0.36	1.99	3.03
U.S. Beet: East	1,425	−0.79	0.91	—	0.05
West	1,220	−1.57	2.71	—	0.04
U.S. Cane: Florida[f]	728	—	4.23	—	—
Hawaii	944	—	0.99	—	—
Louisiana[f]	539	—	0.75	—	—
Puerto Rico[f]	263	—	0.00	—	—
Texas[f,g]	67	—	2.59	—	—
Sub-Total (U.S.A.)	5,186	—	1.77	—	—

Source: Based on the author's computations.

[a] Including 356,000 tonnes from French Overseas Departments.

[b] Domestic price, except for Communist nations for which world free-market was used.

[c] Fertilizer price only.

[d] For yield only: elasticity of 1.00 assumed for model and for weighted average below.

[e] From land-area equation.

[f] From simulated output at 10 cents per pound sugar price.

[g] From an assumed supply schedule.

where:

> HA = thousand hectares of cane
> PP^* = average of real price of sugar exported at times $t - 1$ and $t - 2$
> PMX = highest value of PP^* ever attained
> β_0, β_1, γ = parameters
> and t = year subscript

This equation makes cane investment a response both to the recent price of exports, in real terms, and to the highest price of such exports ever attained. When PP^* is less than PMX there is a short-run, inelastic response to changing prices. When PP^* is equal to PMX, that is, price is at a new high, more elastic responses may occur although the maximum response that this function allows is limited to an elasticity of one.[3] The elasticities derived from this equation for the sample period (usually 1950–1972) are shown in Table 6–5. They are called "indicative" elasticities because they are calculated on the assumption that $(HA_t/PP_t^*) = (HA_{t-1}/PP_{t-1}^*)$.

The long-run elasticities seem to be "reasonable" in magnitude (from 0.2 to 1.0), but the seven negative short-run elasticities, implying an increase in supply as export price falls (over a limited range), require an explanation. To some extent pooled pricing, under which returns to producers are held constant regardless of export prices, may be the cause.[4] In addition, some fixed asset theories would be consistent with an expansion of output when prices fall once capital has been committed (Johnson and Quance, 1972). Four of the negative short-run elasticities are close to zero and therefore not of great importance. Indeed, the important features are that the long-run elasticities are of acceptable magnitude and *larger* than the short-run elasticities.

Demand

The demand for sugar was examined in seventy-three countries in two distinct ways. First, time-series data were analyzed for each country whenever possible. Second, the time-series and cross-section data were pooled and "international" equations were estimated, with each country having its own intercept to allow for differences in taste. Three different kinds of equations were estimated, semilogarithmic, double logarithmic, and Ramsey, of which the semilogarithmic was used in the model. This form is given in Equation (6–15) in the specification used for pooled time-series and cross-section estimation:

$$Q_{it} = \sum_{j=1}^{N-1} w_j + \beta_0 + \beta_1 \log Y_{it} \qquad (6\text{--}15)$$

$$+ \beta_2 \log P_{it} + E_{it}$$

where

> Q is kilogram per head of sugar consumed in raw value
> w is a dummy variable equal to zero unless $j = i$
> Y is real income per head (thousands of 1972 dollars)
> P is real price per kilogram of raw sugar at retail (1972 dollars)
> E is a disturbance term
> $\beta_0, \beta_1, \beta_2$ are parameters
> i denotes i^{th} country ($i = 1 \ldots N$)
> j denotes j^{th} country ($j = 1 \ldots N$)
> t denotes year
> N denotes number of countries

Corrections were made in estimating individual time series for autocorrelation and in the international equations for both autocorrelation and heteroscedasticity.

The results from pooled international estimation using the semilogarithmic function are summarized in the form of average price and income elasticities in Table 6–6 at various price and income levels. This method of presentation shows very clearly how both income and (absolute value of) price elasticities fall as price falls and as income rises. The figures in brackets are some of the cross-sectional estimates of Viton and Pignalosa (1961) for 1956 converted to a 1972 basis; they exhibit a more compressed set of values but are of the same order of magnitude. For countries for which time-series estimation gave reliable results, these were used in the model. Otherwise, the pooled results were used.

RESULTS FROM THE MODEL UNDER ALTERNATIVE POLICIES

This section presents the results from simulating the world sugar economy in long-run equilibrium in order to discover the effects of alternative policies. It is divided into two parts: first, the values of the endogenously determined variables—wholesale price, quantity supplied, and quantity demanded—are given; second, the prices and quantities are converted, via producers' and consumers' surplus, to

Table 6–5.   Sugar Cane Area Investment Elasticities

Country	Short-Run Investment Elasticity	Long-Run Investment Elasticity
Argentina	0.295	0.943
Australia	0.011	0.539
Barbados	0.383	0.835
Bolivia and Chile[a, b]	−0.006	0.212
Brazil	0.281	0.676
China-Taiwan	0.308	0.424
Colombia	0.508	0.807
Cuba	0.039	0.485
Dominican Republic[c]	−0.159	0.579
Fiji	0.121	0.726
Guatemala	0.464	0.844
Guyana	−0.034	0.701
India[c]	0.225	0.526
Indonesia	0.190	0.244
Iran[a]	0.359	0.508
Jamaica	0.448	0.840
Japan[a, b]	0.295	0.455
Mauritius	0.100	0.716
Mexico	0.610	0.931
Nicaragua	−0.131	0.836
Peru	0.543	0.874
Philippines	0.408	0.923
South Africa	−0.679	0.178
Thailand	−0.219	0.368
Trinidad and Tobago	0.036	0.736
Venezuela	−0.451	0.877
Central America[a]	0.417	0.850
Paraguay and Uruguay	0.306	0.461

Source: Based on the author's computations.
[a]Dependent variable is Q_t/PP_t^* rather than HA_t/PP_t^*.
[b]Includes some sugar beet also.
[c]Hectares growing and not hectares harvested.

welfare losses and gains. It should be noted that the supply functions were estimated in relation to a variety of domestic and international prices that were converted into 1974 dollar values for solution of the whole model. Similarly, the demand functions were estimated in relation to retail prices, and in solving the model, these were converted to prices at the wholesale level.[5] The spatial equilibria take account both of transportation costs and trade distortions and were computed at projected 1974 population and income levels.

Equilibrium Prices and Quantities

The model was solved for each of thirteen different combinations of policies, ranging from a fully distorted set, reflecting the high level of

Table 6–6. Price and Income Elasticities at Various Price and Income Levels from the Semilogarithmic Equation (Income in Dollars, 1972, and Price in Cents per Pound 1972)

Price Elasticities

		Income				
Price	100	200	500	1,000	3,000	5,000
10	-0.880	-0.511	-0.329	-0.259	-0.194	-0.173
20	-2.254	-0.791 (-0.582)[a]	-0.426 (-0.360)	-0.316 (-0.310)	-0.224 (-0.235)	-0.197
30	-26.205	-1.165 (-0.762)	-0.515 (-0.461)	-0.362 (-0.355)	-0.246 (-0.260)	-0.214
40	—	-1.753 (-0.913)	-0.614 (-0.532)	-0.404 (-0.395)	-0.265 (-0.281)	-0.228
50	—	-2.879	-0.699	-0.444	-0.282	-0.241
60	—	-6.060	-0.801	-0.483	-0.297	-0.252

Income Elasticities

		Income				
Price	100	200	500	1,000	3,000	5,000
10	1.041	0.605	0.389	0.306	0.229	0.205
20	2.667	0.936 (0.545)[a]	0.504 (0.337)	0.373 (0.290)	0.265 (0.220)	0.233
30	31.000	1.379 (0.713)	0.609 (0.431)	0.428 (0.332)	0.291 (0.243)	0.254
40	—	2.074 (0.854)	0.715 (0.498)	0.478 (0.370)	0.313 (0.263)	0.270
50	—	3.406	0.827	0.525	0.333	0.285
60	—	7.169	0.947	0.572	0.351	0.298

Source: Based on the author's computations.

[a]Figures in brackets are the cross-sectional estimates of Viton and Pignalosa for 1965 converted to a 1972 basis.

protection that existed in 1974 in the developed countries, to completely free trade. Rather than giving the results for each individual country, the results in prices for the United States, European Economic Community, and Cuba and quantities for the United States, European Economic Community, and the whole world are summarized in Table 6–7.

The six policy variables of Table 6–7 require a short explanation. A plus (+) in the diagram denotes a policy in operation and a minus (−) the abandonment of a policy. The "U.S. Sugar Act" policy included quotas of 4,882,000 tons, a 0.625 cents per pound tariff, and the banning of nonquota imports. The "EEC Levy" policy denied entry to the European Economic Community of raw sugar at less than the threshold price of 14.62 cents per pound and countervailing charges insured compliance with the policy. The "Cuban Quotas" policy directed 2,745,000 tons of Cuban exports to Communist countries. The "Commonwealth Quotas" policy directed 1,383,000 tons to be delivered from Commonwealth countries (excluding Australia) to the United

Table 6–7. Policy Experiments and Long-run Equilibria

Experiment Number	*U.S. Sugar Act*	*EEC Levy*	*Cuban Quotas*	*Common- wealth Quotas*	*Other Tariffs*	*Export Tax*
I	+	+	+	+	+	−
II	−	−	−	−	−	−
III	−	+	+	+	+	−
IV	+	−	+	+	+	−
V	−	−	+	+	+	−
VI	−	+	−	+	+	−
VII	10% VTAR	+	+	+	+	−
VIII	−	−	−	+	+	−
IX	+	+	+	−	+	−
X a	+	+	+	+	+	2¢/lb.
b	+ 0.625¢/lb.	+	+	+	+	6¢/lb.
c	FTAR 0.625¢/lb.	+	+	−	+	10¢/lb.
d	FTAR	+	+	−	+	20¢/lb.
1973	+ 0.625¢/lb.	+	+	+	+	−
1974	FTAR	+	+	−	+	−

Source: Based on the authors' computations.
Notes: VTAR denotes ad valorem tariff. FTAR denotes specific tariff.

Table 6–7. (Continued)

Experiment Number	Prices			
	Free-Market New York	U.S. Domestic New York	EEC (France)	Cuban Domestic
I	7.76	11.89	12.79	6.72
II	10.85	10.72	11.36	9.81
III	10.23	10.33	12.56	9.19
IV	9.17	11.82	9.87	8.13
V	11.24	11.13	10.31	10.20
VI	9.78	9.53	12.83	8.74
VII	9.86	11.01	12.74	8.82
VIII	10.40	10.22	10.78	9.36
IX	7.43	11.86	13.83	6.39
X a	9.07	11.91	12.84	6.03
b	10.13	11.88	12.61	3.09
c	13.77	14.48	13.78	2.73
d	16.24	16.24	14.59	1.36
1973	11.68	11.42		
1974	31.03	29.50		

EEC Threshold Price is 14.6172¢/lb.
Prices are c.i.f. in 1974 cents/lb.

Table 6–7. (Continued)

Experiment Number	United States		E.E.C.		World
	Imports	Domestic Production	Imports	Domestic Production	Production and Consumption
I	4882	5987	1383	9303	78535
II	5674	5216	2808	8112	77575
III	6380	4544	1383	9305	77818
IV	4882	5991	3918	7140	77627
V	5718	5148	3587	7451	77393
VI	6902	4013	1383	9295	77820
VII	5954	4951	1383	9296	78301
VIII	6263	4644	3275	7663	77134
IX	4882	5990	366	10196	78830
X a	4882	5991	1383	9305	78752
b	4882	5990	1383	9292	77391
c	3443	7375	322	10223	76245
d	1443	9322	− 204	10717	75281
1973	4831	5731	313	10177	78095[a]
1974	5188	5398	1036	9237	78909[a]

Quantities are in thousand metric tons of raw sugar.
[a]Production.

Kingdom. The "Other Tariffs" policy imposed all other specific and ad valorem tariffs known to exist. Finally, the "Export Tax" policy imposed a tax on exports from all cane-producing countries, ranging from 2 to 20 cents per pound, as a representation of the possible effect of a cartel of exporters.

Before proceeding to a discussion of the individual results in Table 6–7, two general comments will be made. First, under all of the different policies the volume of world production is relatively constant. This results not only from the low magnitudes of changes in price that are induced by the alternative policies, but also from the ease with which beet production may be substituted for cane production. Even under a huge export tax of 20 cents per pound (Xd), the volume of world production is not greatly curtailed but its geographical distribution merely changes. Second, prices are considerably lower than those existing in 1974, even under the imposition of a large export tax by cane exporters. This suggests that relatively low average prices are likely to continue for some time.

The differential impact of each policy will be examined by comparing it with the appropriate alternative. The first such comparison is between the historical set of policies (I) and *completely free trade* (II). Surprisingly, world production would decline by 960,000 tons under free trade. The underlying cause is the increase in free market price, from 7.76 to 10.85 cents per pound, and the associated increase in sugar prices in exporting countries, while prices decline in previously protected importing nations. Since the price elasticity of demand is higher in the exporting nations as a group than in the importing nations, the high prices reduce consumption by more in the exporting countries than the lower prices increase consumption in the importing countries. The net effect in equilibrium is a small decline in world production (and consumption). The effect of free trade on U.S. and EEC prices and production is less than might have been expected. In both regions some domestic production is replaced by imports and the domestic price falls to meet the free market price (which has risen). Imports to the United States increase by 792,000 tons or 16 percent and to the European Economic Community by 1,505,000 tons or 103 percent.

The second comparison is between policy set (I) and a set in which there is *no U.S. Sugar Act* (III). Note that Cuban sugar was allowed entry to the United States in this experiment, unlike the current (1978) situation. World production and consumption decline slightly (by 717,000 tons). U.S. and free market prices become synonymous, but the free market price rises much more (+2.47 cents) than the U.S. domestic price falls (−1.56 cents). The hypothesis of Sanchez (1972) that the U.S. Sugar Act raised free market prices is rejected by this experiment—the converse is true. Because the U.S. domestic price falls more than it would under free trade, imports rise correspondingly more. As compared with the benchmark I, imports rise 1,498,000 tons or 31 percent and domestic production declines 1,443,000 tons or 24 percent.

The third comparison is between the benchmark (I) and the *unilateral end of its protective levy by the European Economic Community* (IV). Just as with the abolition of U.S. protection in III, the free market price is raised (by 1.41 cents), but in this case the EEC price (as measured in France) falls considerably (by 2.92 cents), indicating that the United States influences world price more than does the European Economic Community. The consequent decline in EEC production is quite large, being 2,162,000 tons or 23 percent, while imports expand correspondingly by 2,535,000 tons or 183 percent. World production remains remarkably constant under this as under each of the other policies.

The fourth comparison is between the benchmark (I) and the *simultaneous abolition of trade barriers by the United States and European Economic Community* (V). The major effect is to raise the free market price even more than under free trade. U.S. prices are slightly higher than under free trade,[6] but EEC prices fall and there is a corresponding decline in EEC production. The implication of experiment V, as compared with III and IV, is that orchestrated reduction of trade barriers by the United States and European Economic Community would lead to smaller problems of domestic adjustment than the unilateral reduction of trade barriers by either region alone.

The fifth comparison is between the unilateral ending of the U.S. Sugar Act (III) and the *simultaneous ending of the U.S. Sugar Act and Cuba's Quota Agreements* (VI). Cuban sugar may now enter the United States in larger amounts. Also the free market price (as measured at New York) and the U.S. domestic price are both lower under VI than under III. U.S. domestic production suffers its severest decline, by 1,974,000 tons (33 percent) as compared with the benchmark (I). U.S. imports rise similarly by 2,020,000 tons (41 percent) as compared with I.

The sixth comparison is between III, the policy set with no U.S. Sugar Act, and VII, *a policy set in which the United States imposes a 10 percent ad valorem tariff on sugar*. The effect is very slight. There is a small decline in free market price, a small rise in U.S. domestic price, and a correspondingly small replacement of imports by domestic production in the United States.

The seventh comparison is between free trade (II) and the *continua-*

tion alone of the Commonwealth quotas and other countries' tariffs (VIII). All prices fall in this set relative to free trade and consequently U.S. and EEC domestic production also fall, but the magnitude is small.

The eighth comparison is between I and the *ending of the Commonwealth Sugar Agreement (IX).* Free market price declines slightly, but the EEC price rises somewhat and the latter region becomes almost self-sufficient in sugar, importing a mere 366,000 tons. The importance attached by the United Kingdom in continuing the Commonwealth Sugar Agreement on behalf of the Commonwealth exporters is seemingly justified by this experiment.

The final comparisons are between the benchmark set (I) and sets with similar policies except for the addition of an *export tax of varying magnitude by the cane exporting countries (X a, b, c, d,).* Export taxes of 2, 6, 10, and 20 cents per pound were considered. At taxes of 10 and 20 cents the U.S. Sugar Act and Commonwealth Sugar Agreements were no longer functional (*c* and *d*). Taxes of 2 or 6 cents per pound would merely be impositions on importers from the free market such as Japan and Canada; hence, they would be similar in effect to previous international sugar agreements. The free market price would not rise to the level of the U.S. or EEC prices, thus avoiding disruptions in those markets. However, an export tax of 10 cents per pound, if also levied on the United States and European Economic Community, would raise prices in these two regions and encourage domestic production. Several traditional exporters of cane would cease to export, for example, Argentina, Brazil, Colombia, Guatemala, Mexico, Nicaragua, Peru, South Africa, Thailand, Venezuela, and Central America. The relatively elastic supply of domestic sugar in the United States and European Economic Community and the inelastic supply of the cane exporters result together in the easy substitution of domestic for imported sugar and only a small reduction in output worldwide. This effect is even more pronounced when a 20 cent tax on exports is imposed, the European Economic Community, now becoming a net exporter and the United States importing a mere 1,443,000 tons (a reduction of 70 percent). Australia, Barbados, China-Taiwan, Dominican Republic, Fiji, Guyana, Jamaica, Philippines, and Trinidad and Tobago are now added to the list of countries ceasing to export sugar; only Cuba is left.

These results may be more easily digested by observing in Table 6–8 the production effects of the five most interesting policies in relation to the benchmark policy set (full distortions) number I. This table also lists the effects on production in the six major Latin American sugar-exporting nations. Note that countries have been grouped under

Table 6–8. Summary of Changes in Production Relative to the Benchmark (I) Set of Policies

Region	Free Trade II		No U.S. Protection III		No EEC Protection IV		No EEC or U.S. Protection V		10 cent per lb. Export Tax X_c	
	Thousand Tons[a]	%	Thousand Tons	%	Thousand Tons	%	Thousand Tons	%	Thousand Tons	%
Argentina	+ 111	+ 7.4	+ 77	+ 5.2	+ 90	+ 6.0	+ 96	+ 6.4	− 423	− 28.3
Brazil	− 24	− 0.4	+ 26	+ 0.4	+ 9	+ 0.1	+ 11	+ 0.2	− 876	− 14.0
Cuba	− 20	− 0.3	− 26	− 0.3	− 10	− 0.2	− 14	− 0.2	− 1205	− 19.3
Dominican Republic	− 109	− 10.7	− 65	− 6.4	− 10	− 1.0	− 122	− 11.9	− 386	− 37.8
Mexico	+ 44	+ 1.4	+ 51	+ 1.6	+ 107	+ 3.5	+ 37	+ 1.2	− 883	− 28.9
Peru	− 2	− 0.2	− 17	− 2.0	− 8	− 1.0	0	0.0	− 312	− 37.6
EEC	− 1193	− 12.8	0	0.0	− 2164	− 23.3	− 1856	− 20.0	+ 916	+ 9.8
U.S.S.R.	+ 1149	+ 11.0	+ 338	+ 3.2	+ 632	+ 6.1	+ 829	+ 8.0	+ 1657	+ 15.9
United States	− 773	− 12.9	− 1443	− 24.1	0	0.0	− 840	− 14.0	+ 1385	+ 23.1
Developed Countries	− 1228	− 3.0	− 1006	− 2.4	− 1419	− 3.4	− 1711	− 4.1	+ 3150	+ 7.6
Less-Developed Countries	+ 268	+ 0.7	+ 289	+ 0.8	+ 510	+ 1.4	+ 569	+ 1.5	− 5441	− 14.6
Cane-Sugar Exporters	+ 269	+ 0.9	+ 61	+ 0.2	+ 3	0.0	+ 63	+ 0.2	− 7724	− 25.0
World	− 960	− 1.2	− 717	− 0.9	− 908	− 1.2	− 1142	− 1.5	− 2290	− 2.9

Source: Based on the authors' computations.

[a] All tons are metric and in raw value.

headings that are not necessarily mutually exclusive; for example, Cuba is both a cane sugar exporter and a less developed country.

1. The effect of free trade is to diminish U.S. and EEC production by about 13 percent and to enhance that of the Soviet Union by 11 percent, leaving production elsewhere largely unaffected. The effect on the Latin American producers is minor. The Dominican Republic suffers an 11 percent decline in production, as it was given highly preferential treatment by the U.S. Sugar Act. Conversely, Argentina's production expands because it was only given a small U.S. quota.
2. An end to U.S. protection forces a 24 percent decline in U.S. production. The effect on Latin American countries is similar to that for free trade in terms of production, that is, rather small.
3. An end to EEC protection causes a 23 percent decline there, mainly affecting France and the Netherlands. Argentina and Mexico appear to have small production gains from such a change to policy.
4. A combined end to U.S. and EEC protection causes 14 percent and 20 percent declines in the two regions, respectively, and encourages production in the Soviet Union to the extent of 8 percent. The effects in Latin America are similar to those for free trade.
5. A 10 cent export tax on cane sugar causes a 25 percent contraction in the output of the cane sugar exporting nations. Only those exporters with small domestic markets continue to export. Of the Latin American countries that means that only Cuba and the Dominican Republic continue to export sugar.

Overall, no policy leads to an even moderate change in the international distribution of production between less developed and developed countries, even if the cane sugar exporters impose a large tax on exports, in which case their share of production falls dramatically. The experiments suggest that the gains to exporters from freer trade will not be derived from increased output but from a higher price. Before drawing welfare implications (which combine the effects of quantity and price), some comments on tariffs and transportation costs will be made. The saving in worldwide transportation costs that occurred under free trade (II) as compared with a fully protected market (I) is estimated to be $240 million or 23 percent, the costs being $819 and $1,059 million, respectively. The major adjustment in the direction of trade that is implied is, not unexpectedly, the redirection of Cuban sugar to fill almost all of the U.S. import requirements. The current direction of trade is highly disadvantageous to Cuba.

Welfare Implications of Long-Run Equilibria

In Table 6–9 comparisons are made, in terms of summed producers' and consumers' surplus and government revenues, between the benchmark solution I (full distortions) and the four most important alternatives: free trade (II), no U.S. Act (III), no EEC protection (IV), and a 10 cent export tax by cane exporters (Xc). All calculations are relative to the benchmark or most likely solution, I. In order to simplify the calculations, the supply and demand functions were assumed linear over the appropriate ranges and the small changes in tariff revenue that accrue to importers under III, IV, and Xc were assumed negligible relative to I.[7]

Considering free trade, II, the net world gain would be $330 million, of which $324 million would go to less developed countries. The largest single beneficiary would be Cuba, the largest exporter, who would gain $392 million. Since Cuba would gain more than the overall gain to less developed countries, it follows that on the average other such countries would lose under this policy. The table shows that the effect on the main Latin American exporters is, however, favorable. Argentina, Mexico, and Brazil would gain substantially while Peru would lose. Other less developed losers under this policy, not shown in the table, include countries in the Near and Far East,[8] India, the Central American countries, Indonesia, and many African countries. These losers consist of two kinds. First, those countries that had highly preferential treatment under the U.S. Act and Commonwealth Sugar Agreement have a loss of government or producer revenue. Second, importing LDCs now have to pay a higher price for their sugar, hence their losses. The explicit effects of U.S. and EEC policy are evaluated below.

Looking at the net situation in the developed countries of the West, the European Economic Community would gain $70 million, most of which would accrue to the United Kingdom ($55 million) and Italy ($21 million). Together producers in the European Economic Community would lose $300 million and consumers would gain $370 million. The United States as a whole would gain $66 million resulting from a gain to consumers of $273 million, a loss to producers of $140 million, and a loss of tariff revenue of $67 million. The big losers in this and all situations of freer trade are Japan and Canada, where losses are $107 million and $64 million, respectively. These two nations have regularly profited from the low price that resulted from protection elsewhere.

Considering unilateral action by the United States in ending its Sugar Act (experiment III), there would be an overall world loss of $20 million. In this experiment Cuban sugar was allowed access to the

Table 6–9. Summary of Gains in Thousands of 1974 Dollars

Region	Free Trade II	No U.S. Protect. III	No EEC Protect. IV	No U.S. or EEC Protect. V	10 Cent Tax Xc
Argentina	+ 16,823	– 6,618	+ 13,939	+ 11,983	– 19,852
Brazil	+ 36,559	– 9,636	+ 43,495	+ 21,541	– 97,541
Cuba	+392,285	+313,664	+179,238	+441,811	+551,795
Dominican Republic	– 1,113	– 15,986	+ 25,826	+ 6,200	– 34,835
Mexico	+ 22,771	+ 5,007	+ 36,442	+ 23,637	– 84,661
Peru	– 23,261	– 31,631	– 599	– 24,923	– 52,225
EEC	+ 70,059	0	+184,331	+140,848	– 32,873
U.S.S.R.	– 31,917	– 12,368	– 37,143	– 59,791	+ 3,740
United States	+ 66,406	+ 33,125	0	+ 26,004	–245,142
Developed Countries	+ 1,402	– 90,572	+ 49,089	– 40,468	–440,934
Less Developed Countries	+328,557	+ 71,951	+123,022	+147,277	–482,635
Cane-Sugar Exporters	+638,622	+171,703	+405,622	+432,133	–454,574
World	+329,959	– 20,053	+172,111	+107,380	–923,569
Free-Market Price[a]	10.85	10.23	9.17	11.24	13.77

Source: Based on the author's computations.

[a] Cents per pound f.o.b. New York.

United States, and hence Cuba had a large gain of $314 million, which was offset by the $377 million that was the gross premium previously paid by the United States to quota-holding countries. For example, Argentina, Brazil, Dominican Republic, Peru, and the Philippines lose under this policy because of the end of the U.S. quotas. The losses are not great, however. Importers from the free market, particularly Japan and Canada, are again the main losers. Turning to the United States, the net gain from an end of the sugar act is estimated to be $33 million, resulting from gains to consumers of $330 million and losses to government of $67 million and to producers of $230 million.

The third welfare comparison concerns experiment IV, the unilateral end of protection by the European Economic Community. There is an estimated international gain of $172 million, divided into $123 million to the LDCs and $49 million to the developed countries. As before, the gainer of greatest magnitude is Cuba, benefiting by an estimated $179 million. Because of the increase in world free market price, exporters of sugar gain and importers lose. However, because there is no longer any Commonwealth premium, since all countries receive the same price from the European Economic Community (although the experiment maintained 1,383,000 tons of Commonwealth imports to the United Kingdom), Commonwealth countries such as Barbados, Guyana, Jamaica, Mauritius, and Trinidad and Tobago suffer small losses. The premium transferred to favored nations under the Commonwealth Sugar Agreement was estimated to be worth $126 million. The major Latin American exporters, except Peru, gain substantially from access to the EEC market. The European Economic Community itself also has large gains of $181 million, chiefly due to the consumer gain of $709 million, while the producers' loss is $525 million. The gains would particularly accrue to the importers in the European Economic Community, that is, to the United Kingdom ($120 million), Italy ($41 million), and Ireland ($26 million).

The fourth set of welfare measurements was made in experiment V in which both U.S. and EEC protection cease. The international gain of $107 million is less than under unilateral EEC action because there was previously an international gain from the U.S. Sugar Act. However, gains to LDCs of $142 million exceed those under unilateral action by the European Economic Community or United States, mainly because the free market price is raised more by this bilateral action. Cuba is again the chief beneficiary, to the extent of $442 million. So large a gain by Cuba implies that other LDCs lose under this policy. The major Latin American exporters, except Peru, are gainers in this particular policy situation. The European Economic

Community as a whole gains an estimated $141 million under this policy, but the United States a mere $26 million.

The final welfare measurements of this kind were made for policy Xc, a 10 cent per pound export tax that is imposed by all cane sugar exporters. It has already been noted that many exporters would simply become producers for their domestic markets under this policy, and as a group, they are estimated to lose $455 million. As under other policies, however, Cuba is a large gainer, this time to the extent of $552 million. Other substantial gainers are China ($107 million) and the large beet producers of Eastern Europe, mainly East Germany ($154 million), Czechoslovakia ($152 million); and Poland ($92 million). The total world loss would be a huge $924 million, resulting both from the cessation of exports by certain countries such as the Philippines (loss of $156 million) and from the higher free market price to be paid by all importers. Under this policy developing countries as a group would lose $483 million and developed countries $441 million. The major Latin American exporters, apart from Cuba, have their share of these losses, including $98 million by Brazil and $85 million by Mexico. The United States would lose $245 million because of the high cost of 3,443,000 tons of imports, but the European Economic Community would lose only $33 million because of its low dependence on imported sugar (only 322,000 tons).

POLICY IMPLICATIONS FOR LATIN AMERICAN COUNTRIES

The policy experiments of this chapter have addressed two kinds of questions relevant to Latin American nations. First, how much do they gain or lose from the systems of preference and protection practiced now, or in the recent past, by the United States and the European Economic Community. Second, how effective would concerted action by cane sugar exporters be in raising the price of sugar and improving their (grossly measured) welfare?

The policy of the United States until 1975, with its country-specific quotas on imports, was a curious mixture of aid and protection. The domestic industry was protected from low free market prices while substantial transfers were made to many Latin American countries through the allocation of quotas. The net effect on the United States itself was minimal, while quota-holders gained an estimated $177 million (net) per annum.[9] With the obvious exception of Cuba, whose sugar continues to be banned from the United States, most Latin American countries did not lose from the U.S. Sugar Act. This may be contrasted with the effect of EEC policy on Latin America, which is definitely harmful. The key difference between U.S. and EEC policies lies in the distribution of tariff revenue. By using auctioned quotas or a tariff, the United States could have captured the $377 million that was the gross transfer to quota-holders. The European Economic Community does make transfers to a few Commonwealth countries, but its variable levy is so high that other imports do not occur—instead the European Economic Community disrupts the world market by subsidized exports.

Turning to the second question, a cartel of cane sugar exporters is likely to be ineffective. The elastic international supply of beet sugar insures that a restriction on cane sugar exports, at least at the level equivalent to a 10 cent per pound export tax, hurts the exporters (except Cuba) as much as the importers. Therefore, there is little likelihood of a strong cartel developing—the motivation of widespread gains in income is lacking. A minor restriction of exports, however, such as that accomplished under the international sugar agreements, might raise the free market price slightly while not affecting the U.S. and EEC prices (assuming the latter to have protective policies). The new international sugar agreement, especially as it includes the United States, may therefore be able to achieve a minor increase in price during surplus periods (such as the present).

On the whole the findings of this research are not very optimistic for the Latin American countries. The latter have allowed their sugar industries to expand following high-price periods only to find themselves thereafter with excess capacity. Similarly, the policy process in the European Economic Community has achieved the same shortsighted results. International sugar agreements shut the stable door after the horse has bolted—there is a new agreement whenever there is excess capacity. Latin America can gain by concerted action to limit expansion following high prices and by pressing the European Economic Community, through UNCTAD and GATT to dismantle its system of protection. Similarly, pressure should be put on the United States so that it does not lapse into protection.

SUMMARY AND CONCLUDING COMMENTS

A spatial equilibrium model of the world sugar economy has been developed to compare the effects of alternative national and international policies. Its main conclusions concerned the impact of U.S. and EEC policy on cane sugar exporting nations and the ability of such exporters to use concerted action to improve their welfare (as measured by Marshallian surplus). It was found that U.S. protectionism in the past had been largely offset by the implicit allocation of tariff revenue to quota suppliers, particularly in Latin America. EEC protectionism, on the other hand, had a greater effect on international welfare, and its cessation would be correspondingly more important for cane sugar exporters as a group. These effects resulted not so much from changes in world production or its international distribution, although beet sugar production was shown to contract under freer trade, as from changes in the price at which sugar was traded internationally.

The country that is most heavily penalized by the present international system of sugar marketing is Cuba, mainly because of the cost of transporting its sugar to the Soviet Union, Eastern Europe and the Far East. Freer trade by the United States and the European Economic Community, assuming no discrimination, is particularly in Cuba's interest.

As to concerted action by cane sugar exporters, the possibilities found were limited to an increase of a few cents per pound (which could still be 20 to 50 percent). Beet sugar production in Western Europe and the United States is sufficiently price elastic to preclude any greater advances in price. The new international sugar agreement, which has rather modest price objectives, might be able to achieve such a price advance.

NOTES

1. Equations 6–1 and 6–2 will be expanded by including other exogenous variables in addition to price later in this section.

2. Equation 6–8 implies that actual shipments may exceed the quota. However, if so desired, the shipment may be limited to the quota by imposing a heavy tariff on additional imports; such a procedure was used in the United States.

3. Subsequent work, with this restriction removed, led to mixed results (see Gemmill, 1978).

4. This is particularly the case in South Africa, as explained by Frans Oosthuizen, Local Market Manager of the South African Sugar Association.

5. See Gemmill (1976: Table 8–1) for retail/wholesale margins used, which included taxes on consumption.

6. While New York U.S. prices rise from II to V, U.S. production does not rise due to slightly lower prices in the other U.S. regions.

7. The welfare measure is Marshallian surplus, summed over all individuals in any one nation. The limitations of such a measure are well known. For a review of the concept of surplus, see Currie et al. (1971). A breakdown into separate producers' and consumers' surplus and government revenue may be found in Gemmill (1976).

8. See Table 6–3 for countries grouped under this and other headings.

9. $377 million in government revenue plus $368 million in consumers' surplus less $568 million in producers' surplus.

BIBLIOGRAPHY

Adams, F.G., and J.R. Behrman. 1976. *Econometric Models of World Agricultural Commodity Markets.* Cambridge, Mass.: Ballinger Publishing Co.

Bates, T.H. 1965. "The World Sugar Economy and U.S. Supply Policy." Ph.D. thesis, University of California at Berkeley.

Currie, J.M.; J.A. Murphy; and A. Schmitz. 1971. "The Concept of Economic Surplus." *Economic Journal* 81 (December): 741–99.

Gemmill, G.T. 1976. "The World Sugar Economy: An Econometric Analysis of Production and Policies." Ph.D. thesis, Michigan State University.

———. 1978. "Asymmetric Cobwebs and the International Supply of Cane-Sugar." *Journal of Agricultural Economics* 29, no. 1 (January): 9–22.

House of Lords (U.K.). 1977. *Select Committee on Commodity Prices.* London: Her Majesty's Stationary Office.

International Sugar Organization. 1977. *Sugar Yearbook, 1976.* London.

Johnson, G.L., and L. Quance. 1972. *The Overproduction Trap in U.S. Agriculture.* Baltimore: Johns Hopkins Press for Resources for the Future.

Sanchez, N. 1972. "The Economics of Sugar Quotas." Ph.D. thesis, University of Southern California.

Tewes, T. 1972. "Sugar: A Short-Term Forecasting Model for the World Market, with a Forecast of the World Market Price for Sugar in 1972/73." *Business Economist* (Oxford), pp. 89–97.

U.S. Naval Oceanographic Office. 1964. *Distances Between Ports.* Washington, D.C.: U.S. Government Printing Office.

Viton, A., and F. Pignalesa. 1961. "Trends and Forces of World Sugar Consumption." Commodity Bulletin No. 32. Rome: United Nations Food and Agriculture Organization.

Zusman, P.; A. Melamed; and I. Katzir. 1969. "Possible Trade and Welfare Effects of EEC Tariff and 'Reference Price' Policy on the European Mediterranean Market for Winter Oranges." Giannini Foundation Monograph No. 24. California Agricultural Experiment Station, Berkeley, California.

Part III

Modeling the Relationship between Commodity Markets and National Economies in Latin America

7

F. GERARD ADAMS and ROMUALDO A. ROLDAN

An Econometric Approach to Measuring the Impact of Primary Commodity Fluctuations on Economic Development: Coffee and Brazil

That fluctuations in primary commodity export market have significant impacts on the economies of the producing countries is intuitively clear and widely accepted. But there is little consensus on the direction and significance of these impacts on economic growth and development. Do fluctuations in primary commodity markets slow down or accelerate the economic growth? This is a difficult question to answer not only because of the conflicting empirical results, but also because of the multiplicity of ways in which the developing economies

Manuel Lasaga made contributions in a number of areas of this research. Computational and programming aspects were handled by Armando Gayoso.

are affected by their primary commodity export industries. In many countries these industries account for a disproportionate share of employment, wage income, export earnings, and government revenues. Fluctuations in the value of primary commodity production and export that may originate in the world market or in the developing producing economy itself have the potential for affecting the growth path through a number of channels. This chapter is concerned with delineating these channels of influence and with establishing quantitative dimensions for the effects. As an illustration, we focus on coffee production and marketing in relation to the economy of Brazil. The relationships between the coffee sector and the national economy are established econometrically and integrated into a macromodel of the Brazilian economy. Various alternative scenarios for coffee production and exports illustrate the nature of the impacts throughout the macroeconomy and the potential effects on Brazilian growth.

STRUCTURAL APPROACH TO COMMODITY MARKET—MACROECONOMY INTERACTIONS

A structural representation of the linkages between world commodity markets and the economy of the producing country is an essential ingredient to an analysis of the impact of commodity market fluctuations. The numerous empirical studies of the correlation between export market performance and economic growth reach equivocal conclusions.[1] Moreover, their ad hoc regression approach obscures the ways in which the economy of the producing country is affected. What, for example, are the forward and backward linkages; what are the impacts on fiscal and external balance; what is the effect on income distribution? Only an explicitly structural analysis, which disentangles the channels of impact and feedback in the economy, can provide a satisfying representation of the relevant phenomena.

Such an analysis must be quantitative in order to measure the various effects and to evaluate their combined impact. Econometric modeling is an ideal tool for this purpose. It is possible, within the limits of the available data, to represent the linkages explicitly and to establish their parameters.

A number of econometric model studies have recognized the impact of particular export-producing sectors in the context of developing country models. These studies include work by Lira in Chapter 8 on copper in Chile, Palma (1976) on petroleum in Venezuela, Jul (1976) on Brazil and the coffee industry, and Acquah (1972) on Ghana. Only the last of these studies is explicitly focused on the impact of the world commodity market on growth of the producing economy. It showed that fluctuations in the world cocoa market generated internal fluctuations in the Ghanaian economy and that, if these fluctuations could be smoothed, the growth potential would be increased. In the other studies the linkage between the commodity market and the producing economy is quite limited, and only a limited range of interactions is considered. Thus, the models explore the relation between commodity production and employment and revenues, but they do not study the concept of the commodity-producing sector as an "engine of growth" for the other parts of the economy. They do not recognize the two-way relationship between the producing country and the world commodity market. Nor do they take into account the possibility for policy intervention by the producing country to smooth the impact of commodity market fluctuations or even to intervene in the operation of the market. These are important considerations, as we shall see.

An essential point in this work is to provide more than a broad aggregative link between the world commodity market and the country economy. Instead, in the context of country macromodels, the specific commodity-producing sector must be broken out and the linkages to the other sectors of the economy must be represented in the model structure. We will refer to this as the micro aspect. It is frequently the more difficult modeling task to accomplish. While the theory of sectoral behavior and linkage is not complex, the data requirements may be hard to meet. Needed are detailed statistics, preferably in time-series form at the sector level. Even when these are available, they require reconciliation with aggregate statistics. Often the timing will be different (crop years rather than calendar years), the units will be different (bags of coffee as compared to deflated value data), and trade statistics may not correspond (customs data as compared to quantity export data). In all cases, the commercial, technical, and government regulation aspects must be known and integrated into the model. It is essential, for example, to use realistic producer prices in the supply function rather than a world market price since the price realized by the producer after exchange (including domestic currency taxes, handling, and transport costs) may be very different from the world price. There are also special challenges to microsector modeling. These will be considered when we discuss the coffee sector and its linkages to the Brazilian macromodel below.

Another important consideration is the recognition that the relationships between the country model and the world commodity market are two-way linkages. If the exporting primary producing sector plays only a small role in the world market, it is possible to carry on the analysis in what is sometimes called a "satellite" model. This means that the world commodity market influences the country economy, but there is no significant backward influence from what happens at the country level to the world commodity market. However, if the producing sector is relatively important in the world commodity economy there will be important feedbacks. Brazilian coffee has traditionally accounted for one-fourth to one-third of world coffee production. A frost in Brazil will affect the Brazilian harvest and it will influence the world price of coffee. Indeed, such an event may be beneficial to Brazil. The 1975–1976 frost sharply increased Brazilian earnings from coffee exports. The two-way interaction is likely to have important dynamic aspects—a price rise today will influence supply and price many years later.[2] It is essential to develop the capability for two-way interaction between the producing country model and the world commodity market. The phenomena examined in Chapter 8 have been studied on a one-way basis, assuming that the world market impacts on the domestic sector, but other analyses are likely to require a fully interactive model system.

The potential for domestic policy response is another complicated element. It would be easy to assume that there are no ways in which the producing country can respond to fluctuations in commodity markets. There are probably few cases where the producing country can influence the world commodity market with unilateral policy actions—the case of Brazil and coffee is said to be one exception. But commodity market fluctuations may not always be allowed to affect the domestic economy without policy intervention. Domestic policy may be used to offset fluctuations, for example, in export taxes, neutralization of foreign exchange earnings, and trade restrictions. The patterns of impact on the domestic economy of the producing country may be quite different from what would be apparent from simple simulations that disregard government intervention.

STRUCTURE OF THE BRAZILIAN
ECONOMETRIC MODEL

As a central vehicle for the present study, we have used an econometric model of Brazil developed at Wharton EFA and the University of Pennsylvania. This model, originally developed as a doctoral dissertation, is currently the basis of the Wharton EFA Brazilian forecasting service. In this section, we describe the structure of the macromodel. In subsequent sections, we elaborate the coffee sector and the linkages from this sector to the macromodel.

This model recognizes the need to modify standard macromodel structures to incorporate particular constraints or features of a developing economy such as Brazil. This point is illustrated in particular by the formulation of the private investment function that, besides utilizing elements of the flexible accelerator theory, incorporates the availability of capital goods imports as an explanatory variable, recognizing the dependence of capital formation on machinery and technology not available internally but only through the international markets. The interest rate, usually introduced in the investment function to reflect the cost of capital, is not appropriate in a country such as Brazil where capital markets are not fully developed and interest rates have been subject to artificial ceilings. In those circumstances, investment funds are allocated through credit rationing, and a credit flow variable seems more appropriate than a measure of the cost of capital.

The functions for government and private consumption depend basically on a relevant measure of income—tax revenue for the government and disposable income for private consumption—while inventory accumulation depends on output variations and some measure of speculative behavior. Another component of the aggregate demand, government investment, is considered an exogenous variable in the model and a main channel through which fiscal policy is carried out. However, an important part of government-sponsored investment, that of quasi-public enterprises, which has become increasingly important in the last decade, is included in private investment.

In the foreign trade block of the model, the treatment of coffee exports deserves a special mention and will be discussed in the next section. Exports of manufactures are determined endogenously as a function of a world trade activity variable and of relative exporters' prices (after adjustment for exchange notes). Other commodity exports are determined exogenously. Imports have been divided into four separate categories: consumption goods, raw materials, capital goods, and fuels. Each one of them is endogenously determined as a function of a proper relative price variable, some domestic activity variable (such as industrial output for raw materials), and the capacity to import. The capacity to import is an important consideration in a country like Brazil where trade policy management is used to maximize the productive potential of imported goods. Payments to foreign factors, particularly in recent years the interest on the foreign debt, is another strategic variable that is explained endogenously.

The productive structure of the economy has been disaggregated into four sectors: the coffee sector (with which we will deal in the next section), the noncoffee agricultural sector, the industrial sector, and the services sector. Agricultural sector value added is specified in the model basically as a supply function whose arguments are relative prices of farm products both in current and lagged terms (which incorporate the formation of price expectations) and government investment in order to take into account the improvement in infrastructure such items as roads, irrigation, and flood control. The latter play an important role in determining the output capacity of the agricultural sector in developing countries.

The specification of the behavioral equation for the industrial sector differs considerably. It is demand-driven, having as independent variables total consumption, total investment, exports of manufactures, and a measure of import substitution taking place in the economy. This type of formulation for the industrial sector value added assumes that productive capacity constraints are not effective. This is in accord with the persistent underutilization of industrial capacity found in Brazil as in other developing economies. The present formulation must be though of as a reduced form equation of an input-output system in which value added can be expressed as a transformation of input-output technical coefficients and the final demand vector. The services sector has a somewhat similar formulation, although here we recognize explicitly the intermediate character of the demand of many of the services, e.g., transport and commerce.

The employment and income distribution sector of the Brazilian macromodel distinguishes the urban wage bill (urban meaning the activity of the industrial and services sector), the nonwage urban income, and the total rural income. The urban wage rate entering the determination of the urban wage bill is assumed to be an exogenous variable largely to reflect the strong controls that government policy has exerted on this variable. In practice, the movement of this variable should reflect indexing for increases in consumer prices and labor productivity gains. But, as is well known, Brazilian indexing is "imperfect," and wage policy contains a large component of government decision about the appropriate distribution of the gains of economic progress.[3]

Urban employment is obtained through an equation for urban labor productivity whose arguments are the present and lagged values of the urban wage rate and the level of the industrial and services value added. Wage income is then computed from urban employment and the wage rate. Nonwage urban income is determined as a function of total urban sales and a markup factor of the industrial and services sector product prices over the urban wage rate. The rural income (obtained directly from the agricultural value added) is added to the urban income to obtain disposable income, after allowing for direct taxes and net government transfers.

The money supply is treated in the forecast model in a substantially exogenous way, making the change in the monetary base an exogenous monetary policy variable. For simulation purposes, endogenous treatment of the money supply becomes essential. We will discuss the way this has been done.

The model determines one central price to which other model prices and deflators are linked. The basic price considered is the gross domestic product price deflator. In its determination, monetary as well as cost-related variables are taken into account. Price increases are viewed as a function of increases of the money supply relative to output, of increases in the urban unit labor costs, and of the increases in indirect taxes and price of imported goods. Finally, the government sector of the model determines the main sources of government revenue: direct and indirect taxes.

LINKAGES OF THE COFFEE MARKET TO THE BRAZILIAN ECONOMY

The linkages between a commodity-producing sector and the macroeconomy are relatively straightforward. We will limit ourselves here to an enumeration of the main impacts, emphasizing the ones that seem more relevant for the case under study. The empirical estimates will be considered in detail in the next section.

The principal impacts of the coffee sector and the macroeconomy can be summarized as follows:

1. The production-income link. Variations in coffee output affect the gross domestic product of the economy, disposable income, and may affect export earnings[4] and government revenues.
2. Production-employment and input linkages. Additional coffee production impacts on labor requirements and on needs for inputs from other productive sectors of the economy.
3. Export value-balance of payments effect. The value of exports (resulting from changes in volume exported or of international price) have significant impact on the Brazilian balance of payments and, consequently, on the ability to import.
4. Export tax revenue. Taxes are imposed on coffee exports and their impact on the coffee fund revenues is of importance. The latter disburses part of its revenues to the government where they may affect public spending.
5. Monetary effects. Monetary effects are through the impact of coffee earnings on foreign exchange receipts and the net balance of the coffee fund operations.

6. Investment impacts. Coffee activity affects the level of aggregate investment. In view of the simultaneity of the model and its numerous complex dynamic feedback channels, the variations in the coffee market has broad effects on the economy. For Brazil, coffee now represents a relatively small sector, particularly compared to its dominance half a century ago. Consequently, we expect it to have only a relatively small impact on the aggregate economy. This situation would make it relatively easy for Brazilian policymakers to neutralize the impacts originating in the coffee sector.

MODELING THE COFFEE SECTOR AND ITS INTERACTIONS WITH THE MACROMODEL

In the following pages, we present the econometric estimates of the direct linkages between the coffee sector and the macroeconomy. The simultaneous nature of the model also insures the existence of widespread indirect linkages whose operation can be traced back to consider the general macromodel structure conceptually. These indirect linkages will be noted where appropriate, and their magnitudes can be measured in the dynamic multiplier analysis of the following section.

In the disaggregation of the coffee production activity, our model has used the specifications utilized by Derek Ford in the world coffee model.[5] Ford distinguishes five different productive zones according to geographical areas: Espiritu Santo, Minas Gerais, Parana, Sao Paulo, and other states. The yield and acreage that jointly determine production in each region are calculated endogenously. The general functional form for acreage in region i is as follows:

Acreage$_i$ = f (ratio of producers coffee price index over agricultural price index other than coffee, dummy variables)

Relative prices are introduced in these equations with lags of up to ten years in order to reflect both the formation of price expectations and the lag between the planting decision and the time trees become productive.

The yield equations conform to the following general form:

Yield$_i$ = f (time trend, rainfall index, dummy variables)

Brazilian statistics do not provide data on the intermediate inputs required by the coffee sector. This has precluded the introduction of such a variable as one of the elements determining the industrial sector value added. As for the services sector, however, coffee enters explicitly in its determination, demanding marketing, transport, and other services both for the actual production process and for the activities required to carry out the exports of coffee. These two influences are registered in the following behavioral equation for the services sector by means of the introduction of the agricultural sector value added and the total volume of foreign trade, variables that include coffee production and coffee exports, respectively.

$$X3R = 0.89155 \ X2R + 0.74422 \ X1R$$
$$(7.44) \qquad\qquad (14.88)$$

$$+ \ 0.0348 \ KR$$
$$(4.00)$$

$$+ \ 0.000523 \ (MCGIFR + EGR)$$
$$(3.39)$$

$$\bar{R}^2 = 1.00 \qquad DW = 1.97 \qquad SEE = 0.736$$

where

$X3R$	= services sector value added
$X2R$	= industrial sector value added
$X1R$	= total agricultural sector value added
KR	= capital goods
$MGCIFR$	= total imports
EGR	= total exports

Coffee-related employment is highly seasonal, and statistical information about it is unavailable. We have chosen to utilize a priori information that relates labor requirements per unit of output ($LACF$) to various yield levels (International Coffee Organization, 1972). Employment requirements (LCF) in the coffee sector are then calculated

$$LCF = LACF * PRCFTON$$

where

$$PRCFTON = \text{volume of coffee production}$$

Wages in the coffee sector (WCF) correspond closely with minimum wages in the different production zones and are assumed to be exogenously determined by general government wage policy.

The wage bill ($WBILLCF$) for the coffee sector is then calculated

$$WBILLCF = WCF * LCF$$

and the wage share of the coffee sector value added ($WXCFC$) is then obtained from

$$W/XCFC = WBILLCF/XCFC$$

where

$XCFC$ = value added of the coffee sector, nominal terms

The next set of equations relate to domestic consumption of coffee and volume of exports. Domestic consumption ($CDCF$) is determined by relative coffee prices ($VACFR$) and disposable income ($YDFR$).

$$ln\ CDCF = 2.19256 + 0.17713\ ln\ YDFR$$
$$ (3.22) \qquad (1.17)$$
$$- 0.3077\ ln\ VACFR + 0.8739\ ln\ CDCF\ (-1)$$
$$ (2.01) \qquad\qquad (7.42)$$
$$\overline{R}^2 = 0.79 \qquad DW = 2.46 \qquad SEE = 0.076$$

As for exports, different specifications are possible. First, one assumes that exports (ECF) are exogenous to the model, determined in world markets by broad demand and price considerations. This alternative implies that production in excess of exports and domestic consumption will find its way into inventory accumulation ($CHICF$):

$$CHICF = PRCFTON - ECF - CDCF$$

Second, one assumes that coffee exports are determined within the model by internal policy measures regarding private and officially held inventories. This approach would apply, for example, if a country simply marketed the excess of coffee production over domestic requirements. It would also apply in the situation, sometimes visualized in Brazil, where sales from or purchases by the official coffee stockpile are used to determine the volume of coffee exports. In this alternative we have

$$ECF = PRCFTON - CDCF - CHICF$$

The distinction between these two alternatives becomes a significant issue when the country model is linked to a world commodity model, a case in which they can be regarded as two opposite views of the determination of the volume of exports (there are, of course, a

number of intermediate alternatives). For our practical purposes—
dealing here only within the framework of a single country model—we
have chosen the first formulation in which we additionally distinguish
private and officially held inventories. Making these inventories an
exogenous policy-determined variable, the changes in private coffee
inventories ($CHICFP$) become the variable calculated through the
identity

$$CHICFP = PRCFTON - CDCF - ECF - CHICFG$$

where

$CHICFG$ = change in government coffee inventories

The coffee export tax system in Brazil was centered around the
existence of an overvalued exchange rate for exports in general. The
difference between this rate and a higher one for imports was retained
by monetary authorities, and much of it was used to finance the
purchase of coffee for the stockpile. This policy had an adverse impact
on the generation of alternative sources of foreign exchange. It was
abandoned by 1961 when the exchange rate and coffee pricing policy
were separated.

The present system establishes a tax per bag of coffee exports, called
"contribution quota," whose proceeds are not for direct fiscal use. They
are managed as an independent fund by monetary authorities. This
coffee fund also handles resources derived from the sale or purchase of
government-held stocks and a number of programs dealing with technology improvements in the coffee sector, financing programs of er-
radication of coffee trees or replantings, and so on.

The total coffee export taxes ($CFCCONT$) are calculated as a product of the coffee export tax rate ($CONTRRATEC$) times the volume of
coffee exports.

$$CFCCONT = CONTRRATEC * ECF$$

The coffee export tax rate is assumed in the model to be an exogenous
policy-determined variable. As it will be shown later, this variable also
plays an important role in determining the level of coffee producers'
prices and, hence, indirectly affects the level of output. Since these tax
revenues are earmarked for the coffee fund, their impact on the rest of
the economic system depends on the net balance of the coffee fund
operations ($CFACCNET$). This balance results as the difference between export tax revenues, net stock sales, and other coffee fund
outlays

$$CFACCNET = CFCCONT + SSTOCKNET - CFACCNETEXP$$

where

$$SSTOCKNET \quad = \text{net sales of coffee stocks}$$
$$CFACCNETEXP = \text{net expenses of the coffee fund}$$

The net sales of coffee stocks are merely the changes in official coffee inventories valued in current terms. The net expenses of the coffee fund are calculated endogenously in the model as a function of the revenues accruing to the fund:

$$CFACCNETEXP = 12.15 + 0.9578\ (CFCCONT + SSTOCKNET)$$
$$\qquad\qquad\ \ (0.03) \quad (4.23)$$

$$\overline{R}^2 = 0.53 \quad DW = 1.07 \quad SEE = 1006.8$$

The net balance of the coffee fund has a direct effect in the expansion of the monetary base and, hence, money supply. A surplus will have a contractionary effect on the monetary base and vice versa. The balance will also have a fiscal impact increasing indirect taxes, and through this channel, coffee export revenues can find their way into having an impact on government expenditures. The change in the monetary base ($FDMBC$) has been made endogenous to the model to allow the registration of the monetary impact of the coffee export tax system. It is treated as a "behavioralized" identity in which the arguments are the change in foreign reserves ($BOPC$), and the credit from monetary authorities to government ($FCRDGMAC$), to the private sector ($FCRDPMAC$), to the commercial banks ($FCRDCBMAC$), and the net balance of the coffee account ($CFACCNET$):

$$FDMBC = 393.43 + 0.490\ BOPC$$
$$\qquad\quad (1.54) \quad (8.72)$$
$$+ 0.886\ FCRDGMAC + 0.655\ FCRDPMAC$$
$$\ \ (6.46) \qquad\qquad\quad (12.20)$$
$$+ 2.565\ FCRDCBMAC - 0.615\ CFACCNET$$
$$\ \ (3.76) \qquad\qquad\qquad (2.38)$$
$$\overline{R}^2 = 0.99 \quad DW = 2.37 \quad SEE = 548.6$$

In view of the relative magnitudes of the variables involved, although the causalty is well established, the elasticity of $FDMBC$ with respect to $CFACCNET$ is small, only $- 0.0035$.

The positive fiscal impact of the coffee export taxes is registered on the indirect taxes (*TINDC*) by the following behavioral equation:

$$TINDC = 0.00082599\ CFACCNET + 0.0225023\ X123C$$
$$(1.10) \qquad\qquad\qquad (0.76)$$
$$+\ 0.0898424\ X123C(-1) + 0.109539\ X123C(-2)$$
$$(9.93) \qquad\qquad\qquad (4.05)$$
$$+\ 0.07859\ X123C(-3)$$
$$(3.30)$$
$$\overline{R}^2 = 0.99 \qquad DW = 1.90 \qquad SEE = 1.924$$

The included Almon Lag is <2,4 *FAR*>

where

$$X123C = \text{value of total output}$$

Here again, since the magnitude of *CFACCNET* is small compared with *TINDC*, the elasticity obtained is only of 0.0007.

The coffee price determination in the model is another area in which we find linkages to the rest of the economy as well as to the coffee world markets. There are two coffee-related prices whose determination is of interest within the country model: the Brazilian export price in dollars and the Brazilian producers' price. The first determines the dollar export revenues obtained by coffee. This price does not coincide with the prices quoted in international markets because of discounts or premiums that are added to the quoted price and because of lags between the sales contracts and actual delivery of the coffee. Consequently, the export price is determined as a function of the coffee price quoted in the New York market (*PNYBRCFD*):

$$ln\ VECFD = 0.1997 + 0.9535\ ln\ PNYBRCFD$$
$$(8.88) \qquad (23.48)$$
$$\overline{R}^2 = 0.97 \qquad DW = 1.73 \qquad SEE = 0.412$$

The determination of the producers' price takes into account a number of considerations. This price will be influenced by the Brazilian export price and the export tax rate. In particular, we have considered the producers' price to be a function of the difference between the export price—translated into cruzeiros (*VECFD/C*)—and the coffee export tax rate. The price equation also considers a stock adjustment element in which the relevant variable is the ratio of coffee sales (exports plus domestic consumption) over total domestic stocks ($S/STOCKCF$), and production costs. The latter are represented, for lack of anything better, by the gross domestic price deflator ($PGDP$). The resulting equation is as follows:

$$ln\ VACFC = 3.276 + 0.204\ ln\ (VECFD/C - CONTRRATEC)$$
$$(6.59)\quad(1.16)$$

$$+\ 0.4340\ ln\ S/STOCKCF + 0.9813\ ln\ PGDP$$
$$(2.32)\qquad\qquad\qquad(6.61)$$

$$\overline{R}^{\,2} = 0.99\qquad DW = 2.33\qquad SEE = 0.136$$

Finally, we have tried to isolate the effect of the income originating in the coffee sector on private consumption. The real disposable income generated in the coffee sector would be the appropriate variable to include from a theoretical point of view. However, the chronic tendency to overproduction and the consequent accumulation of inventories not only in the hands of government agencies but more significantly in the hands of producers makes the income generated by current production activity inadequate to measure the purchasing power originated in the sector. When excess production occurs, part of the "income" generated immediately finds its counterpart as inventory accumulation. Inversely, when the market situation makes possible a depletion of inventories, the proceedings are added to the disposable income stream and are subject to the usual saving-consumption decision process. To register this particular condition, we have included as an argument in the consumption function the sales of coffee (SCF)

$$CPR = -7.2986 + 0.8425\ YDFR + 0.005978\ SCF + 0.04227\ PCP^*$$
$$(1.28)\quad(89.70)\qquad\qquad(1.86)\qquad\qquad(1.68)$$

$$\overline{R}^{\,2} = 0.95\qquad DW = 2.16\qquad SEE = 2.164$$

where

$YDFR$ = real disposable income of the economy
PCP^* = percentage change private consumption implicit deflator

The consumption elasticity for SCF is 0.068.

One additional linkage does not need elaboration since it is already an integral part of the Brazilian macromodel. This is the impact of the coffee exports on export earnings and on the ability to import. This latter variable is explicitly introduced in the import equation for consumption goods and capital equipment, finding through this last variable an impact on the rate of capital formation of the Brazilian economy.

A final adaptation of the Brazilian macromodel has been to make government investment—traditionally an exogenous, policy-determined magnitude—an endogenously determined variable, as a function of total government revenues, in order to register more fully the impact, however small, of coffee export taxation on the government expenditure patterns. The equation used for that effect is

$$IGR = 2.205 + 0.142315 \ TGREVR$$
$$(4.71) \ \ (14.54)$$
$$\overline{R}{}^2 = 0.93 \quad DW = 1.42 \quad SEE = 0.878$$

where

$$TGREVR = \text{government revenues in real terms}$$

DYNAMIC MULTIPLIER ANALYSIS

The simultaneous nature of the model insures the existence of widespread indirect or secondary linkages among different variables of the country model and its coffee sector. The full extent of the interaction between the coffee sector and the rest of the economy is captured by solving the model in a simultaneous fashion. The dynamic multiplier analysis establishes numerical magnitudes for these linkages.

The experiments that follow have been designed to illustrate different aspects of the interaction between the commodity-producing sector, the developing economy, and the world commodity markets. In each case, multipliers are calculated by comparing the results of a disturbed solution (multipliers solution) with a base solution.

The first experiment will deal with an increase of 10 percent in the volume of Brazilian coffee production for the production figures obtained in a control simulation for every year of the simulation period. This increase in production is translated into inventory accumulation, and exports therefore remain unchanged. The second assumes the same increase in coffee production, but this time the increase is fully translated into export expansion. In both cases, we are making simplifying assumptions about world coffee markets, in particular, that world coffee prices are not affected by these changes in Brazilian variables.

These two scenarios may not be entirely realistic from the perspective of the interaction of the Brazilian economy and the world commodity markets. However, maintaining coffee exports constant allows us to concentrate solely on the magnitude of domestic economy linkages between the commodity-producing sector and the rest of the economy. These are regarded as key variables in development economics, used to explain the existence of a dualistic economic structure in a particular developing economy. The second simulation example, allowing exports to grow by the amount of the production increase, makes it possible to examine the next issue, that is, whether the expansion of the commodity exports make possible higher rates of growth for the domestic economy above the rates that the purely domestic production effect implies.

The next two experiments focus on the impact of coffee market developments external to Brazil. For this purpose, we utilize the world coffee model, even though a full simultaneous linkage between the two models is not yet available.

A world coffee simulation in which a blight in coffee production in Africa is considered provides a simultaneous determination of the higher world price needed to equilibrate demand with lower supplies, and the corresponding increase in Brazilian exports, that helps to compensate the drop in African supplies to the world market. The third experiment consists in introducing exogenously in our Brazil model, the new international prices and the resulting coffee exports for Brazil.

A fourth simulation evaluates the impact of the coffee export tax as an economic policy mechanism that Brazil can operate to compensate or isolate the economy from fluctuations in the external markets. And finally, we consider the effects of an offsetting monetary policy.

Autonomous Increase in the Volume of Coffee Production

Table 7–1 presents the main multipliers of the simulation in which coffee production has been exogenously increased by 10 percent over the figures attained in a base solution for each year of the simulation period.[6] The main channels by which the impact is transmitted to the rest of the economy is the generation of demand for transport and commercial services from the tertiary sector. The increase in output generates consumer demand and higher investment that, in turn, also calls for additional increases in production. Increased economic activity also implies larger tax revenues that make possible an expansion of government outlays on consumption and investment.

The extent of the linkages between the Brazilian economy and its coffee sector can be summarized by the result that shows a 0.44 percent (yearly average in the simulation period) increase in the economy's

Table 7–1. Average Percentage Differences Between Disturbed and Base Solutions (10% Higher Coffee Production Over the Base Solution—Dynamic Simulation 1976–1987)

		% Difference
GDPR	Gross Domestic Product	0.44
PGDP	Deflator Gross Domestic Product	−0.05
CPR	Real Private Consumption	0.50
IPR	Real Gross Private Investment	0.45
CGR	Real Government Consumption	0.34
IGR	Real Government Investment	0.56
X2R	Industrial Output	0.36
X3R	Services Output	0.40
TDC	Direct Taxes	0.59
TINDC	Indirect Taxes	0.36
LCF	Coffee Sector Employment	3.69
VACFC	Coffee Producers Price	−7.47
MKCIFR	Capital Goods Imports, real terms	0.98
ECF	Coffee Export, real terms	0.0
S/STOCKCF	Ratio of Coffee Sales Over Stocks	15.85

Source: Based on the authors' computations.

gross domestic output when coffee production increases by 10 percent (also yearly average). Coffee production accounts roughly for 0.8 percent of the gross domestic product in the sample period. This implies that the direct impact of the increase in coffee output accounts for merely 0.08 percent of the 0.44 percent increase in the gross domestic product. The difference of these two magnitudes gives an idea of the indirect repercussions that the coffee activity has on the rest of the economy.

Other results in Table 7–1 suggest that the higher level of coffee production generates a slightly larger output response from the services sector than from the industrial sector. This fact is explained partly by the more direct technical linkages and input requirements existing between coffee production and the generation of services such as transport, storage, and commerce. Our results show 3.69 percent higher employment in the coffee sector at the higher production level. This estimate is, in fact, a lower bound, since we have assumed in this simulation that the increase in coffee production was generated solely by an increase in the yield per hectare instead of by a combination of higher yield and expanded acreage. Expanded acreage would produce greater labor requirements.

For the aggregate demand categories, Table 7–1 shows that the expansion in economic activity, as a consequence of the higher coffee output, has a large impact on government investment, followed by private consumption, private investment, and government consumption.

The producers' coffee price appears to decrease by 5 percent in the simulation period. This result is due mainly to the excess supply situation domestically because higher production does not have a counterpart in greater exports. As a result, there is excessive accumulation of stocks. The ratio of total coffee sales over stocks increases by an average of 15.9 percent in this simulation.

Exogenous Increase in Coffee Production with Corresponding Expansion of Coffee Exports

The assumption that the increase in production goes completely into exports implies that coffee exports increase by 17 percent in the simulation period, both in volume and value. The average annual increase in coffee revenues is $528 million, which implies approximately a 2.2 percent increase in total annual export revenues.

As the foreign trade variables are allowed to operate in this solution, the main channels through which they have an impact on the domestic economy are the increased capacity to import and the increase in government revenues accruing through the coffee export taxes.

The increased capacity to import stimulates capital equipment purchases abroad that are seen to increase by 2.0 percent on average in this simulation. This makes possible a higher rate of capital formation in the economy with its corresponding multiplier effect on general economic activity. Other imports—raw materials, fuels, and consumption goods—also increase. Coffee export tax revenues increase by the same percentage as coffee exports, making possible larger expenditures in government current consumption and government investment. The expansion of these aggregate demand elements also has a positive multiplier effect on the level of general economic activity.

The combination of the increased coffee output and export of the additional output increases the impact of the coffee sector on the economic system. Gross domestic product is greater on an average of 0.81 percent in this simulation, as compared with only 0.44 percent obtained from the simulation that assumes coffee output expansion without an increase in exports.

The monetary effects of the increase in coffee export tax revenues through the coffee account are not significant. Although there is an increased collection of coffee export taxes because of the higher export volume, the higher domestic coffee prices make necessary larger disimbursements to finance the accumulation of official coffee stocks. This results in a larger deficit for the coffee account and, hence, in an expansionary effect on the monetary base. Tax rates and export tax revenues can be increased to give a surplus in the coffee account that could have a contractionary effect on the monetary base. However, in the context of this simulation, the monetary impact of the coffee account is negligible. It is offset by other developments taking place simultaneously in the economy, in particular, by the increase in foreign reserves resulting from the more favorable trade situation.

The expansion of the money supply that results from higher foreign reserves in this experiment has an inflationary impact. Measured by the gross domestic product deflator in Table 7–2, it is shown to be an average of 0.77 percent higher than in the control solution. This situation can be contrasted with the first simulation in which the foreign trade situation remains unaltered for the control solution. As shown in Table 7–1, the prevailing effect on prices is then in a downward direction (−0.05 percent), resulting from an increase in productivity and thus creating lower cost pressures.

International Coffee Price Increase and Brazilian Export Expansion

A consistent set of assumptions about international coffee price movements and changes in Brazilian coffee exports can be obtained through a simulation of the world coffee model. The scenario of that simulation consisted in assuming a blight for African coffee production

Table 7–2. Average Percentage Differences Between Disturbed and Base Solutions (10% Higher Coffee Production over the Base Solution and Corresponding Higher Export Expansion—Dynamic Simulation 1976–1987)

		% Difference
GDPR	Gross Domestic Product	0.81
PGDP	Deflator Gross Domestic Product	0.77
CPR	Real Private Consumption	1.27
IPR	Real Gross Private Investment	0.74
CGR	Real Government Consumption	0.55
IGR	Real Government Investment	0.74
X2R	Industrial Output	0.72
X3R	Services Output	0.80
TDC	Direct Taxes	1.54
TINDC	Indirect Taxes	1.54
LCF	Coffee Sector Employment	4.68
VACFC	Coffee Producers Price	4.72
MKCIFR	Capital Goods Imports, real terms	2.01
ECF	Coffee Export, real terms	17.43
S/STOCKCF	Ratio of Coffee Sales Over Stocks	9.09

Source: Based on the authors' computations.

beginning in 1979 and continuing all through the rest of the simulation period. This scenario then results in higher world prices and expanded Brazilian exports. Based on Table 7–3, column (1), world coffee prices are on average 26.5 percent higher than in the control solution for the period 1979–1987. The volume of Brazilian coffee exports increases by 8 percent on the average, and 34.6 percent in revenues over the base solution. By the same token, total export revenues are higher by 4 percent over the base solution figures.

The higher international prices and the increase in export sales drive producer prices up by 10.7 percent over the base solution figures. Higher prices bring a decrease in domestic coffee consumption (−6.1 percent) and an expansion of coffee production by an average of 1.3 percent over the base solution numbers.

The increase of 0.31 percent on an average for the gross domestic product over the control solution, shown in Table 7–3, column (1), summarizes the net positive impact derived by Brazil from this particular set of events assumed to take place in the world markets.

Coffee Export Tax Policy

Brazil has applied a vast array of policy measures with varying degrees of success, in order to offset some of the destabilizing influences that world market conditions could introduce in the economy. Limitation of the coffee acreage through the eradication of coffee trees has been the most direct measure to limit the expansion of production. Domestic coffee consumption has been guaranteed at low prices by the establishment of export quotas and other mechanisms. The impact of

Table 7–3.   Average Percentage Differences Between Disturbed and Base Solutions (Increase of International Coffee Prices and Export Expansion—Dynamic Simulation 1979–1987)

		Without Economic Policy Intervention (% Difference)	With Export Tax Policy (% Difference)
GDPR	Gross Domestic Product	0.31	0.23
PGDP	Deflator Gross Domestic Product	1.71	2.49
PNYBRCFD	New York Price Brazilian Coffee	26.46	26.46
VACFC	Coffee Producers Price, Brazil	10.74	8.77
PRCFTON	Coffee Output	1.30	0.99
LCF	Coffee Sector Employment	1.27	0.97
CDCF	Domestic Coffee Consumption	−6.11	−4.62
ECF	Coffee Exports, Volume	8.00	8.00
ECFD	Coffee Exports Dollar Terms	34.60	34.60
S/STOCKCF	Coffee Sales Over Stocks	9.05	10.42

Source: Based on the authors' computations.

these direct administrative measures can be introduced in a simulation exercise, but we have preferred to deal here with the manipulation of the coffee export tax rate, that is, a more market-oriented policy measure.

In the experiment analyzed previously, the higher level of the world coffee price ultimately leads to a supply response in Brazil. Since planting and maturing of coffee trees is involved, the new supply does not reach the market for many years, possibly at a time when additional coffee production is no longer needed. In the absence of some kind of market intervention by Brazilian authorities, this could accentuate the decline in world coffee prices or force the coffee fund to make large stockpile purchases. Consequently, it may be desirable to reduce incentives for coffee planting by offsetting the higher world coffee price through a higher coffee export tax. Distributional considerations may also suggest that Brazilian authorities might levy a higher export tax.

The simulation analyzed previously assumed a coffee export tax (cruzeiros per 60-kilo bag) to be constant for the period. We have assumed in the present simulation that besides the price increases in world markets and larger Brazilian coffee exports, there is an active tax policy aimed at keeping the tax at a fixed percentage (15 percent) of the coffee export price (translated in cruzeiros). In Table 7–3, column (2), we present the results of this simulation, which can be compared with the results of the previous simulation that appears in column (1). Domestic coffee prices increase less rapidly; consumption appears to decrease less; and the effect on production is to decrease the production expansion. The results show that export tax policy can be an important policy instrument. It can presumably be utilized to eliminate completely the coffee price impact in the internal economy and, therefore, keep production and domestic consumption at the same levels as in the base solution, or at some intermediate levels.

Coffee Export Tax Policy and Sterilization of Foreign Reserves

As we have mentioned previously, the increase in coffee exports will result in higher inflation as the more favorable trade situation is translated into accumulation of reserves. This experiment will assume that monetary authorities, besides raising the coffee export tax as in the last experiment, will offset the monetary expansion caused by the increase in reserves, thus sterilizing the additional reserves.

A lower rate of inflation stimulates additional aggregate demand, resulting on the average in a larger rate of growth when compared with the control solution than the rate attained by the simulations in

Table 7–4. Comparisons of Solutions with Various Policy Options and an Increase in International Coffee Prices and Export Expansion (Average Percentage Differences Between Disturbed and Base Solution Dynamic Simulation 1979–1987)

Experiment	Gross Domestic Product (GDPR) (% Difference)	Deflator of Gross Domestic Product (PGDP) (% Difference)
No Economic Policy Intervention	0.31	1.71
Coffee Export Tax Policy	0.23	2.49
Coffee Export Tax Policy plus Offsetting Monetary Policy	0.43	1.00

Source: Based on the authors' computations.

which the expansion of the money supply is left unchecked. A comparison between the last three solutions is made in Table 7–4.

CONCLUSIONS

The computations described in this chapter indicate that fluctuations in the coffee market have a magnified impact on the macrostatistics of the Brazilian economy. Increases in coffee output or in the value of coffee exports translate into a higher real product with an effect on other parts of the economy—on income, government revenues, secondary and tertiary sector activity, investment, foreign exchange earnings, imports, and so on. Aggregate growth is increased by more than the contribution of greater coffee output.

In order to establish the nature and magnitude of these effects, we have modeled the coffee sector and have traced through the linkages from this sector to other parts of the Brazilian economy. These computations suggest that the principal linkages operate through:

1. The effect of coffee production on requirements for tertiary sector output.
2. The impact of earnings from coffee production on consumer demand.
3. The impact of coffee export tax payments on the government revenues and subsequently on government spending for consumption and investment.
4. The effect of increased foreign exchange earnings (in cases where the value of coffee exports increases) on imports and subsequently on capital formation and on higher prices.

The predominant effects in the present version of the model system are through the demand linkages although there is some supply impact from capital formation. The predominance of the demand effect is not altogether surprising. The Brazilian macromodel does not contain a capacity constraint in the industrial and tertiary sector output functions, reflecting the significant underutilization that occurs in Brazil as in many other developing economies. The simulations thus assume either that a capacity constraint, as in the industrial and service sectors, does not operate or that a sufficient supply side response occurs but is not modeled explicitly.

The results described above suggest a number of priorities of the next stage of the Coffee-Brazil project. Concerning model specification, we are reasonably content with the specifications obtained. In general, they seem to describe the structural aspects of the Brazilian coffee sector and its linkages to the rest of the economy. Some relatively small model modifications may improve the system, though it is unlikely that they will produce very different simulation results. These changes involve:

1. Further elaboration of the supply side aspects of the model. As we have indicated, the supply side constraints have not been operational in Brazilian industry because of underutilization although it would be useful for simulation purposes to make additional efforts to model these phenomena.
2. Endogenization of the wage rate. The latter is normally a policy variable, but for simulation purposes it will be useful to explain wages endogenously in terms of growth of productivity and the consumer price level.
3. Attempts to link income distribution in some broad measures. Needless to say, this poses some serious problems of data development.

In addition, we expect shortly to establish the computer system to permit fully linked simultaneous simulation of the coffee model and the Brazil model. This is basically a programming task, since the two systems already exist in compatible form. It is an important step because it will make possible simulations of production and policy changes in Brazil that take into account their impact on the world market. It will also facilitate simulations of changes in world market conditions and their impact on the Brazilian economy. Such a system is necessary for stabilization scenarios. The simultaneous system will also be useful in tracing out the dynamics of the interaction of the world economy and the Brazilian coffee market. This is particularly interesting because of the long lags between changes in coffee prices and the response of coffee production.

As soon as possible, the linked system will also contain models for other coffee producers, Central America and the Ivory Coast. Finally, we expect to focus, using the above system, on a variety of policy simulations. These simulations fall into two classes:

1. Simulations of world coffee market policy and its impact on the developing economy. In particular, the policy questions to be investigated involve various stabilization alternatives and their impact on the growth path of the producing countries.
2. Simulation of alternative policy responses by the producing country. In this connection, we may envision policies intended to affect the world market—for example, the purchases or sales by the Brazilian Coffee Fund Stockpile. In addition, we may consider the impact of offsetting macropolicies such as neutralization of foreign exchange earnings. Finally, as in the discussion above, we may consider policies that have direct distributional impact such as the coffee export tax.

NOTES

1. See the discussion by Lord in Chapter 9.
2. For a discussion on such dynamics, see Adams and Behrman (1978) and Ford (1977).
3. However, for simulation purposes an endogenous wage rate equation is being formulated.
4. We will consider alternative cases where variations in coffee output are offset by inventory changes and where they affect Brazilian coffee exports.
5. This is important from the point of view of consistency once we run the coffee and the Brazil model simultaneously.
6. The base solution is one in which the econometric model projects a reasonably steady growth path for the Brazilian economy for the period 1976–1987. The alternative simulations are, of course, run for the same period.

BIBLIOGRAPHY

Acquah, Paul. 1972. "A Macroeconomic Analysis of Export Instability in Economic Growth (The Case of Ghana and the World Cocoa Market)." Ph.D. dissertation, University of Pennsylvania, Philadelphia.

Adams, F. Gerard, and Jere R. Berhman, eds. 1978. *Econometric Modeling of World Commodity Policy*. Lexington, Mass.: Lexington Books.

Adams, F. Gerard, and Romualdo A. Roldan. 1978. "Econometric Studies of the Impact of Primary Commodity Markets on Economic Development in Latin America." Paper prepared for the NBER Conference on Commodity Markets, Models and Policies in Latin America, Lima, Peru, May.

Ford, Derek J. 1977. "Coffee Supply, Trade and Demand: An Econometric Analysis of the World Market, 1930–1969." Ph.D. dissertation, University of Pennsylvania, Philadelphia.

Jul, Ana-Maria. 1976. "A Macroeconometric Forecasting Model for Brazil." Ph.D. dissertation, University of Pennsylvania, Philadelphia.

International Coffee Organization. 1972. "Coffee In Brazil." Report 1119/72(E). London.

Lira, Ricardo. 1974. "The Impact of an Export Commodity in a Developing Economy: The Case of the Chilean Copper 1956–1968." Ph.D. dissertation, University of Pennsylvania, Philadelphia.

Palma-Carillo, P.A. 1976. "A Macroeconometric Model of Venezuela with Oil Price Impact Applications." Ph.D. Thesis, University of Pennsylvania.

8

RICARDO
LIRA

The Impact of Copper in the Chilean Economy

The purpose of this chapter is to describe the interrelationship between the copper sector and the rest of the economy in Chile and to analyze the possible impact on the economy of changes taking place in the copper sector. The chapter thus rests on a macroeconometric model that is both descriptive and useful for simulating the impact of fluctuations in the copper sector. The study first centers on exogenous price changes and later on changes in three policy variables: tax rates, exchange rates, and investment. Although the empirical analysis is somewhat dated, the methodology employed should be of help in the design of government policies relating to the copper sector.

Chile is endowed with an important portion of the world's reserves of copper. The main part of its production is extracted from three large mines; exports from these mines fluctuated between 38 percent and 66 percent of the total exports of the economy during the period 1956–1968. In this same period government receipts from these mines fluctuated between 6.3 percent and 17.1 percent of total government receipts. The three mines (Chuquicamata, El Salvador, and El Teniente) were owned by foreign interests during this period. Both because of their relative importance in total Chilean copper production and because of the great differences in technology and legal treatment as compared with the smaller mines, policy analysis is focused on these

This paper is based on the author's Ph.D. dissertation. Several articles also based on this dissertation were published in Spanish (1975a, 1975b). The author wishes to thank Professors F. Gerard Adams and Jere Behrman.

three mines. According to Chilean law, they belonged to what was called the "Gran Mineria del Cobre" (copper large-scale mining).

In the next section, the model is presented and briefly discussed. It is then solved numerically, and the solution is compared with the actual values for the period 1956–1968. In order to gain insight into the functioning of the model, some simulations of changes in the noncopper sector are presented. The third section is devoted to a simulation of possible impacts of an exogenous copper price change. These results depend largely on how the Chilean government would react to such changes. Finally, the fourth section presents simulations of the impact of changes in policy variables related to the copper sector. Here the results depend not only on the government's reaction, but also on the reaction of the copper companies through their investment policies.

THE MODEL

General Features

The present study has called for a model that can describe in a simplified way the impact of the copper sector on the economy as well as can evaluate the behavior of what are considered the most important variables in that sector. They are (a) the prices of copper, (b) investment in copper, (c) tax rates on the copper companies, and (d) discriminatory exchange rates in the copper sector. It would have been preferable to build a detailed model of the copper sector and to link it with an existing macroeconometric model of Chile.[1] While such an exercise has been performed in Chapter 7, the preliminary nature of this study required a small and more manageable two-sector model.[2]

The model finally adopted possesses the following characteristics:

1. The economy is divided into two sectors. One sector comprises large-scale copper mining, defined by Chilean law as the "Gran Minería del Cobre." The other sector features the rest of the economy.
2. The price of copper is taken as exogenous. The model is designed to simulate the effect of different sets of copper prices. While changes in Chilean supply are assumed not to affect the world price of copper, one can also interpret the simulated prices as those prevailing "after" the reaction of Chilean supply has taken place. A more complete model would endogenize copper prices, linking the model with a model of the world copper market.
3. The noncopper sector is demand-based. Except for the fact that it is linked to the copper sector and possesses a few other special fea-

tures, it basically works as a Keynesian model. The corresponding copper sector is supply-based. A major simplification adopted has been the leaving out of sales of copper to the national manufacturing industry, both because such sales are minimal and because descriptive data are lacking. The only link from the noncopper to the copper sector is through the exchange rate.

4. From the point of view of foreign trade, the copper sector produces a net inflow of foreign exchange and the noncopper sector a net outflow. These flows are summarized with one equation for each sector; all consumers are assumed to belong in the noncopper sector.

5. The change in money supply is related to the government deficit and the change in foreign reserves, two variables that depend a great deal on copper. The change in money supply, in turn, affects the level of prices.

6. To simplify the model, only one price deflator is employed.

The model consists of twenty-eight equations; eleven are stochastic, and seventeen are definitions. Two of the definitions contain a parameter imposed with the help of extraneous information. Owing to limitations in the data, the period of estimation varies in different equations, the longest being 1950–1971. The method of estimation used is ordinary least squares.[3] For the sake of comparison, we also estimated the consumption function by two stage-least squares; the results are presented in note 4.

Figure 8–1 describes the flows between the sectors of the model. One can see how consumption, investment, government, and the foreign sector converge to determine income. The copper sector enters through government and foreign trade. Both total investment and investment in copper are exogenous. Investment in copper affects production capacity in some of the simulations. Production capacity, together with the world price of copper, determine the production of copper. The definitions of the variables and the data sources are presented in the chapter Appendix.

The Equations

In presenting the equations of the model, a detailed discussion of the underlying hypotheses has been omitted. In parentheses next to each heading are presented the period of estimation and the $\bar{R}^2$. In parentheses below the coefficients of the stochastic equations are the values of the t-statistic. The Durbin-Watson values do not suggest autocorrelation.

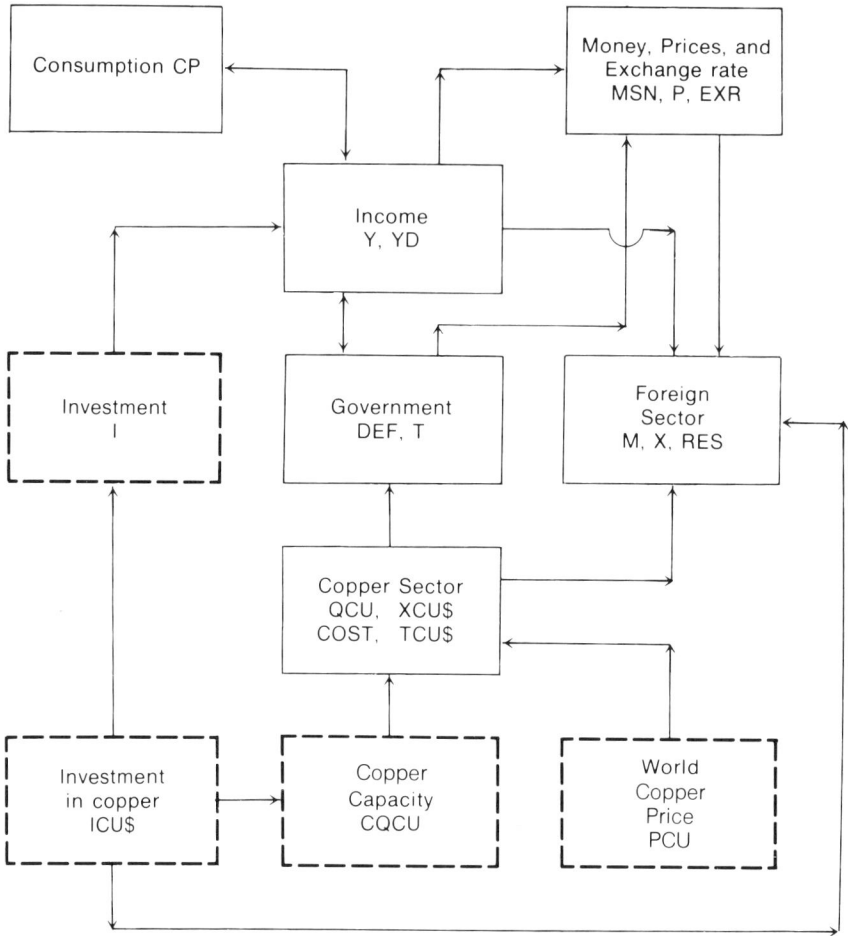

FIGURE 8-1. Sectoral Flows in the Chilean Economy

Noncopper Sector

Consumption

$$\textit{Private consumption } (1956\text{--}1969, \ \overline{R}^2 = 0.95) \qquad (8\text{--}1)$$

$$CP = -1.0236 + 0.2027 \ YD + 0.3041 \ YD_{-1}$$
$$(-1.32) \quad (16.82) \qquad \quad (16.82)$$

$$+ \ 0.3041 \ YD_{-2} + 0.2027 \ YD_{-3}$$
$$(16.82) \qquad \qquad (16.82)$$

In this equation real private consumption is a function of permanent or expected real disposable income. It was estimated using the Almon Lag technique with a second degree polynomial and restricted to have a coefficient equal to zero in the periods $t + 1$ and $t - 4$. This procedure causes the coefficients to be symmetrical.[5] The estimated long-run propensity to consume is 1.0137, but it is not significantly different from one. No doubt the Chilean propensity to consume is quite high.[6] However, one suspects that deficiencies in the Chilean national accounts make its estimated value even higher.

Government: Taxes from copper companies appear with the copper sector equations.

Government deficit:

$$DEFN = -TCU\$ \cdot EXRCU - TO \cdot P + CG \cdot P + IGN \quad (8-2)$$
$$+ SUB + TRGP \cdot P + TRGX \cdot P$$

A positive value of *DEFN* corresponds to a deficit and a negative value to a surplus.

Other taxes $(1950-1971, \overline{R}^2 = 0.97)$ $\hspace{3cm}$ (8-3)

$$TO = -2.2802 + 0.3945 \ Y$$
$$(9.95) \quad (26.96)$$

TO comprises all noncopper government receipts.

Money Supply, Prices, and Exchange Rate:

Change in money supply $\hspace{7cm}$ (8-4)

$$DMSN = 1.5 \ (DEFN + NFFEO\$ \cdot EXR$$
$$+ NFFECU\$ \cdot EXRCU) + DMSEX$$

Part of the change in money supply is endogenous and the rest, represented by *DMSEX*, is exogenous. The terms inside the parentheses constitute an approximation of the Central Bank's new money issues. This amount gets amplified by the banking multiplier, which is assumed to be constant at a value of 1.5, an approximation to the sample average. I decided not to get into accounting complications regarding the money supply and instead adjust the endogenous variable by the difference, represented by *DMSEX*. Also note that in Chile banks usually do not hold excess reserves, and thus the multiplier is well determined by the minimum legal required reserves.

Money supply (8–5)

$$MSN = MSN_{-1} + DMS$$

Rate of change in prices $(1952–1969, \overline{R}^2 = 0.79)$ (8–6)

$$\dot{P} = 0.8240 \; (MSN/\dot{P}OP) + 0.3384 \; (MSN/\dot{P}OP)_{-1} - 2.8449 \; (\dot{Y}/POP)$$
$$(6.16) \qquad\qquad (2.56) \qquad\qquad (-3.99)$$
$$- 0.5594 \; (\dot{Y}/POP)_{-1} - 0.2030 \; DUMSP$$
$$(-0.80) \qquad\qquad (-3.03)$$

Chilean inflation has been both high and erratic. The dummy added to the equation $(DUMSP)$ corresponds to the beginning of the Alessandri and Frei administrations. It takes the value of one in the years 1960 and 1965 when notable attempts to reduce inflation took place. According to this equation, the increases in money supply translate completely to prices in two periods.[7]

Level of prices (8–7)

$$P = P_{-1} \; (1 + \dot{P})$$

Rate of change of the exchange rate $(1952–1969, \overline{R}^2 = 0.50)$ (8–8)

$$E\dot{X}R = 1.0201 \; \dot{P}/100$$
$$(8.86)$$

Exchange rate (8–9)

$$EXR = EXR_{-1} \; (1 + E\dot{X}R)$$

Foreign Sector: Imports

Total imports (8–10)

$$M = MCONS + MKO + MKCU + MINTCU\$ \; (EXRCU/P)$$

Imports of consumption goods $(1953–1968, \overline{R}^2 = 0.93)$ (8–11)

$$MCONS = -0.1965 + 0.6 \; MCONS_{-1} + 0.05 \; (CP + CG)$$
$$(-0.79) \qquad (2.97) \qquad\qquad (2.61)$$
$$+ 0.0003 \; RES_{-1} - 0.0006 \; (PMC \; EXR/P)$$
$$(0.71) \qquad\qquad (-1.03)$$

Note that this is a partial adjustment equation with an adjustment coefficient of 0.4. The level of reserves at the end of the previous period represents the restrictions to imports when foreign reserves are scarce; these are lowered as the conditions improve. At the mean, the long-run elasticities are 2.3 for consumption; -0.6 for relative prices; and 0.09 for reserves. In spite of some low t-statistics, the equation explains well the behavior of *MCONS*. The estimates of the parameters of foreign reserves and prices are approximately the same that appear in many different specifications with higher t-values.

Imports of capital goods $(1953\text{--}1968, \overline{R}^2 = 0.88)$ $\hspace{2em}$ (8–12)

$$MK = 0.46\ MK_{-1} + 0.22\ (IP + ICU\$\ EXRCU/P$$
$$\hspace{0.5em}(2.26)\hspace{3em}(2.40)$$

$$+ IGN/P) + 0.0008\ RES_{-1} - 0.0004\ (PMK\ EXR/P)$$
$$\hspace{3em}(2.20)\hspace{3.5em}(-1.44)$$

The adjustment coefficient is 0.54, imports adjusting faster than consumption goods. The long-run elasticities are 1.3, 0.2, and -0.4 for investment, reserves, and prices, respectively.

Imports of intermediate goods $(1950\text{--}1968, \overline{R}^2 = 0.78)$ $\hspace{1em}$ (8–13)

$$MINT = 0.102 + 0.96\ COEFM$$
$$\hspace{0.5em}(1.50)\hspace{1em}(8.04)$$

The elasticity for COEFM is 1.07 at the mean.

Imports of capital goods for the noncopper sector $\hspace{2em}$ (8–14)

$$MKO = MK - MKCU$$

Imports of intermediate goods for the noncopper sector $\hspace{1em}$ (8–15)

$$MINTO = MINT - MINTCU\$\ EXRCU/P$$

Foreign Sector: Exports

Total exports $\hspace{2em}$ (8–16)

$$X = XO + XCU\$\ EXRCU/P$$

Other Relations in the Foreign Sector

Net flow of foreign exchange in the noncopper sector $\hspace{2em}$ (8–17)

$$NFFEO\$ = (XO - MCONS - MKO - MINTO)\ P/EXR + OF\$$$

I have added the variable $OF\$$, calculated as a residual, to account for all other noncopper flows and to correct for the data deficiencies.

Change in foreign reserves   (8–18)

$$DRES\$ = NFFECU\$ + NFFEO\$$$

Foreign reserves   (8–19)

$$RES\$ = RES\$_{-1} + DRES\$$$

Income

Income   (8–20)

$$Y = CP + CG + IP + IGN/P + ICU\$ \, EXRCU/P$$
$$+ \, X - M + DSTOCK - INFP + ADJ$$

Disposable income   (8–21)

$$YD = Y - TCU\$ \, EXRCU/P - TO + TRGP + SUB$$

Copper Sector

Production of copper (1950–1970, $\bar{R}^2 = 0.87$)   (8–22)

$$QCU = 0.89 \, CQCU + 0.867 \, PCU\$ - 86.5 \, DUMND$$
$$ (20.11) (1.50) (-4.52)$$

For each level of production capacity the given short-run supply function has a very low price elasticity of 0.07 at the mean. Fisher and Cootner (1971) have estimated a supply function similar to this. Instead of capacity they used one-year lagged production, achieving a short-run and a long-run elasticity of approximately 0.112 and 0.402, respectively. The dummy *DUMND* takes a value of unity in the years immediately before the New Treatment Law of 1955 (1953–1954). In those years the legal treatment of the companies tended to depress production.

Exports of copper   (8–23)

$$XCU\$ = QCU \cdot PCU\$ - DSCU\$ - ADXCU\$$$

The variable $ADXCU\$$ adjusts production according to changes in stocks in Chile.

Costs in national currency $(1950-1969, \overline{R}^2 = 0.79)$ (8–24)

$COSTCH\$ =$
$$\exp(-7.2 - 1.5\,GORE + 0.9\,DUMND)\,(QCU)^{2.6}\,(P/EXRCU)$$
$$(-1.12)\ (-1.45)\qquad(3.51)\qquad\qquad\qquad(3.30)$$

With constant factor costs and a constant grade of ore, this function corresponds to a Cobb-Douglas production function where the sum of the exponents is 1/2.6 (see Dhrymes 1970: 232–34).

Costs in foreign currency $(1950-1969, \overline{R}^2 = 0.67)$ (8–25)

$$COSTEX\$ = -22.1807 + 0.5377\,COSTEX\$_{-1} + 0.0777\,QCU$$
$$(-2.98)\qquad(3.88)\qquad\qquad(3.36)$$

The adjustment coefficient is 0.46; the elasticities for production are 1.3 for the short run and 2.8 for the long run at the mean.

Imports of intermediate goods for the copper sector (8–26)
$$MINTCU\$ = 0.5\,COSTEX\$$$

The coefficient of 0.5 on $COSTEX\$$ was derived from extraneous information.

Copper taxes $(1950-1969, \overline{R}^2 = 0.94)$ (8–27)

$TCU\$ = 18.5578 + 0.8134\,\hat{T\!R} \cdot PCU\$ \cdot QCU$
$\qquad\quad(1.19)\quad(12.94)$
$$- 0.3511\,\hat{T\!R} \cdot CINDX \cdot QCU$$
$$(-4.10)$$

The taxation of the companies was basically a profit tax, but given the complication of the tributary system, a stochastic specification was chosen with both a proxy for the tax rate $(\hat{T\!R})$ and for the tax base (value of production minus costs). The costs are based on a unitary cost index $(CINDX)$.

Net flow of foreign exchange from the copper sector (8–28)
$$NFFECU\$ = TCU\$ + COSTCH\$ + 1/2\,ICU\$ + WUS\$$$

Control Solution

By setting the equation residuals equal to zero, one can solve the model using the Gauss-Seidel iterative method. Using for the lagged endogenous variables the solution values, a dynamic solution is obtained for a given number of years. The control solution of the model is a dynamic deterministic solution for the period 1956–1968. The model converges in six to eight iterations. Table 8–1 summarizes the mean, root mean square, and the ratio of these two magnitudes for the control solution. The solution is quite satisfactory in the sense that it approximates the actual values for the major macroeconomic aggregates: income (Y), disposable income (YD), and private consumption (CP), and for the two important variables in the copper sector: production (QCU) and exports of copper ($XCU\$$). For the remainder of the variables in the model the results are satisfactory.

The net flow of foreign exchange variables do much better than expected. The net flows from the copper sector ($NFFECU\$$) appear to be consistently overestimated and from the noncopper sector ($NFFEO\$$) to be consistently underestimated. These two variables

Table 8–1. Mean, Root Mean Square Error, and Ratio of the Control Solution

	Mean	*RMS*	*RMS/MEAN*
1 CP	11.5649	0.518	0.045
2 DEFN	0.3937	0.292	0.742
3 TC	3.8032	0.296	0.078
4 DMS	0.3381	0.385	1.139
5 MS	1.2490	1.445	1.157
6 $\dot{P}$	30.0651	13.419	0.446
7 P	0.6972	0.100	0.143
8 E$\ddot{X}$R	0.3492	0.194	0.556
9 EXR	2.2658	0.825	0.364
10 M	2.1699	0.262	0.121
11 MCONS	0.7308	0.085	0.116
12 MK	0.7836	0.194	0.248
13 MINT	0.6556	0.064	0.098
14 MKO	0.7119	0.194	0.273
15 MINTC	0.6013	0.068	0.113
16 X	2.1619	0.309	0.143
17 NFFEC$	−321.1850	105.176	0.327
18 DRES$	6.0154	96.906	16.110
19 RES$	99.3691	163.995	1.650
20 Y	15.5254	0.633	0.041
21 YD	13.1166	0.417	0.032
22 QCU$	490.1299	20.907	0.043
23 XCU$	326.8152	15.431	0.047
24 COSTCH$	156.9230	54.160	0.345
25 COSTEX$	32.0153	3.809	0.119
26 MINTCU$	16.0077	1.904	0.119
27 TCU$	115.8615	21.280	0.184
28 NFFECU$	327.1973	56.466	0.173

Source: Based on the author's computations.

perform much better after readjusting them by using a better defini-tion of their components. That is, one can subtract half of the invest-ment in copper from the first variable and add it to the second, follow-ing the original model specification. This redefinition does not affect the rest of the results because these flows are always aggregated together. The variables subject to larger errors are those formed as small differences of large variables, that is, government deficit (*DEFN*), change in money supply (*DMS*), and change in foreign re-serves (*DRES$*), and those with accumulated errors, that is, money supply (*MSN*) and foreign reserves (*RES$*).

Multiplier Analysis

To test the sensitivity of the model when changes in some exogenous variable takes place, I have made a series of simulations of the noncop-per sector. The variables selected for the analysis are of a traditional Keynesian type: change in investment, change in taxes, autonomous change in private consumption, and change in exports. The only link from the noncopper to the copper sector is through the exchange rate. Had it been exogenous, the noncopper sector could have been simulated separately. To interpret the results, one has to keep in mind that the model assumes that aggregate supply adjusts immedi-ately to aggregate demand.

1. *Once and for all increase in government investment*

With a shock consisting of a once and for all increase in government investment of E°10 million I found an investment multiplier (*MIG* = $\Delta Y / \Delta IG$) of 1.3. Seventy percent of the income impact takes place in the first year; the complete impact appears after the fourth year. The low value of the multiplier, which contrasts with the very high propen-sity to consume, is explained by the high tax rates (40 percent) and the high response of imports to changes in income.

2. *Increase in government investment*

In this case the shock, consisting of an increase in government investment of E°10 millions (in 1965 values), is repeated every year, starting in 1956. The average increase in income is E°20 million (1965). The multiplier for this type of shock, defined as the ratio of the average increase in income to the average increase in government investment, is equal to 2. But during the simulation period, income has increased at a declining rate, suggesting a higher multiplier over a longer period, maybe around 2.6. The level of prices is consistently lower than in the control solution because the effect of income is stronger than the effect of the increase in money supply. The increase in government deficit (*DEFN*) is not as high as the increase in government investment because receipts are increased with income.

3. *Increase in noncopper taxes*

The shock is an increase of E°100 (1965) every year, starting in 1956.[8] Decrease in income is an average of E°180 million. Nevertheless, the lower government deficit translates into a lower money supply; the level of prices is higher than in the control solution because of the decrease in income. It is very interesting to observe the final effect on noncopper taxes. In the first period the decrease in income is small; therefore the negative indirect effect on noncopper taxes is also small. Instead of the E°100 million intended, taxes increase by only E°91 million in the first year. As the impact on income continues to increase, the negative effect on taxes becomes larger. The government's attempt to increase taxes fails in the long run. In the last year the increase is only E°2 million out of the E°100 million intended.

4. *Autonomous increase in private consumption*

The shock is an increase of E°1 billion (1965) every year, starting in 1956. The average multiplier and the last year multiplier are virtually the same as in the second simulation (government investment), 2.0 and 2.5, respectively. The government deficit decreases very strongly because receipts increase with income. The lower increase in money supply and the higher income act together to achieve a lower price level.

5. *Increase in noncopper exports*

With an increase of E°100 million in noncopper exports every year starting in 1956, income increases during the first four years, then decreases from 1960 to 1962, and finally increases slightly from 1963 to the end. The average increase in income is E°21.7 million; the first year increase is E°112 million, compared with only E°2 million in 1968. This phenomenon is explained by the rapid increase in imports. What happens in the economy is that the foreign reserve position improves as exports increase, but imports, which are very sensitive to the level of reserves, start to increase also, counteracting in part the effect of exports in aggregate demand.

Summary of Results of the Multiplier Analysis: The traditional Keynesian multiplier is quite low because of the high leaks, the high tax rate, and the high response of imports to income. The multiplier for continuous shocks is possibly twice as high. If income is actually constrained by demand, prices should decrease as deficit government expenditures increase. In the long run the government fails to increase taxes if the new receipts are sterilized. Finally, imports, which are very sensitive to increases in foreign reserves, counteract very quickly the effect on aggregate demand caused by increases in exports.

THE IMPACT OF WORLD COPPER PRICE CHANGES ON THE CHILEAN ECONOMY

The price of copper is one of the variables whose impact on the Chilean economy is of primary interest. Its fluctuations in the world market are very wide and have a strong impact on the highly dependent Chilean economy. In our model the price of copper is taken as exogenous, but one can simulate different prices and see what their impact would have been. This study could be complemented with a study on the world market capable of forecasting the world price.

In recent years Chile has been selling its copper at a price called the "price of Chilean Producers," fixed by the Chilean Copper Corporation (CODELCO). This price has been temporarily set equal to the price at the London Metal Exchange. Although a change in this policy is not foreseen in the near future, this has not been the situation in the past. During the second World War, all the Chilean copper was exported to the United States, which resulted in a low price. After the end of the war, the price ceiling was removed, and Chilean copper was sold at a much higher price, fixed by the large U.S. producers. At the beginning of the Korean War the U.S. government fixed the price again, but this time there was an agreement between the United States and the Chilean government to set the price 3 cents per pound higher (27 cents per pound instead of 24 cents). The additional 3 cents did not go to the companies, but directly to the Chilean government. After a year under this agreement, Chile decided not to renew it and began to fix the price directly. The Chilean copper was sold at more than 35 cents per pound, but the companies continued to receive 24 cents. This experience did not end happily. Chile was unable to adapt to the new situation when the demand pressure slowed down. Stocks started to pile up. Finally, the New Treatment Law of 1955 allowed the companies to sell the copper directly, but the government reserved the right to intervene to insure that they were selling at the highest market prices.

Simulation analysis is used to evaluate the impact of price changes on copper production (QCU) and on copper exports ($XCU\$$). For example, had the copper price been 10 cents higher every year during the simulation period, the copper supply would have been 8,674 metric tons higher every year, and the value of the exports of copper would have been an average of $115.1 million higher (in 1956—$102.3 million higher and in 1968—128.2 million higher). Similarly, the cost of production in foreign currency ($COSTEX\$$) is easy to calculate, and consequently the imports of intermediate goods ($MINTCU\$$). But to see the effect of a price change on the cost in national currency ($COSTCH\$$), it is necessary to make use of the complete model, which computes a new exchange rate.

It is much more complicated to see the effect on the rest of the economy, which not only requires a simulation with the complete model, but also assumptions about how the Chilean government is to react when prices change. Many of these assumptions are built into the model, one of the most important being the way of regulating imports according to the foreign reserve constraint. The given specification of the import functions seems to describe well the government reaction during the simulation period. But this is a policy tool whose use is very important in the design of governmental economic policy. It has been and continues to be greatly discussed among Chilean economists. The present contribution to this discussion is to show what is likely to happen to aggregate demand, based on the underlying assumptions of the model.

Another important decision that must be made by the government is how to use the receipts from an increase in the price of copper (in this case set at 10 cents). The model assumes that the Central Bank buys the foreign currency from the government, who uses it to relieve its deficit (the budget is not separated into national and foreign currency). This appears to be so because of the need to counteract inflation. The simulations presented here are based on two alternative assumptions: (1) the government acts the way described by the model, sterilizing the additional receipts when copper price increases; and (2) the government increases its expenditures by exactly the same amount as the additional receipts. The results obtained are radically different.

1. *Government maintains the original expenditures*
   In this case GNP increased at the beginning of the period, but then decreased after 1960. The average decrease for the period was E°12.7 million (1965). The increase in exports is counteracted in two ways: (1) by an increase in imports, owing to a better situation in the foreign reserves, and (2) by the sterilization of the portion of the increase in exports corresponding to higher taxes from copper. The increase in imports alone is not enough to produce the decline in GNP because it is only part of the increase in exports. Alternatively, the sterilization of the tax increases alone is not enough to produce the decline in GNP, because what is being sterilized is again part of the increase in exports.

But the sum of these two effects is sufficient to produce the decrease in GNP found in this simulation.

2. *Government increases its expenditures by the amount of the additional receipts*

In this case the only counteracting effect is that of the induced increase in imports. A higher GNP occurs every year during the simulation period. The average increase is E°290.3 million (1965).

THE IMPACT OF GOVERNMENT POLICY CHANGES

Let us now analyze the impact of the three macro policy variables: changes in investment, taxation, and the exchange rate. The government could fix the tax rates of the companies and could impose discriminatory exchange rates on them. But these two policies would affect the willingness of the companies to invest in Chile. Many times during the sample period, negotiations between the government and the companies took place. On two occasions these negotiations changed substantially the legal treatment of the companies. First in 1955 with the New Treatment Law and later, in the second half of the 1960s, with the process of partial nationalization. Sometimes negotiations failed, as at the beginning of the 1960s, when the companies wanted to expand production capacity. They requested a guarantee by the government not to increase the tax rates for a long period of time. Since the government did not accept this condition, expansion did not take place.

The practice of fixing lower exchange rates for the copper companies was ended by the New Treatment Law of 1955, but it was again applied, to a lesser extent, in the 1960s. For example, in 1951 the average exchange rate of copper was E°0.019 per dollar, and for the rest of the economy it was E°0.057. Since the companies purchase all their imports with their own exchange, the real discrimination would be the difference between the actual exchange rate for the copper sector and the parity exchange rate. I presently refer only to the nominal discrimination.

Increasing the tax rate was always a temptation to the Chilean government. It would alleviate the government deficit and increase the inflow of foreign exchange. From the point of view of internal politics, it would be a popular measure. Of course there was the fear that the expansion of production capacity would be inhibited, but this temptation was not always resisted. For example, in the early 1960s a devastating earthquake was a reason to establish an additional reconstruction tax on the copper companies.

Of these three variables, the tax and the exchange rates are properly government policy variables. Investment was a variable controlled by the companies although it was influenced by the government policies. The Chilean government could also invest in copper, thus making investment also a government policy variable.

Here we do not study the interrelationship between these three policies, but simply conduct the simulation analysis by assuming different relations between tax rates and investment, and between exchange rates and investment. To avoid varying the relation between investment and changes in production capacity, two additional assumptions are made:

1. Assumption 1: every million dollars of investment increases production capacity by 500 metric tons per year.

2. Assumption 2: every million dollars of investment increases production capacity by 1000 metric tons per year.

These values come from the observation of specific expansion programs undertaken in Chilean large-scale copper mining. For large projects, it seems that the following patterns appear to exist. A lag of two years occurs until investment becomes materialized in increased production capacity; and one-half of the investment is spent on imports of capital goods and one-half on payments in Chile.

Simulations follow in seven groups. In the first three groups I change only one variable, assuming that the other two remain unchanged. In the last four, changes in investment are assumed in response to either discriminatory exchange rates or changes in the tax rate. The seven groups of simulations are as follows:

1. Higher investment
2. Higher tax rates
3. Discriminatory exchange rates
4. Discriminatory exchange rates and lower investment
5. Higher tax rates and lower investment
6. Tax rate equal to 100 percent and zero investment by the companies
7. Tax rate equal to 50 percent and higher investment

Because of space limitations, only a sample of the total simulation runs can be discussed. The results selected are based on assumption 1. In addition government expenditures do not vary with changes in government receipts.

1. *Higher investment*
The impact of the new investment on the economy will depend not only on its magnitude, but also in the way it is spread over time.

Results are presented for two cases: (a) that the total investment is completed in one year, and (b) that the investment is equally distributed among the simulation periods.

a. *Additional investment of $200 million in 1956*

Beginning with the third year, production capacity will be 100 thousand metric tons higher than historical levels, and production will be 89,100 metric tons higher. Exports will increase between 50 and 105 million dollars. Taxes on copper will average $15 million higher. The accompanying improvement in foreign reserves will induce an increase in imports. As the government sterilizes the new receipts, the combined counteracting effect produces a decrease in aggregate demand averaging E°200 million (1965). The only years in which income increases are the first, third, and fourth. In the first year investment increases, but neither imports (except capital goods for the copper sector) which react with a lag to the change in reserves nor taxes from copper sales increase. In the second year there is no investment injection; production capacity has not yet increased; but imports are higher and so are the noncopper taxes. This produces a decline in aggregate demand. In the third and fourth years we already have the increase in exports that predominate over the counteracting forces. In the fifth year, however, income is lower than in the control solution.

b. *Additional investment of $20 million every year*

The difference from the previous simulation is that new investment now enters the economy every year. Income increases until 1962 and decreases from 1963 on. The result is an average decrease of E°46 million (1965). The depressing forces take more time to predominate.

2. *Higher tax rates*

An additional tax of 10 percent introduced to our model through the proxy for the tax rate (TR) will have a variable effect on $TCU\$$, because this variable is determined stochastically. The increase in taxes will be between 9 percent and 14.5 percent, with an average of around 12 percent. Income decreases an average of E°95.4 million (1965). Both foreign reserves and imports are higher during the simulation period. The government gets additional receipts that are sold to the Central Bank and used to diminish the deficit. But as income is depressed, so are noncopper taxes; the final result is a very slight decrease in government deficit.

3. *Discriminatory exchange rates*

With a lower exchange rate, the companies have to spend more dollars to cover the same expenses in national currency. Thus, an exchange rate 50 percent lower would have meant an increase in the dollar value of the costs in national currency ($COSTCH\$$) between \$123.4 million and \$293.6 million, averaging around \$200 million. With this additional inflow of foreign exchange, reserves are increased substantially. At the end of the period, in spite of the high increase in imports, the level of reserves is nearly five times that in the control solution. Aggregate demand diminishes an average of $E°847.5$ million (1965) because of the increase in imports.

4. *Discriminatory exchange rates and lower investment*

The effect of a discriminatory exchange rate is now made dependent on how the companies would have reacted through their investment. Because it is difficult to guess the reaction of the companies, different assumptions were made about the decrease in investment. The magnitude of the results changes, but not their nature. Suppose that an exchange rate 50 percent lower would have induced the companies to invest 20 percent less in Chile. The result would have been to end up in 1968 with a production decrease of 18.6 percent. Had the investment been 50 percent lower, production in 1968 would have been 46.8 percent lower. In the first case the dollar value of the costs in national currency would still be higher, but this increment averaging \$80 million is lower. In the second case this variable is higher during the first four years and lower than in the control solution from then on. Returning to the first case, the level of reserves is higher for the whole period except for the last year. This produces an increase in imports, which depresses income by $E°500$ million (1965). In 1968 imports are \$41 million lower, a consequence of the lower income.

5. *Higher tax rates and lower investment*

If the introduction of an additional tax of 10 percent had induced the companies to decrease investment by 20 percent, production would have declined an average of 52.2 thousand metric tons. In this case copper taxes increase the first six years, but later production is sufficiently lower to cause them to decrease, resulting in an average decrease of \$0.4 million. On the other hand, the lower production implies a lower cost in national currency of \$57.4 million. The result is a great deterioration of foreign reserves, which in turn induce imports to decrease significantly. The lower investment is able to produce a very slight decrease in income during the first three years, but afterward income increases, ending with an average increase of $E°65$ million (1965).

6. *Tax rate of 100 percent and zero investment by the companies*

A 100 percent tax rate is very similar to nationalizing the copper companies without giving them any compensation. Thus, the proxy for the rate (TR) is set equal to 100 percent and this comes very close to taxing the entire profits of the companies. Of course the companies do not make any new investment in Chile. In this group two cases are analyzed: (a) investment is zero, and (b) the government obtains money from abroad and makes an investment of $100 million in 1956.

a. *Zero investment*
Production declines an average of 41.5 thousand metric tons. In spite of this reduction, the government gets additional receipts from copper averaging $28.8 million. This increase in taxes is too low to prevent the deterioration in the level of foreign reserves, which induces a decline in imports. But the decline in disposable income, together with the decline in exports, produces a decrease in aggregate demand.

b. *Government invests $100 million in 1956*
Production capacity is higher between 1958 and 1962, but it is lower from 1963 to the end. The average loss in production is 3.8 thousand metric tons. It is assumed that government finances the investment with a long-term foreign loan so money is not taken from reserves. Despite foreign reserves being higher most of the years as taxes are increased, this increase is not enough to keep imports higher, because the decline in disposable income tends to predominate in depressing imports. The decline in exports and investment is stronger than the decline in imports, giving a net decrease in income.

7. *Tax rate equal to 50 percent and higher investment*
A tax rate of 50 percent would probably have been an incentive to the companies to invest more. Being conservative, let us assume that investment would have been 10 percent higher. In this case production would increase, ranging from 4.2 thousand metric tons in 1958 to 49.2 thousand metric tons in 1968, with an average of 26.3 thousand metric tons. But as the tax rate is lower, there is an average decrease in taxes of $21.7 million. In terms of foreign reserves, the increase in production is not enough to compensate the lower tax receipts, but the increase in disposable income, perhaps together with the time structure of the increases and decreases in reserves, produces an average increase in imports. Exports increase far more than imports, which together with the increase in disposable income and investment, produce an increase in income.

SUMMARY AND CONCLUSIONS

I have developed a model of the Chilean economy describing the interrelationship between the copper sector and the rest of the economy.

The model used for the noncopper sector is essentially Keynesian. This means that the emphasis is placed on the demand side. Aggregate demand is what determines real income; aggregate supply plays the passive role of adjusting to aggregate demand. The validity of the results has depended, among other things on (1) the state of the economy in terms of the responsiveness of aggregate supply to adjust to increases in aggregate demand, and (2) the realism of the assumptions made regarding government behavior. When aggregate demand decreases, as in most of the simulations, one may well expect that supply decreases will follow. Although the specification of the model has not permitted the testing of more sophisticated assumptions about government behavior, further development of the model could easily accomplish this task. In effect, simulation analysis conducted along these lines could be of great help to the Chilean government in designing its copper related policies.

NOTES

1. Jere Behrman (1976) has constructed a larger, more general model of the Chilean economy that could be used in future exercises.

2. Some of the advantages and disadvantages of establishing such a linkage are reported in Chapter 7.

3. Behrman (1976) justifies using primarily ordinary least squares in estimating his model for the Chilean economy in the following way:

> The expected returns of adopting more sophisticated methods are less than the expected costs of doing so given the nature of the data, some questions about the robustness of alternative estimators, and the opportunity costs of sophistication in estimation procedure in terms of exploring various model structures.

4. Using 2SLS:

$$CP = -2.0277 + 0.2198 \ YD + 0.3297 \ YD_{-1}$$
$$(-2.79) \quad (19.53) \quad\quad (19.53)$$
$$+ \ 0.3297 \ YD_{-2} + 0.2192 \ YD_{-3}$$
$$(19.53) \quad\quad\quad (19.53)$$
$$\bar{R}^2 = 0.95$$

The long-run propensity to consume from this equation is 1.0990.

5. In this case

$$P(\tau) = \beta_0 + \beta_1\tau + \beta_2\tau^2 \qquad \tau = 0, 1, 2, \ldots, n$$

where n, the maximum lag, is 3. Constrained to have $P(t + 1) = P(t - n - 1) = 0$, we have

$$P(\tau) = -\beta_2 \left| n + 1 + n\tau - \tau^2 \right|$$

See Dhrymes (1971).

6. Jere Behrman (1976) estimated a log-run propensity equal to 0.956.

7. The sum of the relevant coefficients is around 1.15, but not significantly different from one.

8. To indicate that most of the solutions values are based on 1965 values, I simply have placed the base year in parentheses (1965) where relevant.

APPENDIX

*1. Endogenous Variables**

	Name	Description	Units	Source
1	CP	Private Consumption[1]	Billion E°1965	Nat'l Acct.
2	DEFN	Government Deficit[5]	Billion Current E°	1
3	TO	Other Taxes[6]	Billion E°1965	2
4	DMSN	Change in Money Supply	Billion Current E°	
5	MSN	Money Supply (M_1)[7]	Billion Current E°	3
6	P	Rate of Change in GNP Deflator	Percentage	
7	P	Implicit GNP Deflator[8]	1965 = 1	4
8	EXR	Rate of Change in Exchange Rate	Per Unity	
9	EXR	Exchange Rate[9]	E° per US$	5
10	M	Imports	Billion E°1965	Nat'l Acct.
11	MCONS	Imports of Consumption Goods[10]	Billion E°1965	6
12	MK	Imports of Capital Goods[10]	Billion E°1965	6
13	MINT	Imports of Intermediate Goods[10]	Billion E°1965	6
14	MKO	Imports of Capital Goods for Noncopper[11]	Billion E°1965	7
15	MINTO	Imports of Intermediate Goods for Noncopper[12]	Billion E°1965	8
16	X	Total Exports[1]	Billion E°1965	Nat'l Acct.
17	NFFEO$	Net Flow of Foreign Exchange from Noncopper Sector[13]	Million US$	9
18	DRES$	Change in Foreign Reserves	Million US$	
19	RES$	Foreign Reserves[14]	Million US$	10
20	Y	Gross National Product	Billion E°1965	Nat'l Acct.
21	YD	Disposable Income[15]	Billion E°1965	11
22	QCU	Production of Copper Net Content[2]	Thousand MT	Codelco
23	XCU$	Exports of Copper. Fob.[3]	Million US$	Bal. de Pagos
24	COSTCH$	Costs of the Copper Company paid in National Currency[2]	Million US$	Codelco
25	COSTEX$	Costs of the Copper Company paid in Foreign Currency[2]	Million US$	Codelco
26	MINTCU$	Imports of Intermediate Goods for Copper Sector[16]	Million US$	12
27	TCU$	Taxes from Copper Comp.	Million US$	Codelco
28	NFFECU$	Net Flow of Foreign Exchange from the Copper Sector[17]	Million US$	13

2. *Exogenous Variables**

No.	Code	Description	Unit	Source
1	ADJ	Adjustment for Changes in the Terms of Trade[1]	Billion E°1965	Nat'l Acct.
2	CG	Government Consumption[2]	Billion E°1965	Bal. de Pagos
3	CINDX	Index of Principal Metal Mining Expenses[4]	1958 = 100	
4	COEFM	Imports of Intermediate Goods Required According to Input-Output Table Coefficients[18]	Million E°1965	ODEPLAN [18]
5	CQCU	Production Capacity of the Copper Companies. Net[19]	000 Metric Tons	CODELCO [19]
6	OF$	Other Flows of Foreign Exchange[20]	Million US$	Nat'l Acct. [20]
7	DMSEXN	Exogenous Change in Money[21] Supply	Million Curr. E°	Bal. de Pagos [21]
8	DSCU	Change in Stocks[1]	Billion E°1965	
9	DSTOCK	Change in Stocks of Copper in Chile[3]	Million US$	
10	DUMND	Dummy, Pre-New Deal Years	1953, 1954 = 1	
11	EXR	Exchange Rate for National Accounts[1]	E°per US$ 1	
12	EXRCU	Average Exchange Rate for the Copper Companies[2]	E°per US$ 1	
13	GORE	Grade of ore of Kennecott's mines in Chile[22]		Bal. de Pagos [22]
14	IGN	Government Investment[23]	Billion Curr. E°	Nat'l Acct. [23]
15	ICU	Investment in Copper[24]	Million US$	Nat'l Acct. [24]
16	INFP	Net Payment to Foreign Production Factors	Billion E°1965	
17	IP	Private investment[25]	Billion E°1965	CODELCO [25]
18	MKCU	Imports of Capital Goods for the Copper Sector[26]	Billion E°1965	
19	MS	Money Supply (M_1)	Billion E°1965	
20	PCU	Price of Copper[29]	US$ per pound	
21	PMC	Unit Value Index of Imports of Consumption Goods	1947 = 100	
22	PMK	Unit Value Index of Imports of Capital Goods	1947 = 100	
23	POP	Population[28]	Million of Persons	
24	RES$	Foreign Reserves	Million US$	
25	SUB	Government Subsidies[29]	Billion E°1965	
26	TR	Proxy for Tax Rate[29]	Per Unit	
27	TRGP	Net Transfers from Govt. to Households[1]	Billion E°1965	
28	TRGX	Net Transfers from the Govt. Abroad[1]	Billion E°1965	
29	WUS	Wages Pd. in Foreign Currency by Copper Companies[2]	Million US$	
30	XO	Noncopper Exports[30]	Billion E°1965	
31	ADXCU	Adjustment for Copper Export	Million US$	
32	DUMSP	Dummy, Stabilization Policies	Million US$	

Notes on the Data Sources

[1]ODEPLAN (annual).

[2]CODELCO: Data furnished by CODELCO (Copper Corporation of Chile).

[3]Balanza de Pagos: *Balanza de Pagos de Chile* (annual).

[4]U.S. Bureau of Mines. Annual. The national accounts of 1950–1959 were adjusted because of changes in compilation.

[5]Calculated as the change in total credit received by the government. $DEFN = CR - CR_{-1}$.

[6]Calculated as total government receipts minus taxes from copper; $TO =$ Gov. Receipts $- TCU\$ \cdot EXR/P$.

[7]Part of this series was taken from French-Davis (1971). It was completed with data from the *Boletin Mensual*, Central Bank of Chile. It corresponds to the definition of M_1.

[8]Calculated as nominal income divided by real income; $P = Ynom/Yreal$.

[9]Corresponds to the exchange rate used in the Chilean national accounts, furnished by ODEPLAN.

[10]The percentages calculated from the *Balanza de Pagos* were applied to the total imports of the national accounts.

[11]Calculated as total imports of capital goods minus imports of capital goods for the copper sector; $MKO = MK - MKCU$.

[12]Calculated as total imports of intermediate goods minus imports of intermediate goods for the copper sector; $MINTO = MINT - MINTCU\$ - EXR/P$.

[13]Calculated as noncopper exports minus noncopper imports plus other flows in the noncopper sector.

[14]From French-Davis.

[15]Calculated as income minus government receipts; $YD = Y - TO - TCU\$ \cdot EXR/P + TRGP + SUB$.

[16]Calculated as 1/2 of the costs of the copper companies paid in foreign currency. These costs are distributed more or less in equal parts between imports of intermediate goods and other costs, according to the partial date we were able to get; $MINTCU\$ = 0.5\ COSTEX\$$.

[17]Calculated as taxes from copper plus costs of the copper companies paid in national currency plus investment in copper plus wages paid in foreign currency in the copper sector (WUS\$).

[18]The coefficients of imports of intermediate goods were applied to the value added of each sector. The coefficients are the following: Agriculture: 0.00949; Mining: 0.0558; Construction: 0.0376; Manufacturing: 0.1047; Transportation: 0.0172; Electricity, Gas and Water: 0.0394; Services: 0.00214.

[19]The method of the "trend through peaks" was used.

[20]Calculated as a residual from $DRES - NFFECU\$ - NFFEO\$$.

[21]Calculated as a residual from the money supply equation.

[22]From Kennecott's Reports to the Stockholders.

[23]Calculated as government savings minus government deficit; $IGN = AGN - DEFN$.

[24]From the Chilean Senate's Information Office.

[25]Calculated as total investment minus government investment minus investment in copper; $IP = I - ICU\$ \cdot EXR/P$.

[26]Calculated as 1/2 of investment in copper. From the observation of specific investment projects in the copper sector, I found that around half is spent on imports of capital goods and half is brought to the country as foreign exchange to buy national goods and services.

[27]Calculated as the value of sales divided by the quantity. It is an average price in US$ per pound of copper.

[28]Provided by ODEPLAN.

[29]The tax rates for each of the companies were first calculated following the taxing laws; then a weighted average of the three tax rates was constructed.

[30]Calculated as total exports minus copper exports; $XO = X - XCU\$ \cdot EXR/P$.

BIBLIOGRAPHY

Balanza de Pajos de Chile. Annual. Santiago, Banco Central de Chile.

Behrman, J.R. 1976. "Macroeconomic Policy in a Developing Country: An Econometric Investigation of the Postwar Chilean Experience." Philadelphia: University of Pennsylvania. Mimeographed.

Dhrymes, P. 1970. *Econometrics, Statistical Foundations and Applications.* New York: Harper and Row.

———. 1971. *Distributed Lags, Problems of Estimation and Formulation.* San Francisco: Holden-Day, Inc.

Fisher, F., and P. Cootner. 1971. *An Econometric Model of the World Copper Industry.* Cambridge, Mass.: MIT Discussion Paper No. 70.

French-Davis, Ricardo. "Economic Policies and Stabilization Programs: Chile, 1952–1969." Ph.D. dissertation, University of Chicago, 1971.

Lira, R., 1974. "The Impact of an Export Commodity in a Developing Economy: the Case of the Chilean Copper, 1956–1968." Ph.D. dissertation, University of Pennsylvania.

———. 1975a. "Un Modelo Macroeconométrico de Corto Plazo y de Dos Sectores para la Economía Chilena." *Cuadernos de Economía* 35: 63–93.

———. 1975b. "Simulaciones con un Modelo Macroeconométrico del Impacto del Cobre en la Economía Chilena." *Cuadernos de Economía* 37: 47–104.

ODEPLAN. Annual. *Cuentas Nacionales, 1960–1971.* Santiago: ODEPLAN, 1972.

U.S. Bureau of Mines. Annual. *Minerals Yearbook.* Washington, D.C.

Part IV

Potentials of Stabilizing Latin America's Commodity Earnings

9

MONTAGUE J.
LORD

Commodity Export Instability and Growth in the Latin American Economies

In recent years Latin American has been a major participant in Third World demands for changes in international economic relations. The ensuing debates between the developing nations and the industrialized states have placed high priority on the regulation of international commodity markets. Consequently, when the first concrete proposals for the establishment of a new international economic order were adopted at the Fourth Session of the UNCTAD, the centerpiece of these proposals was the resolution on the Integrated Program on Commodities (UNCTAD, 1976; 1977a).

The central theme of the integrated program has become "to achieve stable conditions in commodity trade, including avoidance of excessive price fluctuations" (UNCTAD, 1976:3). The operational means designated for the stabilization of commodity markets is the "establishment of pricing arrangements, in particular negotiated price

I am indebted to Frank Orlando for helping to develop the analytic technique for the measurement of instability utilized in this chapter. The chapter also benefited from valuable comments on an earlier version by a number of persons, including John C. Elac, Jorge Espinosa Carranza, Walter C. Labys, and Robert C. Vogel. Computer work for the statistical results was undertaken by Nadine Lopez Callejas. The views expressed herein are those of the author and do not necessarily reflect those of the Inter-American Development Bank.

213

ranges" (UNCTAD, 1976:4); these arrangements would operate through supply management, principally in the form of commodity stockpiling or through production controls and export quotas. Since the fall of 1976, the developing and industrialized countries have engaged in a series of negotiations for regulating the international markets of up to eighteen commodities; twelve of which are among Latin America's principal exports (Table 9–1).[1] Although the UNCTAD proposal for the establishment of a common fund to serve as the main financial source of individual commodity stocking agreements has encountered some resistance, the key issue remains commodity price stabilization arrangements.

The focus of the integrated program on commodity price stabilization poses a number of issues for Latin America. First is a question of fact; that is, have Latin America's commodity exports been subject to unstable market conditions from a long-term perspective? Second, where export fluctuations have been severe, what have been their consequences on the economic development of the countries? Third, have commodity prices, rather than quantities, been the significant component affecting unstable behavior in export earnings? Finally, to the extent that export stability is a desired objective of the Latin American countries, can export instability be remedied or foreign exchange earnings be improved through international commodity arrangements as proposed by the integrated program? The importance of these questions has been underscored in the statement by Harry Johnson (1976:332 and 1977:248) on the need to "concentrate on the issue of why commodity prices fluctuate as much as they do, how far and in what respect such fluctuations have the undeniable adverse development effects that UNCTAD lore—and earlier popular beliefs about the development problem—invariably and sweepingly attribute to them, and what if anything can be done to mitigate the fluctuations by tackling the basic causes rather than the symptoms."

This chapter will examine these issues from the point of view of Latin America.[2] It begins by considering the relationship between economic development and export instability and also evaluates the empirical techniques used to measure this relationship. The next part assesses the degree of instability in Latin America's export earnings caused by the regionally significant commodities included in the integrated program and considers the responsiveness of earnings to fluctuations in both export price and volume. The final section deals with the feasibility of international commodity price stabilization arrangements for stabilizing or improving the region's export proceeds. The principal conclusion of this chapter is that neither the degree, the origins, nor the consequences of instability are phenomena common among the Latin American countries but rather are uniquely circumscribed by the particular characteristics of each country and international commodity market. These last two factors determine whether or not a specific country is likely to benefit from global price stabilization schemes for their exports.

NATIONAL EXPORT INSTABILITY

Export instability has been a traditional preoccupation for Latin America because of the dependence of most countries on a relatively few primary commodity exports. To the extent that the markets for these products are unstable, their effect on overall export earnings may constitute a deterrent to national economic growth. The degree of fluctuations in export earnings and the impact on economic development are essential to the understanding of Latin America's support of international commodity stabilization agreements. This section addresses these two issues.

Consequences of Instability

Since most Latin American economies are strongly oriented toward foreign trade, export instability can more readily influence their overall economic performance. It is argued that unstable export receipts induce domestic instability and hinder economic development. When there is limited borrowing capacity and low reserves of foreign exchange, fluctuations in export receipts will cause variations in imports of capital goods. Because of the openness of the economies, these fluctuations in turn, can bring about sharp alterations in the level of investment, output, and employment. Sudden shortfalls in export earnings may retard growth in domestic sectors, whereas sharp increases in export earnings can cause inflationary pressure on the economy. The unreliable nature of these earnings hampers implementation and follow-up of projects that depend on projected levels of foreign exchange earnings and also can create discontinuities in the domestic economic policies of government development programs. Finally, export price volatility will increase uncertainty in investment planning and produce greater risks in investment financing and, thus, higher costs for fixed capital formation.[3]

However, assertions regarding the adverse effects of export instability on the economic growth of primary exporting countries have been questioned by MacBean (1966) on the basis of empirical evidence. His study assessed the relationship between export instability and a number of indicators of economic activity in a cross-section of countries. It concluded that export instability in developing countries, in

Table 9–1. Latin America: Contribution of Principal Commodity Exports to Each Country's Total Value of Merchandise Exports, 1970–1974 Average (Percentages)

	Regionally Significant Non-fuel Exports[a]										Others		
	In UNCTAD List												
	"Core" Products					Other Products							
Country	Coffee	Sugar	Copper	Cotton	Cocoa	Beef	Iron Ore	Soy-beans	Bananas	Bauxite	Maize	Fish-meal	Sub-total
Argentina	—	2.3	—	0.3	—	13.3	—	—	—	—	14.3	0.1	30.3
Barbados	—	31.4	—	—	—	—	—	—	—	—	—	—	31.4
Bolivia	1.6	2.4	—	3.1	—	0.4	—	—	—	—	—	—	7.5
Brazil	20.2	10.5	—	3.3	3.3	2.2	5.9	9.5	0.3	—	1.3	—	56.5
Chile	—	—	69.9	—	—	—	4.6	—	—	—	—	1.6	76.1
Colombia	51.6	3.2	—	3.9	0.1	2.2	—	—	1.7	—	—	—	62.7
Costa Rica	28.5	5.4	—	0.1	1.5	8.8	—	—	26.9	—	—	—	71.2
Dominican Rep.	9.3	48.0	—	—	6.3	1.7	—	—	0.3	4.2	—	—	69.8
Ecuador	11.0	3.7	—	—	7.6	—	—	—	20.1	—	—	—	42.4
El Salvador	42.2	5.7	—	10.9	—	0.7	—	—	—	—	0.4	—	59.9
Guatemala	32.5	5.6	—	10.8	0.1	4.8	—	—	4.4	—	—	—	58.2
Guyana	—	36.1	—	—	—	—	—	—	—	43.5	—	—	79.6
Haiti	37.3	5.5	—	—	3.6	1.8	—	—	—	8.0	—	—	56.2
Honduras	15.9	0.8	—	0.6	—	7.4	—	—	36.5	—	0.2	—	61.4
Jamaica	0.4	11.0	—	—	0.5	—	—	—	3.6	68.1	—	—	83.6
Mexico	5.8	6.0	0.7	6.5	0.4	2.0	—	—	—	—	0.4	—	21.8
Nicaragua	14.7	4.9	—	26.8	—	12.7	—	—	1.1	—	0.3	—	60.5
Panama	1.4	7.7	—	—	—	1.4	—	—	44.7	—	—	1.1	56.3
Paraguay	1.9	0.5	—	7.0	—	10.7	—	9.1	—	—	0.1	—	29.3
Peru	4.2	7.7	19.1	5.1	—	—	5.9	—	—	—	—	19.5	61.5
Trin. & Tobago	0.2	3.4	—	—	0.4	—	—	—	—	—	—	—	4.0
Uruguay	—	—	—	—	—	35.7	—	—	—	—	—	—	35.7
Venezuela	0.3	0.2	—	—	0.2	—	3.2	—	—	—	—	—	3.9
Latin America	9.6	5.5	5.3	2.4	1.1	3.2	2.5	2.1	1.7	1.7	1.9	1.1	38.1

Source: National statistical offices.

[a]The criterion used to define the main primary commodity exports of the region has been those products which during 1970–74 represented an average of at least 1% of the total value of Latin America's merchandise exports.

Table 9-1. (Continued)

| | Other Nationally Significant Non-fuel Exports[b] | | | | | | | |
| | UNCTAD "Core" Others | | Others | | | | Total Main Commod. Exports | Total Merch. Exports |
Country	Tin	Lumber	Prepared Meat	Shell-fish	Wool	Sub-total		
Argentina	—	—	4.9	—	2.1	7.0	37.3	100.0
Barbados	—	—	—	1.6	—	1.6	33.2	100.0
Bolivia	41.3	1.6	—	—	—	41.3	48.8	100.0
Brazil	0.2	0.5	1.1	0.6	0.3	3.8	60.3	100.0
Chile	—	—	—	0.3	0.2	1.0	77.1	100.0
Colombia	—	0.2	—	0.8	—	1.0	63.7	100.0
Costa Rica	—	—	0.1	0.6	—	0.7	71.9	100.0
Dominican Rep.	—	—	—	—	—	—	69.8	100.0
Ecuador	—	—	—	1.7	—	1.7	44.1	100.0
El Salvador	—	—	—	2.2	—	2.2	61.4	100.0
Guatemala	—	0.6	0.5	0.7	—	1.8	60.0	100.0
Guyana	—	—	—	2.9	—	2.9	82.5	100.0
Haiti	—	—	—	—	—	—	56.2	100.0
Honduras	—	13.4	—	1.2	—	14.6	76.0	100.0
Jamaica	—	—	—	—	—	—	83.6	100.0
Mexico	—	—	—	4.0	—	4.0	25.8	100.0
Nicaragua	—	1.9	—	3.0	—	4.9	65.4	100.0
Panama	—	—	—	10.2	—	10.2	66.5	100.0
Paraguay	—	—	12.0	—	—	12.0	41.3	100.0
Peru	—	—	—	—	—	—	61.5	100.0
Trin. & Tobago	—	—	—	—	—	—	4.0	100.0
Uruguay	—	—	—	—	14.8	14.8	50.5	100.0
Venezuela	—	—	—	0.2	—	0.2	4.1	100.0
Latin America	0.6	0.5	0.9	0.8	0.5	3.3	41.4	100.0

[b]Nationally significant products have been defined as those products which during 1970–74 accounted for an average of at least 10% of a country's total value of merchandise exports.

general, has not led to such detrimental effects on the growth of their economies as had been traditionally supposed. Later works of Kenen and Voivodas (1972) and Knudsen and Parnes (1975) corroborated these results. Nevertheless, there has also been much skepticism expressed over the empirical validity of these studies. Maizels (1968), for example, has disputed the statistical interpretation of MacBean; Voivodas (1974) showed the results to be sensitive to the manner in which the equations are formulated; and more recently, Lim (1976) has pointed to the failure of empirical works in this field to provide a theoretical framework for analyzing the relationship between export instability and economic growth.

More conclusive evidence has been found on the significance of export growth as a determinant of economic expansion in developing nations. Hence, Glezakos (1973) tested the effect of export instability on the growth rate of exports and the effect of the growth rate of exports on real per capita income. The results of this more indirect approach tended to support the traditional view that export instability may inhibit the economic growth of developing countries. Nonetheless, even these results do not seem necessarily valid for Latin America on the basis of the cross-national approach used by Glezakos. Although Massell, Pearson, and Finch (1972) have verified the importance of export growth to economic development in Latin America, export instability and growth (for the region's commodities included in the integrated program) have not been found to be significantly related for the twenty-three countries of the region during the 1960–1975 period.[4] These findings are not surprising. Various factors influence the growth rate of exports of the Latin American countries. Because of their structural differences, these may include the highly divergent internal policies among the countries, as well as the geographic destination of the products and conditions in the world markets. Moreover, high levels of instability have often resulted from discontinuities related to domestic expansionary export programs instead of unstable external markets (de Vries, 1977).

Cross-country analysis therefore does not provide a methodologically feasible manner of empirically resolving the issue of the effects of export instability. Its intrinsic limitation, as pointed out by Maizels (1968), presupposes similar domestic economic responses to export disturbances. To the extent that export responses differ, cross-section regression analysis fails to provide a significant relation between unstable export proceeds and economic growth, even though individual country responses may nonetheless be significant. It would therefore seem more valid empirically to test the experiences of each country separately.

This approach has been attempted recently by Rangarajan and Sundararajan (1976). They based their investigation on the use of export-income and export-investment multipliers calculated from aggregate country models. Although export fluctuations invariably increase instability of income, their findings show that the investment and income growth responses of countries to fluctuations in their export earnings vary considerably. For example, of the eleven countries examined, only five achieved an improved income growth rate when export instability declined; four of these were Latin American countries (Argentina, Chile, Colombia, and Mexico). However, in the fifth Latin American country included in the sample (Brazil) the reverse occurred; the average growth rate of income declined with increased export stability. Thus, even though their results cannot be considered conclusive because of the simplicity of the model employed, it does point to the need to examine the domestic impact of export instability on each Latin American country by considering its economic structure, openness, and adjustment response to short-run changes in foreign exchange earnings.

Magnitude of Instability

An equally controversial but closely related issue has been the degree of export fluctuations in the developing countries. This argument has been couched principally in terms of whether the degree of instability in developing countries exceeds that in developed countries. Coppock (1962; 1977), MacBean (1966), and Lawson (1974) found that the experiences of these two groups have not been significantly different. Conflicting results have, however, been reported by Massell (1970), Naya (1973), Glezakos (1973), Mathieson and McKinnon (1974), Knudsen and Parnes (1975), Stein (1977), and Sheehey (1977), all of whom found that developing countries do suffer from more instability than developed countries.[5]

Our primary concern in this chapter is to focus more narrowly on individual country export fluctuations, and specifically with reference to those commodities currently included in the integrated program.[6] As in the analysis of the effects of instability on development, it seems reasonable to presuppose that the degree of instability in Latin America for these commodities would not be accurately revealed by cross-country statistical comparisons. Instead, given the considerable differences in national behavior within the region, comparisons between country experiences in these commodity exports is likely to be more fruitful. Furthermore, it is useful to compare the extent of national export instability in the commodities included in the integrated program with that of the remaining exports not covered by the program. In conjunction with an appreciation of the commodities' contribution to total foreign exchange earnings, it may then be possible to decipher more readily Latin America's interest in the integrated program negotiations.

Export instability is defined as sizeable, short-term movements of exports from their growth trend.[7] In its measurement, the norm most widely adopted for defining the trend has been the arithmetic or geometric growth of exports.[8] These functional forms are given by $X_t = a_0 + a_1 t + u_{1t}$ and $\log X_t = b_0 + b_1 t + u_{2t}$ respectively, where u_t is the unexplained variance. The trend coefficient, T, which is interpreted as the average annual growth rate of the export series, is equal to $(a_1 / \bar{X})*100$ in the linear function, where $\bar{X}$ denotes the mean of the X variable, and to $b_1 * 100$ in the semilog function.

The index of instability, I, may then be defined as the normalized standard error of estimate for the given functional form, that is, the standard error of estimate divided by the arithmetic mean of the observations of the dependent variable.[9] However, since the dependent variable, X, is defined differently in the linear and semilog functions, their standard errors cannot be directly compared. For this reason, comparative instability indices in the past have been derived by imposing the same functional form to the series in a sample, even though an alternative form of the equation may have been preferred (Knudsen and Parnes, 1975:9).

This difficulty can be overcome, however, by a simple transformation of the dependent variable. The linear and semilog functional forms may be compared if the dependent variables have been previously divided by the geometric mean of the series.[10] By transforming and reestimating the equations in this manner, we derive the normalized "transformed" standard error of estimate and our new instability index becomes

$$I' = \frac{\sqrt{\dfrac{1}{n}\sum_{t=1}^{n} u_t'^2}}{\bar{X}'} * 100$$

where $\bar{X}'$ is the arithmetic mean of the transformed dependent variable. In this way, comparative instability indices may be calculated using either the linear or semilog functional form, depending on which equation provides the best fit.[11]

These calculations are presented in Table 9–2 (column 1) for Latin America's export earnings from the regionally significant commodities currently included in the integrated program. The results show a wide dispersion of average year-to-year fluctuations among the countries.

Table 9–2. Latin America: Instability Indices and Growth Trends of Regionally Significant Exports in Integrated Program and of Other Exports, 1960–1975

Country	Exports of Integrated Program Commodities[a]			Other Exports[b]	
	Instability Index (I')	Trend Coefficient	Col(1) ÷ Col(2)	Instability Index (I')	Trend Coefficient
Argentina	27.7	6.1	4.5	18.2	7.4
Barbados	22.3	4.0	5.6	14.4	11.6
Bolivia	15.6	27.5	0.6	14.3	13.6
Brazil	15.5	10.1	1.5	20.2	17.5
Chile	23.7	10.1	2.3	19.7	12.3
Colombia	15.4	5.6	2.8	24.7	13.4
Costa Rica	8.8	9.9	0.9	14.9	17.4
Dominican Republic	28.4	9.3	3.1	33.3	10.6
Ecuador	14.2	8.6	1.6	36.9	14.1
El Salvador	19.1	6.5	2.9	11.9	14.0
Guatemala	15.1	8.4	1.8	8.5	6.8
Guyana	12.1	10.3	1.2	24.1	6.0
Haiti	17.0	1.6	10.6	23.7	7.1
Honduras	14.9	7.0	2.1	15.7	12.3
Jamaica	17.4	9.3	1.8	33.6	7.9
Mexico	16.5	4.2	3.9	13.1	10.6
Nicaragua	11.1	10.7	1.0	9.1	14.2
Panama	14.1	12.2	1.2	31.0	10.5
Paraguay	27.4	22.8	1.2	13.4	9.5
Peru	10.9	5.4	2.0	12.8	9.0
Trinidad and Tobago	28.4	5.1	5.6	26.2	9.8
Uruguay	24.8	12.2	2.0	20.9	3.8
Venezuela	20.5	7.1	2.9	30.0	7.3

Source: Details of the regressions used to calculate instability and trend rates are available from the author on request. Data for the individual commodity export from national statistical offices; that for total merchandise exports from IMF (1977).

[a]Includes products of regional significance included in the Integrated Program as defined in Table 9–1.

[b]Refers to total national merchandise exports less regionally significant products included in the Integrated Program.

The indices of instability range from 8.8 to 28.4, with the frequency distribution skewed to the higher range. In the upper quartile are the Dominican Republic, Trinidad and Tobago, Argentina, Paraguay, Uruguay, and Chile. If consideration is given to the share of the product in total exports as well, it may be seen from Tables 9–1 and 9–2 that the countries for whom these products have accounted for over half of total export proceeds and for whom the index of instability has exceeded the median level of the region are the Dominican Republic, Chile, El Salvador, Jamaica, and Haiti. It is also apparent from Table 9–1 that the largest absolute fluctuations of earnings have occurred where the major export crops are sugar (Dominican Republic, Trinidad and Tobago, Paraguay, and Barbados), beef (Argentina and Uruguay), and copper (Chile). The fact that the countries with the lowest levels of instability depend on exports of one or more of these products suggests that either fluctuations in these markets were moderated by offsetting or more stable movements in other exports of this group of commodities, or volume and price movements of the products have tended to compensate one another.

However, absolute indices of instability conceal different patterns of growth for countries. A country with unstable growth caused by rapidly rising exports would be in a preferred position to one in which earnings fluctuated around a moderate growth trend. Similarly, a country with a given level of instability around a high growth trend would be better off than another with the same level of instability around a much slower growth rate. Column 3 of Table 9–2 indicates the different comparative circumstances that emerge among countries when the instability index is considered within the context of the export growth trend. Whereas Haiti and Mexico have had near average absolute levels of instability for countries in the region, they have ranked among the more severe cases of instability in relation to their comparatively slow growth rates in these exports. In contrast, whereas Paraguay has had one of the highest absolute levels of export fluctuations in the region, its instability has been primarily the result of the rapid growth of its soybean exports during the period.

It is also important to take into account the fact that export instability in Latin America has not been caused solely by fluctuations of products included in the integrated program. Instability in the receipts from other exports may have an equally detrimental effect on some of the economies of the region. In fact, a comparison of earnings fluctuations of all other commodity exports (Table 9–2, column 4) with those of products included in the integrated program reveals that instability of other exports has been higher in over half the countries. Eleven countries have had fluctuation indices in the integrated program commodities that were larger than those in their other exports, but twelve countries have had lower fluctuations. Nonetheless, among those in the first group, earnings fluctuations for the integrated program products were still at least 50 percent higher than for the other commodity exports of five of the countries—Barbados, Guatemala, El Salvador, Argentina, and Paraguay.

Thus, on the basis of the evidence presented so far, it appears that export instability has been a justifiable preoccupation for several Latin American countries. Nevertheless, the national concern is still dependent upon the nature of the variation of these export products. Criteria for the evaluation of this instability may include its comparative absolute levels, the importance of the products to total foreign exchange receipts, its context in the trend growth rates, and its comparison to that of other commodity exports.

Furthermore, whereas export instability has up to now been characterized in terms of earnings fluctuations for selected primary products, the integrated program focuses more specifically on their price volatility. Much attention has been given to the unstable price behavior of the markets for primary commodities. However, Table 9–3 shows that for many of the Latin American countries instability of export earnings has also been caused by volume fluctuations. Indeed, quantum fluctuations have been over one-fifth larger than price fluctuations in eight of the countries, and fluctuation indices of quantum have been roughly equal (± 10 percent) to price fluctuations in four of the countries. Quantum fluctuations may or may not be related to unstable price movements in the commodity export markets. The question remains, therefore, whether the stabilization of prices would also mitigate volume fluctuations and lead to greater and more stable earnings. This issue is treated in the following section.

COMMODITY EXPORT STABILITY

By itself, price stabilization for primary commodities may be desirable for the Latin American countries as a means of reducing the risk of investment planning. Moreover, producers may support greater price stability because it could raise the long-run demand for a product by not inducing risk-averse manufacturers to switch to more price-stable synthetic inputs or by creating permanent shifts in consumer preferences for other food or beverage substitutes during periods of otherwise temporary high prices. Beyond the possible direct benefits, however, it is also important to consider the impact of price stabilization on export earnings, the latter being of a greater concern to the Latin American countries.

Table 9–3.   Latin America: Earnings, Price, and Volume Instability of Regionally Significant Commodity Exports in Integrated Program, 1960–1975

Country	Instability Index (I')		
	Earnings	Price[a]	Quantities[b]
Argentina	27.7	19.1	27.0
Barbados	22.3	23.9	15.6
Bolivia	15.6	23.7	33.7
Brazil	15.5	15.8	9.0
Chile	23.7	16.0	16.5
Colombia	15.4	12.6	7.0
Costa Rica	8.8	7.2	8.7
Dominican Republic	28.4	16.6	13.2
Ecuador	14.2	9.6	13.1
El Salvador	19.1	9.9	7.4
Guatemala	15.1	11.6	9.0
Guyana	12.1	17.6	15.8
Haiti	17.0	18.4	13.3
Honduras	14.9	10.1	16.5
Jamaica	17.4	24.6	11.0
Mexico	16.5	10.8	10.8
Nicaragua	11.1	8.1	9.9
Panama	14.1	10.2	10.6
Paraguay	27.4	24.0	46.6
Peru	10.9	11.8	6.9
Trinidad and Tobago	28.4	25.1	12.5
Uruguay	24.8	17.6	25.3
Venezuela	20.5	18.3	13.9

Source: Details of the regressions used to calculate instability and trend rates are available from the author on request. Data from national statistical offices.

[a]Calculated from the Paasche export price index of the products (1960 = 100).

[b]Calculated from the Laspeyres export quantum index of the products (1960 = 100).

The emphasis of the integrated program on mitigating price, rather than earnings, fluctuations is based on the recognition that market intervention mechanisms in commodity agreements are administratively more feasible for the regulation of prices than they are for regulating earnings.[12] Realizing that revenue stabilization is more desirable than price stability to developing countries, UNCTAD has advocated the expansion of existing compensatory financing facilities as a complementary measure to commodity agreements since price and earnings stabilization may be irreconcilable goals for the export markets of individual countries.[13] Yet the central feature of the integrated program remains the negotiation of international commodity price stabilization agreements, rather than compensatory financing systems. Stockpiling arrangements, which for the "core" products are to be supported financially by a common fund, have been promoted as the key regulatory mechanism for the selected commodity markets since this control system generally introduces fewer distortions in the operation of the markets than do other mechanisms. However, additional regulatory measures, principally export quotas, have also been advanced to operate in conjunction with buffer stocks for the "core" products;[14] other intervention measures have been recommended for the more perishable products. Nonetheless, insofar as the effect on export earnings is concerned, there is theoretically a basic economic (though not administrative) similarity in control instruments that maintain prices within a given range by regulating supplies entering the market.[15]

Impact of Price Stabilization on Export Earnings

The more fundamental issue of commodity market intervention for producers is the impact that price stabilization has on both the overall level and the degree of instability of export earnings. Under a buffer stock arrangement, it can be demonstrated that this impact on the overall level depends on the source of the market disruption and on the degree depends on the price elasticities of supply and demand. Consider, for example, a market described by the linear demand and supply relation[16]

$$Q_d = a_0 - a_1 P + u \qquad a_1 \geqslant 0$$
$$Q_s = b_0 + b_1 P + v \qquad b_1 \geqslant 0$$

where Q_d = demand, Q_s = supply, P = price, a_0, a_1, b_0, b_1 = deterministic constants, and u, v denote stochastic disturbance terms.

In equilibrium, $Q_d = Q_s$, the price will be

$$P = \frac{a_0 - b_0}{a_1 + b_1} + \frac{u - v}{a_1 + b_1}$$

and the export earnings will equal

$$R = PQ_s = \left(\frac{1}{a_1 + b_1}\right)^2 \{b_0(a_0 - b_0)(a_1 + b_1) + (a_0 - b_0)^2 b_1$$
$$+ [2(a_0 - b_0)b_1 + b_0(a_1 + b_1) + (a_1 + b_1)v](u - v)$$
$$+ (a_0 - b_0)(a_1 + b_1)v + b_1(u - v)^2\}$$

For demand-induced disruptions, in which shifts of u and $-u$ take place, the export earnings in the first period at price P_1 (Figure 9–1) are

$$R_{t-1} = \left(\frac{1}{a_1 + b_1}\right)^2 \{b_0(a_0 - b_0)(a_1 + b_1) + (a_0 - b_0)^2 \, b_1$$
$$+ [2(a_0 - b_0)b_1 + b_0(a_1 + b_1)]u + b_1 u^2\}$$

and in the second period at P_2 are

$$R_t = \left(\frac{1}{a_1 + b_1}\right)^2 \{b_0(a_0 - b_0)(a_1 + b_1) + (a_0 - b_0)^2 \, b_1$$
$$- [2(a_0 - b_0)b_1 + b_0(a_1 + b_1)]u + b_1 u^2\}$$

This produces average export earnings of

$$\left(\frac{1}{a_1 + b_1}\right)^2 [b_0(a_0 - b_0)(a_1 + b_1) + (a_0 - b_0)^2 \, b_1 + b_1 u^2]$$

and an average deviation of

$$\left(\frac{1}{a_1 + b_1}\right)^2 \{[2(a_0 - b_0)b_1 + b_0(a_1 + b_1)]u\}$$

For supply-induced disruptions, in which shifts of v and $-v$ occur, the export earnings in the first period at price P_1 are

$$R_{t-1} = \left(\frac{1}{a_1 + b_1}\right)^2 \{b_0(a_0 - b_0)(a_1 + b_1) + (a_0 - b_0)^2 b_1$$
$$- [2(a_0 - b_0)b_1 + b_0(a_1 + b_1) + (a_1 + b_1)v]v$$
$$+ (a_0 - b_0)(a_1 + b_1)v + b_1 v^2\}$$

and in the second period at P_2 are

$$R_t = \left(\frac{1}{a_1 + b_1}\right)^2 \{b_0(a_0 - b_0)(a_1 + b_1) + (a_0 - b_0)^2 b_1$$
$$+ [2(a_0 - b_0)b_1 + b_0(a_1 + b_1) - (a_1 + b_1)v]v$$
$$- (a_0 - b_0)(a_1 + b_1)v + b_1 v^2\}$$

This results in an average export earnings equal to

A. Demand Shifts

D_1 D_0 D_2 S_0

P_2

P_0

P_1

Effect of price stabilization at
$P_0 = (p_1 + p_2)/2$ is to
(a) decrease level of earnings:
$(p_0 \cdot q_0) < [(p_1 \cdot q_1) + (p_2 \cdot q_2)]/2$
(b) stabilize earnings fluctuations:
$(p_0 \cdot q_0) < [(p_2 \cdot q_2) - (p_1 \cdot q_1)]$

q'_1 q_1 q_0 q_2 q'_2

Q

B. Supply Shifts

D_0 S_1 S_0 S_2

P_1

P_0

P_2

Effect of price stabilization at
$P_0 = (p_1 - p_2)/2$ is to
(a) increase level of earnings:
$(p_0 \cdot q_0) > [(p_1 \cdot q_1) + (p_2 \cdot q_2)]/2$
(b) stabilize earnings fluctuations:
$[(p_0 \cdot q'_2) - (p_0 \cdot q'_1)] <$
$[(p_1 \cdot q_1) - (p_2 \cdot q_2)]$

q'_1 q_1 q_0 q_2 q'_2

Q

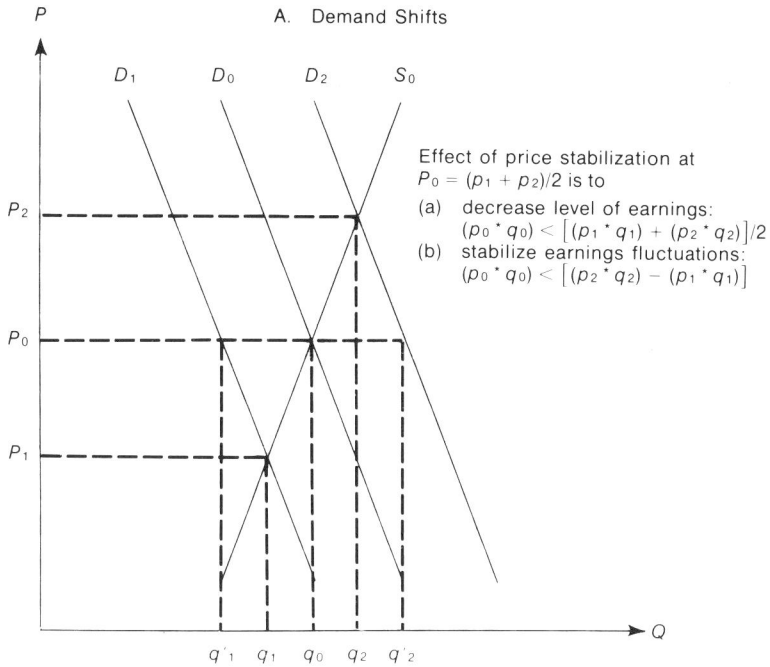

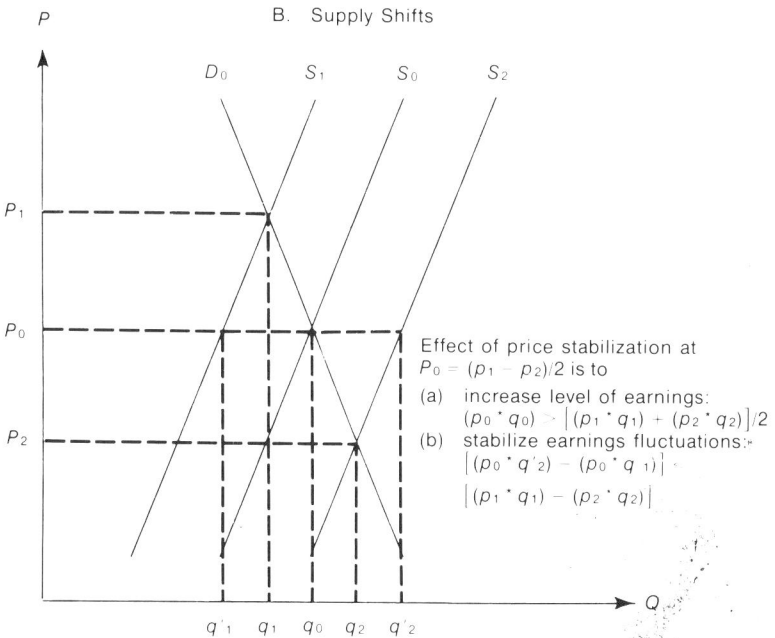

FIGURE 9-1. Impact of Price Stabilization on Export Earnings Under Price-Inelastic Supply and Demand Conditions

$$\left(\frac{1}{a_1 + b_1}\right)^2 [b_0(a_0 - b_0)(a_1 + b_1) + (a_0 - b_0)^2 b_1$$
$$- (a_1 + b_1)v^2 + b_1 v^2]$$

and an average deviation of

$$\left(\frac{1}{a_1 + b_1}\right)^2 [a_0(a_1 - b_1) - 2b_0 a_1]v$$

Under a buffer stock scheme, the price would be maintained at the level needed to equate the nonstochastic components of demand and supply[17]

$$P_0 = \frac{a_0 - b_0}{a_1 + b_1}$$

maintained by the authorities trading from their stock[18]

$$x = v - u$$

When disruptions to the market are brought on by demand shifts, the quantity supplied under a buffer stock scheme would be

$$Q_s = \frac{b_0(a_1 + b_1) + (a_0 - b_0)b_1}{a_1 + b_1}$$

such that average revenue equals

$$P_0 Q_s = \left(\frac{1}{a_1 + b_1}\right)^2 [b_0(a_0 - b_0)(a_1 + b_1) + (a_0 - b_0)^2 b_1]$$

Consequently, price stabilization would reduce average export earnings by[19]

$$\left[\frac{b_1}{(a_1 + b_1)^2} u^2\right]$$

although earnings fluctuations would decline by

$$\left[\frac{2a_0 b_1 + b_0(a_1 - b_1)}{(a_1 + b_1)^2} u\right]$$

On the other hand, when disruptions to the market are caused by supply shifts, the export earnings under a buffer stock scheme in the first period would be

$$P_0 Q_{t-1} = \left(\frac{1}{a_1 + b_1}\right)^2 [b_0(a_0 - b_0)(a_1 + b_1) + b_1(a_0 - b_0)^2$$
$$+ (a_0 - b_0)(a_1 + b_1)v]$$

and in the second period would equal

$$P_0 Q_t = \left(\frac{1}{a_1 + b_1}\right)^2 [b_0(a_0 - b_0)(a_1 + b_1) + b_1(a_0 - b_0)^2$$
$$- (a_0 - b_0)(a_1 + b_1)v]$$

Price stabilization would therefore increase average export earnings by

$$\left[\frac{a_1}{(a_1 + b_1)^2} v^2\right]$$

and fluctuations of export receipts in a stabilized market

$$\left(\frac{a_0 - b_0}{a_1 + b_1} v\right)$$

would be lower than that in a nonregulated market

$$\left[\frac{a_0(a_1 - b_1) - 2b_0 a_1}{(a_1 + b_1)^2} v\right]$$

if supply and demand were sufficiently price inelastic.[20]

Sources of Export Instability

Agricultural market instability, especially for foods, has been principally associated with supply disruptions from natural phenomena (such as weather and disease conditions) and from internal actions taken by governments in price and investment policies. On the other hand, instability in the mineral markets and in some agricultural raw material markets have been mainly related to fluctuations in the level of economic activity of the industrialized countries. Disruptions of both types are aggravated by the high geographic concentration in these product markets,[21] and therefore changes within one of the major exporting or importing countries have a more pronounced effect on those price adjustments needed to balance total supply and demand. This effect is especially serious if preferential trading arrangements or other obstacles to free trade prevent the geographic markets from acting as substitutes for one another.

One way of empirically identifying the source of export instability that has been used by the IBRD (1968) and by Brook, Grilli, and Waelbroeck (1977) consists of regressing trend deviations in the volume exported against price deviations. Since prices and quantities move in similar directions in demand-induced disturbances, a significant positive coefficient would imply that demand shifts were the main cause of instability; conversely, a significant negative coefficient would indicate that supply shifts had been the dominant cause.

Such results are reported in Table 9–4 for both Latin America and the world markets for the regionally significant commodity exports included in the integrated program. For world markets, the results verify the hypothesis of supply related causes for instability in three food products—coffee, cocoa, and bananas. The empirical work of Brook, Grilli, and Waelbroeck (1977) supports these findings. The calculations for iron ore and bauxite also indicate that instability in the two markets for these products has been mainly the result of supply disruptions, which is consistent with the findings of Behrman (1978).[22] Only in the case of copper have demand changes been the major cause of instability in the world market. Of the remaining four products (sugar, cotton, beef, and soybeans), the regression results were inconclusive, suggesting that in those markets both supply and demand shifts have been important.

The results show that on the world market the effect of price stabilization schemes on coffee, cocoa, bananas, iron ore, and bauxite would be to increase aggregate producer earnings; however, in copper the effect would be to lower earnings. Although Behrman's results support these conclusions, his findings indicate that fluctuations in aggregate earnings would be significantly reduced only in cocoa and copper, whereas they would remain about the same in an unrestricted market in coffee, bauxite, and iron ore. In the remaining four products, where no clearly dominant source of instability emerged over the period reviewed, the effect of a price stabilization scheme on aggregate producer earnings cannot be determined from the past behavior of the markets.

For the Latin American countries the pattern is more ambiguous, especially in world markets not dominated by demand-originating disruptions. The significance of supply disruptions in such markets reflects the export experiences of the major producers. Latin American examples include Brazil in coffee, the Central American countries in bananas, and Jamaica in bauxite. In turn, shortages or surpluses in the markets resulting from supply shifts by the major producers have tended to be transmitted to the smaller producers in the form of demand-shift disruptions; this may be observed by the experiences of some of the region's coffee exporters.

Implications for Latin America

What can be inferred from these results about the effects of stabilization schemes on Latin America's export earnings? The principal lesson is that an analysis of the sources of instability at the world market level can be misleading when determining whether a country in Latin America is likely to benefit or not from price stabilization. At best, aggregated analysis of the sources of disruptions is useful when demand shifts dominate a market since they tend to affect all producing countries similarly. For example, in copper the principal source of disturbances for the Latin American exporters has also been attributed to demand shifts. In such instances, the effect of price stabilization on the export earnings of the Latin American producers would also be uniform. The results of Behrman and Tinakorn in Chapter 10 attempt to quantify the region's revenue effects in this commodity. Their simulated buffer stock program for copper shows that Chile and Peru's annual export earnings in copper during 1963–1975 would have fallen by 3.4 and 4.8 percent, respectively, below the level that was otherwise achieved.

In contrast, since supply-induced market instability is generally ascribed to independent output fluctuations of major producers, a price stabilization scheme that responded to supply changes in the market would have a direct effect only on the source of the disturbance. This effect would be to raise the level of earnings of the country but to lower its earnings fluctuations if demand and supply were sufficiently price inelastic. For those Latin American countries responding to external supply-induced market surplus or deficit conditions, the extent of the impact of price stabilization measures would be determined by demand-shift disturbances. Hence, the impact on national export earnings from supply-induced market disturbances cannot be directly ascertained from the effect of price stabilization on aggregate producer earnings.

Moreover, because global price stabilization schemes are unresponsive to domestic output disruptions in countries accounting for a small share of the world markets, they are limited in their capacity to mitigate export fluctuations or to improve the level of foreign exchange earnings in many Latin American countries. Given the relatively high

Table 9–4. Latin America: Principal Sources of Export Quantum Fluctuations of Regionally Significant Commodity Exports in Integrated Program, 1960–1975[a]

A. *"Core" Products*

Coffee		*Sugar*		*Copper*		*Cotton*		*Cocoa*	
Brazil	SS	Barbados	S/D	Chile	DD	El Salvador	DD1	Domin. Rep.	S/D
Colombia	S/D	Brazil	SS	Peru	DD	Guatemala	S/D	Ecuador	S/D
Costa Rica	S/D	Costa Rica	SS			Mexico	SS		
Domin. Rep.	DD	Domin. Rep.	SS			Nicaragua	S/D		
Ecuador	S/D	El Salvador	S/D			Paraguay	DD1		
El Salvador	DD	Guatemala	DD2			Peru	S/D		
Guatemala	DD1	Guyana	DD2						
Haiti	S/D	Haiti	S/D						
Honduras	DD2	Jamaica	DD1						
Mexico	DD	Mexico	SS						
Nicaragua	S/D	Panama	S/D						
		Peru	SS						
World	SS	*World*	S/D	*World*	DD	*World*	S/D	*World*	SS

232

B. *Other Products*

Beef		Iron Ore		Soybeans		Bananas		Bauxite	
Argentina	SS	Brazil	DD	Brazil	DD	Costa Rica	SS	Guyana	S/D
Costa Rica	SS	Peru	SS	Paraguay	DD	Ecuador	S/D	Haiti	SS
Honduras	SS					Honduras	SS	Jamaica	SS
Nicaragua	SS					Panama	SS		
Paraguay	DD								
Uruguay	SS								
World	S/D	*World*	SS	*World*	S/D	*World*	SS	*World*	SS

Source: Details of the fitted equations are available from the author on request.

Note: SS—Supply shifts dominant.

DD—Demand shifts dominant. DD1 and DD2 indicate prices lagged one and two years, respectively.

S/D—Both supply and demand changes important.

The dominant source of quantum fluctuations over the period has been inferred by the sign of the coefficient when quantum deviations from trend were regressed against the product's world unit export price deviations from trend. A statistical significant positive coefficient implies that demand changes (DD) have been the dominant source of instability; a significant negative coefficient indicates that supply shifts (SS) have dominated; an insignificant coefficient suggests that both supply and demand changes (S/D) have been important sources of instability. The test for the significance of the coefficient was at the 90 percent level.

ᵃCalculated for countries in which the commodity is at least 5 percent significant to total merchandise exports, as described in Table 9–1.

degree of supply-associated instability that has characterized the exports of products covered in the integrated program, other remedial measures might be necessary either within the scope of the program or through domestic stabilization policies in the countries themselves.

Thus, although price stabilization schemes may reduce foreign exchange fluctuations, the impact on the level of export earnings is more varied. Under conditions that generally typify Latin America's primary commodity exports, price stabilization in demand-induced disruptions would probably reduce earnings below what they would otherwise be without market intervention. In supply-induced disruptions, price stabilization would benefit only the major exporter(s); it would reduce the revenues of the smaller producers since shortages from the major supplier(s) would be transmitted to them in the form of changes in demand for their exports. On the other hand, importing countries actually derive greater benefit from these schemes than heretofore realized. Kaldor (1976) has suggested that primary commodity price increases are passed on to final products and have a deflationary impact on the effective demand for industrialized countries' goods. Since market imperfections in these countries prevent declines in prices of basic products from having a symmetrically downward effect on final products, any significant change in primary commodity prices eventually has a dampening effect on industrial activity.[23] Furthermore, Behrman (1978) has demonstrated that over a simulated ten-year period the revenue gains from the reduction of inflationary pressure on consuming countries are greater than the earnings to producers as a whole. One, therefore, wonders whether there has been a *volte-face* in the roles at the UNCTAD negotiations. On the one hand, Latin America and other developing countries are becoming frustrated by the failure to complete the preparatory phase on individual commodities as set forth in the conference resolution 93(IV) and to reach any conclusive results on the fundamentals of a common fund;[24] but on the other, there has been speculation that at least for some of the industrialized countries this "setback" is seen as part of their overall bargaining posture, and thus perhaps a diplomatic "success."

CONCLUSIONS

This chapter has examined the rationale for the high priority that Latin America, in conjunction with other Third World nations, has placed on comprehensive commodity market arrangements in attempting to establish a new international economic order. The issue has been approached from three distinct but related dimensions for the regionally significant commodities currently included in the integrated program. The first is whether export instability has been a serious problem in Latin America; the second is the validity of empirical techniques for measuring the consequences of instability; and the third is the efficacy of international agreements for mitigating fluctuations and improving export earnings in the Latin American countries.

On the basis of evidence for the last decade and a half, it appears that the experiences of many of the countries in the region constitute justification for participatory interest in market stabilization schemes for their products in the integrated program. The range of instability has been dramatic but the significance to each country will depend on the criteria used to evaluate these fluctuations. Notwithstanding the absence of an established norm for interpreting instability indices, it is apparent that especially severe export fluctuations have been recorded by countries heavily dependent on export earnings from sugar, copper, and beef, most notably Argentina, Chile, Uruguay, Haiti, and the Dominican Republic.

Important potential gains may consequently be derived by a number of countries in Latin America from international agreements because of the disruptive effects that could otherwise hinder their economic development progress. Empirical evidence has thus far failed to verify the degree to which export instability adversely affects economic growth. This shortcoming has little, if any, relation to the actual nature of the transmission process. Instead, the inability of applied economics to resolve this problem has been attributed primarily to the methodologically defective approach used in testing the hypothesis, which presupposes similar economic responses by all countries to export instability. There is little doubt that export instability can produce serious disruptions in the growth of an economy. Nevertheless, a more systematic case-by-case approach in Latin America will be needed to reveal the national interests in supporting greater export stability.

Yet it is questionable whether a solution to the problems confronting developing countries' exports can be found in comprehensive commodity arrangements as proposed by UNCTAD. The issue focuses on whether it is economically profitable to a sufficient number of countries in Latin America to induce them to exert their political force on the integrated program. Theoretically, depending on the conditions under which price fluctuations take place, the stated goal of price stabilization may or may not be compatible with the more substantive aims of stabilizing and improving export earnings of the Latin American countries.

Empirically, the analysis of those conditions in Latin America's exports indicates (i) that price stabilization would generally not have an adverse effect on earnings instability in the international commodity markets and in most instances would reduce fluctuations; (ii) that if the copper market continues to be primarily subject to fluctuations on the demand side, buffer stock policies would have an adverse effect on the Latin American exporters' foreign exchange proceeds; (iii) that the apparent gains in total export earnings from a buffer stock arrangement for commodities that have responded primarily to changes in world supply conditions accrue to the major producer, but would reduce the amount of foreign exchange earnings of the other exporters because of the concurrent effects on changes occurring in their foreign demand; and (iv) that international commodity price stabilization schemes are unresponsive to export supply fluctuations in the medium- and small-level commodity producing countries of Latin America.

The policy implication is that the benefits from international price stabilization schemes need to be examined separately by each country on the basis of the severity of fluctuations in exports, the potentially disruptive consequences on the economy, and the primary source of the disturbance in the export market. At the regional level, the possible adverse revenue effects of commodity agreements on a fairly large number of countries in Latin America suggests the need for complementary measures in the integrated program that would enable the expansion of compensatory financing facilities to those nations.

NOTES

1. See Lord (1976) for a statistical analysis of the region's export markets for these products.

2. A good analysis of the broader economic issues confronting the developing and industrialized countries in the integrated program negotiations is provided by Michalopoulos and Perez (1977). Comprehensive reviews of the historical development of these issues are contained in Erb and Fisher (1977) and in Vastine (1977); see also Corea (1977), David (1977: 34–41), Fiallo (1977), Fishlow et al. (1978), Grubel (1977: 289–94), MacBean and Balasubramanyam (1976: 158–88), MacLaren (1977), Maizels (1976), Malmgren (1976), and Rangarajan (1978).

3. At the microlevel, Thoburn (1977) has found that this latter effect can induce developing countries to favor capital-intensive techniques for primary commodities, since they are viable at a wider range of prices than are labor-intensive methods of production.

4. The results of the regression were as follows:

$$T_c = 9.75 - 0.04 \, I_c'$$
$$(.19)$$
$$R^2 = .002 \quad D.W. = 2.14 \quad S.E. = 5.98$$

where T is the trend growth of exports in the integrated program commodities, I_e' is their index of instability, and the figure in parentheses is the t-statistic. The variables are defined more specifically below.

5. Beyond generalized comparisons of aggregative magnitudes of instability in low per capita income countries with those in high per capita income countries, there have been attempts to identify specific country characteristics associated with greater or lesser instability. Erb and Schiavo-Campo (1969) found that the economic size of a country (as measured by the gross domestic product and as a proxy of structural economic differences among countries) to be inversely related to instability in the less developed economies. In a similar vein, Mathieson and McKinnon (1974) concluded that openness, measured as the ratio of exports to gross national product, was negatively correlated with instability and thus implied that relatively greater trade of developing countries with advanced countries has had a stabilizing impact on their exports. However, geographic diversification of exports was not found to reduce instability in the investigations of Michaely (1962), Coppock (1962), Massell (1964; 1970), and MacBean (1966). On the other hand, Massell (1970), Knudsen and Parnes (1975), and Stoutar's (1977) findings tend to support the contention that product concentration increases export instability, although this has been questioned by O'Brien (1972) and Katrak (1973). Another interesting finding by Coppock (1962) and Askari and Weil (1974) is that instability in developing countries is a more serious problem with respect to exports of manufactured goods than that for primary commodity exports. Thus, while empirical work in this field has cast doubt on generalizations concerning instability in primary exporting countries, there has been evidence uncovered on patterns in instability associated with developing countries' structural characteristics.

6. Kingston (1973) provides data on total export fluctuations in the Latin American countries for the 1948–1965 period.

7. This definition has been applied equally to price, volume, and earnings fluctuations of exports.

8. Another method has been to measure deviations from a moving average within the period covered. (For a synopsis of indices of export instability used in previous studies, see Knudsen and Parnes (1975: 9–13)). However, the IBRD (1968: 37) study on export fluctuations has noted that preference is usually given to the least-squares method for analyzing fluctuations over a long-term period and to the moving average method in dealing with fluctuations of a relatively short-term nature. For this reason, the former norm has been adopted, given the orientation of the integrated program toward seeking long-term improvements in market conditions for exports of developing countries and the present concern over export instability in the Latin American countries over the past fifteen years.

9. Alternatively, the index has been defined by some researchers as the normalized square of the residuals from the fitted trend. However, this implies the heuristic assumption that larger deviations contribute proportionately more to uncertainty.

10. See Rao and Miller (1971: 107–111).

11. Instability indices are interpreted as follows: a low index implies that year to year changes in exports did not depart much from the trend taken as

the norm; conversely, a high index implies that there were substantial deviations from the trend. Nevertheless, it should be emphasized that such an index is limited by what Sundram (1967) depicts as the average for the period, which thereby conceals differences in the frequency and the regularity of export fluctuations. These could be in the form of short-term fluctuations throughout the period, a sharp peak or trough in an otherwise fairly stable growth, or cyclical movements around the trend.

12. Nevertheless, the difficulty of defining the trend growth rate around which a central agency would monitor price deviations continues to be of important concern in the literature on international commodity arrangements, as exemplified in the writings of Donges (1977: 241–44) and Hoffmeyer (1976). This has, however, been a more general problem related to informational inefficiency of long-run changes in commodity market prices (Smith, 1978).

13. At present, the two major compensatory financing mechanisms are those of the International Monetary Fund (IMF) and the STABEX system established under the Lomé Convention in 1975 for the European Economic Community's present and former possessions. In Latin America, the latter system covers Barbados, Jamaica, and Trinidad and Tobago. See Erb (1977) for a critical discussion of these two mechanisms within the new international economic order deliberations; Goreaux (1977) for an analysis of the IMF mechanisms; Wall (1976) and Alting von Geusau (1977) for an examination of the STABEX system in the context of the developing countries' aspirations for international trade reform; and de Vries (1975) for a general analysis of alternative compensatory financing schemes.

14. The new International Sugar Agreement (negotiated October 17, 1977, for the 1978–1982 period) makes use of export quotas as well as a buffer stock to defend the negotiated price range (UNCTAD, 1977d). Similarly, the present International Cocoa Agreement (effective 1976–1979) relies on the interaction of export quotas and a buffer stock mechanism. In the current deliberations on the other "core" products of regional importance to Latin America, a supplementary control mechanism in the form of export quotas has been proposed in addition to buffer stocks for copper (UNCTAD, 1977b) but not, however, for cotton (UNCTAD, 1977c).

15. See Brown (1975) for a thorough treatment of the variety of national and international mechanisms that have been devised to moderate export fluctuations and French-Davis M. (1968) for a specific analysis of the effects of an export quota system.

16. The nonlinear form of the model is presented in the works of Turnovsky (1978), Sarris and Taylor (1978), and Just, Lutz, Schmitz, and Turnovsky (1977). Extensions of this model have been undertaken by Turnovsky (1974; 1978) for price uncertainty, where supply decisions are based on "adaptive" and "rational" price expectations rather than actual market prices; by Sarris and Taylor and by Just, Lutz, Schmitz, and Turnovsky (1977) for markets with trade barriers; by Hueth and Schmitz (1972) for intermediate and final product trade; by McKinnon (1967) and Hallwood (1977) on the role of private futures markets for price stabilization authorities; and by Newbery and Stiglitz

(1977) for the impact of complete versus partial price stabilization on export earnings.

17. Because of the linearity of the function, this implies that the price would be maintained at the mean of the nonregulated market prices, which for the present case would be $P_0 = (P_1 + P_2)/2$.

18. Note that the expected value of the buffer stock, $E(x)$, is equal to zero.

19. This result was first proven by Grubel (1964) and Snape and Yamey (1963).

20. In all the regionally significant commodity exports included in the integrated program, the extensive survey of available elasticity estimates by Labys and Hunkeler (1974) indicates that supply and demand are price inelastic. Several factors contribute to the price inelastic nature of these products. Supplies tend to respond slowly to price changes as a result of capacity constraints on output expansion, lagged production response to demand changes, low or policy determined minimum levels of inventory holdings, and various institutional rigidities such as credit availabilities; on the demand side, the products mainly for direct human consumption are little affected by price variations over a fairly wide range, while consumption of products that serve as industrial raw materials, insofar as they represent a fairly low proportion of the final product's value, also tend to be unaffected by price changes over a fairly large range. The result is that relatively small changes in the quantity of supply and demand create sizeable increases or decreases in prices, while large price changes induce little response in the quantity of output or consumption, especially in the short run.

21. During the first half of this decade, the concentration ratio of the five leading exporters of these products ranged from 0.51 to 0.97, while that of the five principal importers ranged from 0.41 to 0.79. See Lord (1976).

22. Brook, Grilli, and Waelbroeck, however, found instability in the world bauxite market to be mainly due to demand shifts. This contradiction may be explained by the inclusion of more recent years in the present sample. During 1974–1975, significant structural changes took place among major bauxite producers and resulted in a major downward shift in world supplies.

23. This hypothesis closely resembles that elaborated by Raul Prebisch, who argued that cyclical swings aggravate the terms of trade deterioration of developing countries because wages and prices in the industrialized countries parallel primary commodity price movements during an upswing, causing inflationary pressure. On the other hand, they resist downward movements in a depression as a result of their monopolistic market structures in comparison to more flexible prices and wages in the primary producing sector of developing countries where workers are not unionized. The hypothesis has currently been popularized as the "ratchet-effect" (Cooper and Lawrence, 1975), and its validity has been attacked by Finger and DeRosa (1978) on the grounds that empirical support for downward inflexibility of prices of final products is unsubstantiated.

24. See IDB (1978: 24–31) for a review of the UNCTAD negotiations on the integrated program up to the scheduled ending of the preparatory meetings in February 1978.

BIBLIOGRAPHY

Alting von Geusau, Frans A.M., ed. 1977. *The Lomé Convention and a New International Economic Order*. Leyden: A.W. Sijthoff.

Askari, Hossein and Gordon Weil. 1974. "Stability of Export Earnings of Developing Nations." *Journal of Development Studies* 11, no. 1: 86–90.

Behrman, Jere R. 1978. "International Commodity Agreements: An Evaluation of the UNCTAD Integrated Commodity Program." In F. Gerard Adams and Sonia Klein, eds., *Stabilizing World Commodity Markets: Analysis, Practice and Policy*. Lexington, Mass.: Lexington Books.

Brook, Ezriel M.; Enzo R. Grilli; and Jean Waelbroeck. 1977. "Commodity Price Stabilization and the Developing World." Bank Staff Working Paper No. 262. Washington, D.C.: International Bank for Reconstruction and Development.

Brown, C.P. 1975. *Primary Commodity Control*. Kuala Lumpur and London: Oxford University Press.

Cooper, Richard D., and Robert Z. Lawrence. 1975. "The 1972–75 Commodity Boom." *Brookings Papers on Economic Activity* 3: 671–723.

Coppock, J.D. 1962. *International Economic Instability*. New York: McGraw-Hill.

———. 1977. *International Trade Instability*. Westmead (England): Saxon House.

Corea, Gamani. 1977. "UNCTAD and the New International Economic Order." *International Affairs* 53, no. 2: 177–87.

David, Wilfred L. 1977. "Dimensions of the North-South Confrontation." In William G. Tyler, ed., *Issues and Prospects for the New International Economic Order*. Lexington, Mass.: Lexington Books.

de Vries, Barend A. 1977. "Export Growth in the New World Environment: The Case of Latin America." *CEPAL Review* 3: 93–120.

de Vries, Jos. 1975. "Compensatory Financing: A Quantitative Analysis." Bank Staff Working Paper No. 228. Washington, D.C.: International Bank for Reconstruction and Development.

Donges, J.B. 1977. "The Third World Demand for a New International Economic Order: Government Surveillance versus Market Decision-Taking in Trade and Investment." *Kyklos* 30, no. 2: 235–58.

Erb, Guy F. 1977. "North-South Negotiations and Compensatory Financing." Washington, D.C.: Overseas Development Council. Mimeographed.

Erb, Guy F., and Bart S. Fisher. 1977. "U.S. Commodity Policy: What Response to Third World Initiatives?" *Law and Policy in International Business* 9, no. 2: 479–513.

Erb, Guy F., and S. Schiavo-Campo. 1969. "Export Instability, Level of Development and Economic Size of Less Developed Countries." *Oxford Bulletin* 31: 263–83.

Fiallo, Fabio R. 1977. "The Negotiation Strategy of Developing Countries in the Field of Trade Liberalization." *Journal of World Trade Law* 2, no. 3: 203–12.

Finger, Michael, and Dean DeRosa. 1978. "Commodity-Price Stabilization and the Ratchet Effect." *The World Economy* 1, no. 2: 195–204.

Fishlow, Albert, et al. 1978. *Rich and Poor Nations in the World Economy.* New York: McGraw-Hill.

French-Davis, M. Ricardo. 1968. "Export Quotas and Allocative Efficiency under Market Instability." *American Journal of Agricultural Economics* 50, no. 3: 643–59.

Glezakos, C. 1973. "Export Instability and Economic Growth: A Statistical Verification." *Economic Development and Cultural Change* 21, no. 4: 670–78.

Goreux, L.M. 1977. "Compensatory Financing: The Cyclical Pattern of Export Shortfalls." *IMF Staff Papers* 24, no. 3: 613–41.

Grubel, H.G. 1964. "Foreign Exchange Earnings and Price Stabilization Schemes." *American Economic Review* 54, no. 4: 378–85.

———. 1977. "The Case Against the New International Economic Order." *Weltwirtschaftliches Archiv* 113, no. 2: 284–307.

Hallwood, Paul. 1977. "Interaction between Private Speculation and Buffer Stock Agencies in Commodity Stabilization." *World Development* 5, no. 4: 349–53.

Hoffmeyer, M. 1976. "International Commodity Agreements as Instruments of Price Regulation." In W. Driehuis, ed., *Primary Commodity Prices: Analysis and Forecasting.* Rotterdam: Rotterdam University Press.

Hueth, Darrell, and Andrew Schmitz. 1972. "International Trade in Intermediate and Final Goods: Some Welfare Implications of Destabilized Prices." *Quarterly Journal of Economics* 86, no. 3: 351–65.

IMF. 1977. *International Financial Statistics.* Washington, D.C.: International Monetary Fund. May.

IBRD. 1968. *The Problem of Stabilization of Prices of Primary Products.* Washington, D.C.

IDB. 1978. *Primary Commodity Exports of Latin America: Quarterly Report on Market Developments.* Report 78/9. Washington, D.C.

Johnson, Harry G. 1976. "World Inflation, the Developing Countries, and 'An Integrated Programme for Commodities'." *Banca Nazionale del Lavoro: Quarterly Review* 118: 309–35.

———. 1977. "Commodities: Less Developed Countries' Demands and Developed Countries' Response." In Jagdish N. Bhagwati, ed., *The New International Economic Order: The North-South Debate.* Cambridge, Mass.: The MIT Press.

Just, Richard E.; Ernst Lutz; Andrew Schmitz; and Stephen Turnovsky. 1977. "The Distribution of Welfare Gains from International Price Stabilization under Distortions." *American Journal of Agricultural Economics* 59, no. 4: 652–61.

Kaldor, Nicholas. 1976. "Inflation and Recession in the World Economy." *Economic Journal* 86: 703–14.

Katrak, H. 1973. "Commodity Concentration and Export Fluctuation: A Probability Analysis." *Journal of Development Studies* 9, no. 4: 556–65.

Kenen, Peter B., and C.S. Voivodas. 1972. "Export Instability and Economic Growth." *Kyklos* 23, no. 1: 791–804.

Kingston, Jerry L. 1973. "Export Instability in Latin America: The Postwar Statistical Record." *Journal of Developing Areas* 7, no. 3: 381–96.

Knudsen, O., and A. Parnes. 1975. *Trade Instability and Economic Development*. Lexington, Mass.: Lexington Books.

Krasner, Stephen. 1977. "The Quest for Stability: Structuring the International Commodity Markets." In Gerald Garvey and Lou Ann Garvey, eds., *International Resource Flows*. Lexington, Mass.: Lexington Books.

Labys, Walter C., and J. Hunkeler. 1974. "Survey of Commodity Demand and Supply Elasticities." Research Memorandum No. 48. Geneva: UNCTAD.

Lawson, C. 1974. "The Decline in World Export Instability: A Reappraisal." *Oxford Bulletin of Economics and Statistics* 36, no. 1: 53–65.

Lim, David. 1976. "Export Instability and Economic Growth: A Return to Fundamentals." *Oxford Bulletin of Economics and Statistics* 38, no. 4: 311–22.

Lord, Montague J. 1976. "The Market Structure of Latin America's Main Primary Commodity Exports." In Inter-America Development Bank, *Primary Commodity Exports of Latin America: Quarterly Report on Market Developments*, Report No. 1. Washington, D.C.

MacBean, A. 1966. *Export Instability and Economic Development*. Cambridge and London: George Allen and Unwin Ltd.

MacBean, A., and V.N. Balasubramanyam. 1976. *Meeting the Third World Challenge*. London: Macmillan Press Ltd. for the Trade Policy Research Centre.

MacLaren, D. 1977. "A Critique of the Proposed Agricultural Commodity Trading Arrangements following UNCTAD IV." *National Westminster Bank Quarterly Review*, pp. 45–54.

Maizels, A. 1968. "Review of *Export Instability and Economic Development* by A.I. MacBean." *American Economic Review* 58: 575–80.

——. 1976. "A New International Strategy for Primary Commodities." In G.K. Helleiner, ed., *A World Divided*. Cambridge: Cambridge University Press.

Malmgren, Harold B. 1976. "Sources of Instability in the World Trading System." *Journal of International Affairs* 30, no. 1: 9–20.

Massell, Benton F. 1964. "Export Concentration and Export Earnings." *American Economic Review* 54, no. 2: 47–63.

——. 1968. *Exports and Economic Growth of Developing Countries*. Cambridge: Cambridge University Press.

——. 1970. "Export Instability and Economic Structure." *American Economic Review* 60: 618–30.

Massell, Benton F.; Scott R. Pearson; and James Finch. 1972. "Foreign Exchange and Economic Development: An Empirical Study of Selected Latin American Countries." *Review of Economics and Statistics* 54, no. 2: 208–12.

Mathieson, Donald J., and Ronald I. McKinnon. 1974. "Instability in Underdeveloped Countries: The Impact of the International Economy." In Paul A. David and W. Reder, eds., *Nations and Households in Economic Growth. Essays in Honor of Moses Abramovitz*. New York and London: Academic Press.

McKinnon, Ronald I. 1967. "Futures Markets, Buffer Stocks, and Income

Stability for Primary Producers." *Journal of Political Economy* 75, no. 6: 844–61.

Michaely, Michael. 1962. *Concentration in International Trade.* Amsterdam: North Holland Publishing Company.

Michalopoulos, Constantine, and Lorenzo L. Perez. 1977. "Commodity Trade Policy Initiatives and Issues." In F. Gerard Adams and Sonia Klein, eds., *Stabilizing World Commodity Markets: Analysis, Practice and Policy.* Lexington, Mass.: Lexington Books.

Naya, Seiji. 1973. "Fluctuations in Export Earnings and Economic Patterns of Asian Countries." *Economic Development and Cultural Change* 21, no. 4: 629–41.

Newbery, David, and Joseph Stiglitz. 1977. "The Economic Impact of Price Stabilization." Draft report presented to a seminar on the economic impact of price stabilization of primary commodities, Washington, D.C., Agency for International Development, 23 December.

O'Brien, P. 1972. "On Commodity Concentration of Exports in Developing Countries." *Economia Internazionale* 25, no. 4: 697–717.

Rangarajan, C., and V. Sundararajan. 1976. "Impact of Export Fluctuations on Income—A Cross Country Analysis." *Review of Economics and Statistics* 58, no. 3: 368–72.

Rangarajan, L.N. 1978. *Commodity Conflict: The Political Economy of International Commodity Negotiations.* London: Croom Helm Ltd.

Rao, Potluri, and Roger LeRoy Miller. 1971. *Applied Econometrics.* Belmont, Calif.: Wadsworth Publishing Company, Inc.

Sarris, Alexander H., and Lance Taylor. 1978. "Buffer Stock Analysis for Agricultural Products: Theoretical Murk or Empirical Resolution?" In F. Gerard Adams and Sonia Klein, eds., *Stabilizing World Commodity Markets: Analysis, Practice and Policy.* Lexington, Mass.: Lexington Books.

Sheehey, Edmund. 1977. "Levels and Sources of Export Instability: Some Recent Evidence." *Kyklos* 30, no. 2: 319–24.

Smith, Gordon W. 1978. "Commodity Instability and Market Failure: A Survey of Some Issues." In F. Gerard Adams and Sonia Klein, eds., *Stabilizing World Commodity Markets: Analysis, Practice and Policy.* Lexington, Mass.: Lexington Books.

Snape, R.H., and B.S. Yamey. 1963. "A Diagrammatic Analysis of Some Effects of Buffer Fund Price Stabilization." *Oxford Economic Papers* 15: 95–106.

Stein, Leslie. 1977. "Export Instability and Development: A Review of Some Recent Findings." *Banca Nazionale del Lavoro: Quarterly Review* 122: 279–90.

Stern, Robert M. 1976. "World Market Instability in Primary Commodities." *Banca Nazionale del Lavoro: Quarterly Review* 117: 175–95.

Stoutar, Geoffrey N. 1977. "Export Instability and Concentration in the Less Developed Countries." *Journal of Development Economics* 4: 279–97.

Sundram, R.M. 1967. "The Measurement of Export Instability." Unpublished Mimeographed Report.

Thoburn, John. 1977. "Commodity Prices and Appropriate Technology—

Some Lessons from Tin Mining." *Journal of Development Studies* 14, no. 1: 35–52.

Turnovsky, Stephen J. 1974. "Price Expectations and the Welfare Gains from Price Stabilization." *American Journal of Agricultural Economics* 56, no. 4: 706–16.

———. 1978. "The Distribution of Welfare Gains from Price Stabilization: A Survey of Some Theoretical Issues." In F. Gerard Adams and Sonia Klein, eds., *Stabilizing World Commodity Markets: Analysis, Practice and Policy.* Lexington, Mass.: Lexington Books.

UNCTAD. 1976. "Resolution Adopted by the Conference: Integrated Programme for Commodities." TD/RES/93(IV). Geneva.

———. 1977a. *Proceedings of the United Nations Conference on Trade and Development.* Fourth Session, Nairobi, 5–13 May 1976. Volume I: Report and Annexes. TD/218(Vol. I). Geneva.

———. 1977b. "Report on the Preparatory Meeting on Cotton." TD/B/IPC/COTTON/3. Geneva.

———. 1977c. "Report on the Intergovernmental Group of Experts on Copper on Its Fourth Session." TD/B/IPC/COPPER/5, TD/B/IPC/COPPER/AC/5. Geneva.

———. 1977d. *International Sugar Agreement.* TD/SUGAR.9/10. Geneva.

Vastine, J. Robert. 1977. "United States International Commodity Policy." *Law and Policy in International Business* 9, no. 2: 401–77.

Voivodas, C.S. 1974. "The Effect of Foreign Exchange Instability on Growth." *Review of Economics and Statistics* 56, no. 3: 410–12.

Wall, David. 1976. "The European Community's Lomé Convention: 'STABEX' and the Third World's Aspirations." Guest Paper No. 4. London: Trade Policy Research Centre.

10

JERE R.
BEHRMAN
and PRANEE
TINAKORN

The UNCTAD Integrated Program: Earnings Stabilization Through Buffer Stocks for Latin America's Commodities

In Latin America there is a long history of preoccupation about the impact of fluctuations and secular trends in international primary commodity markets on the domestic economies of producing nations. In Chapter 9, Lord has reviewed the recent Latin American primary commodity export experience and concludes that for a number of Latin American countries this history provides a justification for interest in international stabilization schemes for primary commodities.[1] It is not surprising, therefore, that there has been substantial Latin American support for coordinating efforts among developing nations to improve the functioning of these international primary commodity markets as part of the call for a new international economic order.[2]

The framework for the currently ongoing exploration of new international commodity market arrangements has been established by the UNCTAD IV (1976a, 1976b) proposal and resolution at the Nairobi meetings. The original UNCTAD proposal focused on ten core commodities: cocoa, coffee, copper, sugar, cotton, jute, rubber, sisal, tea, and tin. Several other commodities are also mentioned. Emphasis is on price stabilization and on increasing the real returns among developing country exporters. The UNCTAD proposal is called an integrated commodity program. The main feature of integration is the proposed establishment of a six-billion dollar common fund that would provide financing for the various individual commodity agreements and which would fulfill a catalytic role in stimulating the exploration of new commodity arrangements. It would also attempt to combine and reduce risks, to have more bargaining power in international capital markets than would a set of individual funds for the same commodities, and to require smaller total financing than the aggregate of a set of individual funds because of differences of phasing of cycles across commodity markets.

The impact of the implementation of the proposed UNCTAD integrated commodity program has been a subject of considerable debate. Largely on a priori grounds, critics have claimed that price stabilization would lead to revenue destabilization or reduction in revenues of the producing nations, that the real gainers from price stabilization programs would be consumers and not producers, and that the cost of introducing distortions into international commodity markets outweighs the potential gains. These arguments, however, seem to be based upon particular a priori assumptions about the nature of existing commodity markets and the underlying supply and demand schedules that are not obviously realistic, as is discussed in Behrman (1977). Whether or not some of these criticisms have validity cannot be determined solely on a priori grounds, but only with analysis that takes into account empirical realities of the real world.

In this chapter we investigate what would be the impact of the implementation of the UNCTAD integrated commodity program on Latin America's export earnings. We do not attempt to explore the question of what is the effect of fluctuations in such earnings on the goal attainment of the Latin American economies.[3] Our basic approach is to utilize econometric models of the primary commodity markets of interest to simulate what would happen if the UNCTAD program were implemented. Our study is organized in the following way. In the next section, we consider the role of Latin America in the world exports of the ten UNCTAD core commodities and the role of earnings from these core commodities in total Latin American exports. In the third section, we introduce the assumptions underlying our simulations of international buffer stock commodity agreements along the lines proposed by UNCTAD. In the fourth section, we give aggregate results. In the fifth section, we explore the disaggregated implications for Latin America, and in the last section, we present conclusions.

UNCTAD CORE COMMODITIES AND LATIN AMERICAN EXPORTS

UNCTAD has placed considerable emphasis on the ten core primary commodities which are mentioned above. The question naturally arises: how important are these core commodities in the exports of the Latin American countries? Table 10–1 gives some data relevant to this question:

1) the average percentage importance in total import revenues of each of the ten UNCTAD core commodities for each of the Latin American countries over the 1970–1975 period,
2) the total percentage of each country's exports for which the ten UNCTAD core commodities account, and
3) a measure of the extent to which each country's exports are concentrated among the ten core commodities.[4]

The statistics in this table point to the relatively great importance of coffee, sugar, and copper and to the lesser importance of cotton, tin, and cocoa in Latin American exports. The other four UNCTAD core commodities are of negligible significance and therefore are not considered further in our analysis.

Coffee accounts for over 20 percent of the export value of six countries, over 10 percent of nine countries, and is 8 percent of total Latin American exports. Sugar accounts for over 33 percent for five countries and is 7 percent of the total. Copper is 73 percent of Chile's exports, 23 percent of Peru's, and 5 percent of the total. Cotton is over 10 percent for three Central American countries and 2 percent of the total. Tin is 50 percent for Bolivia and less than 1 percent of the total. Cocoa is also less than 1 percent of the total. Taken together, in the early 1970s the UNCTAD core commodities accounted for almost 25 percent of total Latin American exports.

The statistics in Table 10–1 also point to widely different degrees of importance of the UNCTAD core commodities and the export values across the Latin American economies. On the average, in 1970–1975 these core commodities accounted for almost 75 percent of the total value of exports from Cuba and Chile, over 50 percent of the value of total exports from the Dominican Republic, Bolivia, El Salvador, Guatemala, and Haiti, and over 25 percent of the total value of exports from Nicaragua, Guadeloupe, Peru, Brazil, Barbados, Guyana, Costa

Table 10–1. Average Percentage Importance and Concentration Indices for Ten UNCTAD Core Commodities in Latin American Export Revenues, 1970–1975[a]

Country	Coffee	Cocoa	Tea	Sugar	Cotton	Rubber	Jute	Sisal	Copper	Tin	Total	Concentration Index[b]
Argentina											0	0.00
Bahamas											0	0.00
Barbados				35							35	0.12
Belize											0	0.00
Bermuda											0	0.00
Bolivia										50	50	0.25
Brazil	24	2		7	5						38	0.06
Chile									73		73	0.53
Colombia	26										26	0.07
Costa Rica	27										27	0.07
Cuba				75							75	0.56
Dominican Republic	8	5		52							65	0.28
Ecuador	11	8									19	0.02
El Salvador	38				12						50	0.16
Grenada											0	0.00
Guadeloupe				43							43	0.18

Country											Total	HH index[b]
Guatemala	31			8			11				50	0.12
Guiana											0	0.00
Guyana			35								35	0.12
Haiti	39			8		3					50	0.16
Honduras	16										16	0.03
Jamaica				13							13	0.02
Martinique											0	0.00
Mexico	5			6	7						18	0.01
Netherlands Antilles											0	0.00
Nicaragua	14			6					26		46	0.09
Panama				9							9	0.01
Paraguay					7						7	0.01
Peru	4			8	5				23		40	0.06
Surinam											0	0.00
Trinidad and Tobago				5							5	0.00
Uruguay											0	0.00
Venezuela											0	0.00
Total	8	1	0	7	2	0	0	0	5	1	24	0.01

[a]Calculated from data in IMF (1976).

[b]The Herfindahl-Hirschman index is the sum of the squares of the shares. The higher the index is, the greater is the concentration. The maximum value is one.

Rica, and Colombia. The concentration index suggests a similar pattern, but one that is somewhat different for the relative vulnerability of the various Latin American economies to fluctuations in world commodity markets if those fluctuations are not perfectly correlated across commodities. By this index, Cuba and Chile are by far the most vulnerable of the Latin American economies because of their respective great dependence on sugar and copper. The Dominican Republic and Bolivia are next because of their respective dependence on sugar and tin. Although El Salvador, Haiti, and Guatemala have the same percentage of their total exports originating in the UNCTAD core commodities as does Bolivia, they are probably less vulnerable because of greater diversification among those commodities. On the other hand, Barbados and Guyana with their relative concentration on sugar may be at least as vulnerable as Guatemala, Nicaragua, and Peru, even though each of the latter group of countries has a higher proportion of their total exports accounted for by the UNCTAD core commodities. At the other end of the spectrum, whether one judges by the percentage of total exports that arise from the UNCTAD core commodities or by the index of concentration in these exports, are countries like Argentina, Bahamas, Belize, Bermuda, Grenada, Guiana, Martinique, Netherlands Antilles, Panama, Surinam, Uruguay, and Venezuela. Thus, the impact of the UNCTAD integrated commodity program would vary quite substantially across the various Latin American economies.

To explore to what extent the Latin American economies would benefit or lose from changes in the international commodity markets for the UNCTAD core commodities, it is useful to ask what proportion of total world production of these commodities originates in Latin America. Table 10-2 provides statistics germane to this question, with the percentage of total world production originating in individual Latin American countries and in all of Latin America during the half decade centered on 1970. For all of Latin America these figures are 48 percent for coffee, 26 percent for sugar, 21 percent for cocoa, 17 percent for copper, 11 percent for cotton, 14 percent for tin, and less than 2 percent for the other four commodities.

On an individual country-commodity basis, in only five cases do Latin American economies average as much as 10 percent of world production: Brazil for coffee and cocoa, Colombia for coffee, Bolivia for tin, and Chile for copper. Since the largest figure is only 18 percent for Brazil in coffee, individual Latin America economies acting alone apparently would not have great market power in the total world markets for these commodities. Also note that Brazil accounts for 5 percent or more of world production for four of the core commodities (coffee, cocoa, sugar, and cotton), but no other Latin American country

Table 10–2. Average Percentage Share of Latin American Countries in World Production of Ten UNCTAD Core Commodities, 1968–1972[a]

Country	Coffee	Cocoa	Tea	Sugar	Cotton	Jute	Rubber	Sisal	Copper	Tin
Argentina			2		1					
Bolivia										13
Brazil	18	12		7	5		1			
Chile									12	1
Colombia	14	1			1					
Costa Rica	3									
Cuba				8						
Dominican Republic		2		4[b]						
Ecuador		4								
El Salvador	5									
Guatemala	4									
Jamaica				1[b]						
Mexico	4	1[b]		4	3				1	
Peru				2[b]	1				4	
Venezuela		1								
Total	48	21[b]	2	26[b]	11	0	1	0	17	14

[a]Calculated from data in Jiler et al. (1975). Countries are excluded if they did not average at least 1 percent for one core commodity.
[b]Based on export data, rather than production data, for the countries indicated. Therefore, this is a lower bound.

averages as much as 5 percent for more than one of these commodities. Thus, only Brazil in Latin America would seem to be an important factor in more than one of the possible international agreements for the core commodities.

ECONOMETRIC MODELS OF THE CORE COMMODITY INTERNATIONAL MARKETS AND ASSUMPTIONS UNDERLYING THE SIMULATIONS OF THE UNCTAD COMMODITY PROGRAM

One of the advantages of using model simulations as a tool of policy analysis is that the assumptions underlying the analysis are very explicit. We first describe the econometric models of the UNCTAD core commodity international markets that are the basis of our simulations. We then list and discuss a number of the assumptions underlying the simulations that are presented in the next two sections.

Econometric Models of the UNCTAD Core Commodity International Markets

The econometric models of the UNCTAD core international commodity markets derive from the earlier work of Adams and Behrman (1976), Agosin (1976), and Behrman (1975). The models are quite simple and are estimated from annual data for the 1955–1972 period.[5] They generally have production and demand relations for each kind of economy in each of the major economic groupings: the developed economies, the developing economies, and the centrally planned economies. There is also a global inventory function estimated by Tinakorn (1978) that attempts to capture better speculative inventory behavior than did the comparable functions in the original models of the three sources listed above. Finally, the market price is solved from the short-run equilibrium condition, that is, supply equals demand for current use plus inventory changes.[6] To simulate international buffer stock policies, it is assumed that the buffer stock buys or sells, when the price would fall outside of predetermined price limits. Any such buffer stock activity affects the price through the short-run equilibrium condition just mentioned.

A discussion of the structure of the full set of commodity models is beyond the scope of this chapter, and interested readers are referred to Behrman and Tinakorn (1978b) and to Tinakorn (1978). Instead the structure of only one model, that for coffee, is presented as an example.

Production: The theory underlying the supply side assumes the existence of pressures leading to competitivelike behavior for a large number of relatively small producers. Short-run production (*PRO*) depends on the stock of trees, a time trend (*T*) to represent secular shifts because of technological change, development of supporting infrastructure, and so on, dummy variables for unusual weather conditions (*DS* followed by the relevant years), the expected real coffee price (*PDF*), and a disturbance term. The stock of trees is unobservable, however, and thus the long-run response to the expected real coffee price PDF_{-i}, where *i* refers to the number of years in a lagged response, is substituted into the relation. For the developing (sole producer) countries[7] the relation obtained is:[8]

$$ln\ PRO = -0.023ln\ PDF_{-6} + 0.054ln\ PDF_{-7} + 0.142ln\ PDF_{-8}$$
$$ (-0.3) \phantom{ln\ PDF_{-6} + } (1.0) \phantom{0.054ln\ PDF_{-7} + } (5.0)$$

$$+ 0.153ln\ PDF_{-9} + 0.024\ T + 0.25\ DS\ 6566$$
$$ (3.2) \phantom{0.153ln\ PDF_{-9} + } (3.9) (5.2)$$

$$+ 0.24\ DS\ 60 + 10.470$$
$$ (3.1) (69.5)$$

$$\overline{R}^2 = 0.87,\ SE = 0.068,\ DW = 2.81,\ 1956 - 1973$$

This relation is consistent with a substantial part of the variance in the dependent variable over the sample. There is no evidence of a significant short-run price response, but there is evidence of a significant long-run price response with a long-run price elasticity of 0.33. It is through this long-run price response that the buffer stock program would affect coffee production. Because of the gestation period for new trees, this response occurs only after several years. The pattern of price response reflects the combination of the time required for the formation of price expectations and the gestation period between planting and mature bearing. In addition to the price response, there also is evidence of a significant secular trend and weather impact (as represented by dummy variables for the particularly good conditions in 1960 and 1965–1966).

Demand: The per capita demand for coffee for current use (*D/POP*) is formulated in the traditional manner as a function of deflated coffee prices (*PDF*) and per capita product in the consuming area (*GDP/POP*).[9] Because of differential responses across country types, three such functions are estimated:

Developed economies

$$ln\ (D/POP) = 3.264 + 0.197ln\ (GDP/POP) - 0.237ln\ PDF_{-1}$$
$$\quad\quad\ \ (10.3)\quad\ (3.0)\quad\quad\quad\quad\quad\quad (-6.1)$$

$$- 0.198(ln\ DPF_{-1} - ln\ PDF_2)$$
$$(-3.9)$$

$$\overline{R}^2 = 0.94, SE = 0.030, DW = 2.00, 1955-1972$$

Developing economies

$$ln(D/POP) = 0.567 + 0.400ln(GDP/POP)_{-1} - 0.314[ln\ PDF_{-1}$$
$$\quad\quad\quad (0.5)\quad\ \ (1.8)\quad\quad\quad\quad\quad\quad (-3.4)$$

$$+ ln\ PDF_{-2})/2.0] - 0.242(ln\ PDF_{-2} - ln\ PDF_{-3})$$
$$(-2.2)$$

$$\overline{R}^2 = 0.88,\ SE = 0.060,\ DW = 2.41,\ 1955-1972$$

Centrally planned economies

$$ln(D/POP) = -6.380 + 1.447ln(GDP/POP) - 1.247\ [(ln\ PDF$$
$$\quad\quad\quad (-6.3)\quad\ \ (7.0)\quad\quad\quad\quad\quad\quad (-5.3)$$

$$+ ln\ PDF_{-1})/2.0]$$

$$\overline{R}^2 = 0.97,\ SE = 0.049,\ DW = 1.92,\ 1955-1972$$

These relations, once again, are quite consistent with fluctuations in the dependent variables over the sample period. The determinants are per capita income and deflated prices. The pattern of income elasticities is 0.20, 0.40, and 1.45, respectively. The largest value is for the medium-income country group, which suggests an S-shaped income response with most future potential for expanded demands in the centrally planned[10] and developing regions. The short-run (defined as current year or with one year lag) price elasticities are -0.44, -0.31, and -1.25, respectively. The long-run (defined as complete adjustment) price elasticities are -0.24, -0.31, and -1.25, respectively. It is through these price responses that the hypothetical buffer stock program would affect coffee demands.

Inventories: The level of world desired inventories (STK) adjusts slowly from earlier levels, and therefore the coefficient on the lagged inventory level is significant and fairly large (0.81). In addition there are included possible responses to the level and change in world coffee demand (D), the current deflated cost of acquiring coffee stocks (PDF), the expected deflated price of coffee as represented by lagged values (PDF_{-i}), and dummy variables for unusual speculative activities in 1964 and 1970 (D6470):

$$ln\, STK = 0.814ln\, STK_{-1} + 0.917ln\, D - 1.371ln\, D_{-1} - 1.052ln\, PDF$$
$$(3.5) \qquad\qquad (.08) \qquad\quad (-1.8) \qquad\quad (1.8)$$

$$+\; 0.508ln\, PDF_{-1} + 0.109\, D\, 6470 + 7.05$$
$$(0.9) \qquad\qquad (1.2) \qquad\qquad (1.0)$$

$$\bar{R}^2 = 0.95,\, SE = 0.20,\, DW = 1.43,\, 1952\text{--}1973$$

This relation is also fairly consistent with fluctuations in the dependent variable during the sample period. Next to the slow adjustment of past desired inventory levels noted above, the most important response appears to be the negative one to the current cost of acquiring inventories (with a unitary elasticity). In addition there is some evidence of (probably weaker) responses to changes in world demand ($D - D_{-1}$),[11] the unusual market conditions in 1916 and 1970 (D 6470), and the expected deflated price (with a positive elasticity of 0.5, but with a large standard error). A hypothetical buffer stock program would alter other desired coffee inventories through the cost of acquiring them and possibly through the effect on price expectations and on changes in world coffee demands.

Short-Run Equilibrium: The following short-run equilibrium condition is that total supply (PRO) equals total demand for current use (D), nonbuffer stock inventory additions ($STK - STK_{-1}$), and buffer stock additions (BS):

$$PRO = D + STK - STK_{-1} + BS$$

This is a short-run equilibrium condition because, in addition to some current price responses, there are expectational and adjustment lags in all of the above relations that determine production, demand for current use, and nonbuffer stock inventories. By changing BS the buffer stock agency can alter the current price, which is solved from this short-run equilibrium condition. When the price would fall below (above) a predetermined floor (ceiling) price, the buffer stock agency is assumed below to purchase (sell) enough coffee so that the current price is at the floor (ceiling) level. Because of the lags, in so doing, the buffer stock agency affects not only the current situation, but also the subsequent history of production demands, and thus prices. For this reason the incorporation in the econometric models of the best available estimates of lagged adjustment and expectational formation processes is very important.

Assumptions Underlying Simulations of the UNCTAD Integrated Commodity Program and Its Implications for Latin American Commodity Exports

We now list and discuss a number of the assumptions underlying the simulations presented in the next two sections.

a. *Our econometric models of the international commodity markets approximate well the structures of the markets despite the operations of the UNCTAD integrated commodity program buffer stock.* More explicit implications of this assumption are that limit pricing and the threat of substitution in use continue to make aggregate supply and demand response relations sufficiently good approximations despite the existence of new market power. National policies that alter the relations between international and domestic prices (e.g., marketing boards, export taxes, and import taxes) continue to have the same effects. Nonbuffer stock inventory behavioral relations remain the same despite the existence of buffer stock arrangements. Other parameters and lags remain the same despite the reduction in price instability.

Some of these implications are strong. For example, a priori private inventories might be expected to fall because of reduction in downward speculation (assuming that the buffer stock had sufficient financial reserves) and the assurance of extra supplies from the buffer stock. On the other hand, the reduction in risks of carrying inventories may cause them to rise *ceteris paribus* if inventory holders are risk averse. The sensitivity of the simulations to structural changes in either direction for inventory behavior (or for any other aspect of the model) in principle could be explored, although such an exercise is beyond the scope of this chapter.[12]

b. *Nonstochastic simulations over a recent particular historical period (1963–1975) provide useful information about likely orders of magnitude associated with the operation of buffer stock arrangements.* It would be preferable to calculate the effective values of various policies by conducting Monte Carlo studies drawing on the estimated distributions of the disturbance terms. To do so, however, would involve a large number of simulations and would require resources far beyond those currently available for this work. Therefore, nonstochastic simulations are utilized. Some preliminary work, reported in Behrman and Tinakorn (1977), suggests that ignoring these disturbance terms in the simulations probably is not too misleading because the underlying relations in the models generally have relatively small unexplained variances.

The use of a thirteen-year period starting in 1963 ties the results to a particular historical experience. However, that period is long enough to encompass a wide range of economic conditions (e.g., substantial fluctuations in the world economy). The length of the period, therefore, lessens the extent to which the total results are conditional on the particular choice of years, although the details of the time sequences obviously reflect that choice.

A simulation period as long as thirteen years is also useful because it permits covering enough years to encompass several commodity price cycles of historical duration. Smith and Schink (1976) emphasize the importance of having sufficiently long simulation periods for this very reason, based on their econometric explorations of the tin market. UNCTAD (1975) gives the lengths of price cycles in the 1960–1974 period for nine of the ten core commodities (not including tea). Across all commodities the average is 22 months, but the means for individual commodities range from 13 months for sugar to 34 months for coffee.[13] The maximum length ranges from 26 months for sugar to 79 months for coffee, but for no other commodity is it greater than 51 months. A thirteen-year simulation period thus should cover enough time for several price cycles of the duration historically experienced—although fewer for coffee than for the other commodities. It should be short enough, on the other hand, so that structural changes caused by reduced price fluctuations are not overwhelming. This is so since many of those changes relate to variations in capital stock that require long gestation periods both for decisionmaking and for implementation.

c. *The buffer stock managers operate with sufficient financial reserves and sufficient commodity reserves so that they can buy or sell to keep the annual deflated commodity prices within a ±15 percent bandwidth of the known secular price trends for the 1950–1975 period. No export or production quotas are utilized by the commodity agreements.*[14] This assumption about the operation of the buffer stock has a number of subcomponents that merit comment. The existence of sufficient financial reserves means that the buffer stocks always can buy to defend the price floor, which should discourage destabilizing speculation. The existence of sufficient commodity reserves always to be able to defend the price ceiling should discourage destabilizing upward speculation. The reason for this assumption is to permit the simulation of the ongoing behavior of buffer stock stabilization without overemphasis on the end points of the scheme. However, for some commodities, it does imply that the buffer stock must start the period with initial commodity reserves in order always to have stocks at nonnegative levels.

The presumed knowledge of the secular price trends tends to reduce the cost and increase the profitability of the buffer stock operation in comparison to situations in which large errors are made about secular trends. In our simulations errors are not made because of the confusion between short-run and long-run price movements. In principle, alternative target pricing rules could be examined with these models (lagged moving averages, fixed prices, etc.), but we do not do so in this chapter. Smith (1975), for example, in conducting such explorations for the copper market has concluded that five-year lagged moving averages result in too great cyclical fluctuations and give a poor estimate of the trend. As a result, the buffer stock model follows some bizarre behavior that causes substantial losses. Much better performance occurs when the price target is fixed for long periods of time (e.g., ten years). Of course, such a rule, like the trend rule used here, can be implemented only with very good ex ante expectations about price movements. We report elsewhere on explorations that led to similar conclusions (see Behrman and Tinakorn, 1977, 1978a).

The price target and floors and ceilings are in real terms which is the normal approach. In the absence of money illusions, moreover, long-run equilibrium prices are also in real terms, and the aim of pure price stabilization schemes is to limit the fluctuations around long-run real equilibrium prices.[15]

All of the variables in the models are annual averages. The use of these annual averages may understate somewhat the cost of buffer stock operations. Transaction costs may be incurred during the year because the price otherwise would move above or below the allowable range, and yet the average price may be within the allowable range (thus indicating no transaction costs). This problem probably is more important for agricultural products with strong seasonal cycles (e.g., cocoa).

The bandwidths around the secular price trends that are maintained by the buffer stock operations and the simulations ±15 percent. The choice of bandwidths is important. Credible narrow bandwidths increase price stability, but they may destroy future markets and much of the motive for holding private inventories. They may also reduce (perhaps to large negative numbers) profits from the buffer stock operations since such profits depend primarily on price differences between buying at the floor and selling at the ceiling. Broad bandwidths do not stabilize prices much. In Behrman and Tinakorn

(1977), some results are reported that explore the sensitivity of the outcomes to different bandwidths.

Finally, it should be emphasized that the simulated rules of operation used here for the buffer stocks are quite simple and mechanical. Buffer stock managers might well have more information than is included in these simulations. More flexible rules of operation might be desirable. To the extent that either of these possibilities is true, the mechanical procedures simulated here may overstate the cost of buffer stock operations.

d. *The distribution of benefits or losses to Latin American producers of the core commodities is assumed to be proportional to their respective shares in world production.* The models that are used for the simulations have relations only on fairly aggregative levels (i.e., for all developing county producers or for total world production). There exists a number of studies of supply elasticities at the disaggregated or country level for the UNCTAD primary products (see Labys and Hunkeler, 1974; and Askari and Cummings, 1977). However, the scope of this study did not permit such a disaggregated analysis. Moreover, it is not clear that any international commodity agreement in fact would divide marginal market shares along the lines indicated by historical price responses. Therefore, we have decided to proceed with the simple assumption that the shares indicated in Table 10–2 would prevail if there were an integrated commodity program. This assumption may bias upward our estimate of Latin America's shares in the losses or gains from the future instigation of an international commodity program, since Latin America has had declining shares in the markets of most of these products during the past several decades.

AGGREGATE SIMULATIONS OF THE UNCTAD INTEGRATED COMMODITY PROGRAMS FOR THE CORE COMMODITIES OF INTEREST TO LATIN AMERICA

We now turn to the simulated results of introducing international commodity buffer stock agreements for the six UNCTAD core commodities of interest to Latin American producers under the assumptions discussed in the previous section. Tables 10–3, 10–4, and 10–5 summarize these simulation results. Table 10–3 gives purchases and sales in millions of 1975 dollars by buffer stocks for each of the commodities of interest and the sum of sales and of sales minus purchases across these commodities, all on a year-by-year basis. Table 10–4 gives the annual percentage changes in the quantities supplied and the

Table 10–3. Annual Purchases and Sales in Millions of 1975 Dollars for Buffer Stocks for Six UNCTAD Core Commodities of Interest to Latin America for 1963–1975

Commodities	Initial Value	1963	1964	1965	1966	1967	1968	1969	1970	1971	1972	1973	1974	1975
Cocoa	0	53	0	295	92	27	0	−8	0	24	246	0	0	0
Coffee	0	1387	0	−114	548	0	0	0	−914	0	−77	0	−434	−1342
Sugar	148	−224	0	806	965	762	879	794	1621	908	0	876	1134	1408
Cotton	0	541	251	279	320	491	633	606	626	360	0	0	0	0
Copper	414	193	0	−52	−178	−123	−395	−307	0	0	976	0	0	0
Tin	141	0	0	−202	0	0	0	0	0	0	0	0	0	0
Sum of Purchases–Sales	703	1950	251	1012	1747	1157	1117	1085	1333	1292	1145	876	700	66
Sum of Purchases	703	2174	251	1380	1925	1280	1512	1400	2247	1292	1222	876	1134	1408

Source: Based on the authors' computations.

Table 10–4. Annual Percentage Changes in Quantity Supplied (Q), Price (P), and Producers' Revenues (R) due to Operation of Buffer Stock for Six UNCTAD Core Commodities of Interest to Latin America for 1963–1975[a]

Commodities		1963	1964	1965	1966	1967	1968	1969	1970	1971	1972	1973	1974	1975
Cocoa	Q	0.0	0.0	0.0	0.0	0.0	0.0	0.2	0.8	3.0	7.7	11.9	11.8	2.7
	P	9.4	3.6	88.7	44.1	-3.1	-12.2	-3.1	-0.8	-3.3	11.8	-25.2	-33.6	-21.2
	R	9.4	3.6	88.7	44.1	-3.1	-12.2	-2.9	-0.0	-0.5	20.5	-16.3	-25.7	-19.2
Coffee	Q	0.0	0.0	0.0	0.0	0.0	0.0	-0.4	1.0	2.5	3.5	1.9	2.9	2.2
	P	20.4	0.8	12.7	6.3	7.5	6.4	6.9	-4.8	1.9	-6.7	1.9	-12.0	-18.7
	R	20.4	0.8	12.7	6.3	7.5	6.4	6.5	-3.8	4.4	-3.5	-0.0	-9.4	-17.0
Sugar	Q	0.0	0.0	-1.4	-0.3	7.0	11.2	5.4	-2.3	-3.0	7.5	11.4	0.9	-8.0
	P	-9.6	-3.7	54.1	84.5	24.5	-25.1	-23.1	64.8	92.1	-7.2	-46.3	-8.0	102.6
	R	-9.6	-3.7	51.9	83.9	33.2	-16.7	-18.9	61.0	86.4	-0.2	-40.2	-7.2	86.5
Cotton	Q	0.0	9.4	-2.7	5.6	1.0	6.8	5.4	3.3	6.0	0.3	-2.2	-0.5	-1.2
	P	24.7	-6.7	6.9	0.0	14.5	10.7	2.6	6.9	-3.9	-10.7	-2.6	1.3	4.3
	R	24.7	2.1	4.0	5.6	15.6	18.2	8.1	10.5	1.9	-10.5	-4.7	0.8	3.1
Copper	Q	0.0	0.0	0.0	0.0	0.0	0.6	0.4	0.2	-0.2	-0.4	-0.9	-1.1	-0.7
	P	4.7	3.0	2.0	-1.9	-3.8	-7.2	-8.8	-5.6	-2.4	10.5	8.1	6.2	4.9
	R	4.7	3.0	2.0	-1.9	-3.8	-6.6	-8.5	-5.4	-2.7	10.0	7.2	5.0	4.2
Tin	Q	0.0	0.0	0.1	-0.1	-0.1	0.0	-0.1	0.0	0.0	-0.1	0.0	0.0	0.0
	P	0.0	0.0	-1.5	0.0	0.0	-0.9	0.0	0.0	0.0	0.0	0.0	0.0	0.0
	R	0.0	0.0	-1.4	-0.1	-0.1	-0.9	-0.1	0.0	0.0	-0.1	0.0	0.0	0.0

Source: Based on the authors' computations.

[a]The comparisons are with simulations that are identical except that no buffer stock activity occurs. The averages for these thirteen years are given in columns 5, 6, and 7 of Table 10–5.

Table 10–5. Summary of Basic International Buffer Stock Commodity Program Simulations for Six UNCTAD Core Commodities of Importance to Latin America, 1963–1975[a]

UNCTAD Core Commodities of Interest to Latin America	Value of Buffer Stock Activity[b]		Longest Continuous Period (in Years) of Buffer Stock Activity		Mean Percentage Changes[c] due to Price Stabilization in:			Value of Additional Producers' Revenue[b,c]	Revenue Stabilization Index[d]
	Excluding Final Stock	Including Final Stock	Without Buying	Without Selling	Price	Quantity Supplied	Producers' Revenues		
	(1)	(2)	(3)	(4)	(5)	(6)	(7)	(8)	(9)
Coffee	−494	−413	9	4	1.5	1.0	2.4	1734	0.71
Cocoa	−667	−70	3	6	4.2	2.9	6.7	334	0.24
Sugar	−13877	−6309	12	2	23.1	2.2	23.6	10609	0.22
Cotton	−3735	−643	13	4	3.7	2.4	6.1	8241	0.51
Copper	−508	382	8	6	0.8	−0.2	0.6[f]	−188[f]	0.94
Tin	30	30	13	10	−0.2	−0.0	−0.2	−21	1.00
Average[e]	−19251[e]	−7023[e]	9.7	5.3	5.5	1.4	6.5	20709[e]	0.60

Source: Based on the authors' computations.

[a]Section 3 above presents the assumptions underlying these simulations.

[b]These values are present discounted values using a 5 percent real discount rate and are in millions of constant 1975 dollars.

[c]The comparisons are with identical simulations except that no buffer stock activity is allowed. These data are the averages of those in Table 10–4.

[d]This is the ratio of the standard deviation in real revenues with price stabilization to that without price stabilization.

[e]Total for columns 1, 2, and 8.

[f]The present discounted value is negative even though the mean percentage change in producers' revenues is positive because of the concentration of negative values early in the simulation period.

prices and producers' revenues due to the operation of the buffer stock for the same commodities.[16] Table 10-5 summarizes the activity of the buffer stocks and the impact of this activity on producers' revenues over the thirteen-year period of the simulations. For each of the six commodities of interest it gives: the present discounted value of buffer stock activity with and without including the value of final stocks; the longest continuous period of buffer stock activity without buying and without selling; the mean percentage changes due to the buffer stock price stabilization program in prices, quantities supplied, and producers' revenues; the present discounted value of additional producers' revenues due to the institution of the integrated commodity program; and an index of the extent of revenue stabilization that occurs because of the price stabilization program.[17]

Let us begin by considering the nature of buffer stock activity. As is indicated in Table 10-3, for three of the six core commodities of interest the buffer stock must begin with initial stocks in order always to be able to defend the price ceiling. If there were not such initial stocks for sugar, copper, and tin, the buffer stock authorities would not always be able to defend the ceilings in the initial years because to do so would require greater quantities of commodities than they would have purchased at an earlier time in efforts to defend the floors.

After establishing their initial position, in the subsequent thirteen years of simulated buffer stock operation the buffer stocks intervene in the market forty-two out of seventy-eight possible times, or slightly more than half of the years on the average for each commodity. Such activity is somewhat more frequent for sugar and somewhat less frequent for tin than for the other four commodities. Despite this frequency of intervention in the market, the buffer stocks would, for long periods of time, not be on one side of the market. Columns 3 and 4 in Table 10-5 give the longest continuous period in years of buffer stock activity, respectively, without buying or without selling. The longest period without buying ranges from three years for cocoa to thirteen years for cotton and tin, with an average of 9.7 years. The longest period without selling ranges from two years for sugar to ten years for tin, with an average of 5.3 years. These long periods without being on one side of the market suggest that it might be quite difficult to be sure that the target prices around which the buffer stocks are attempting to stabilize are related to long-run equilibrium values. These long periods also suggest that if international commodity agreements are in effect only for the five-year period suggested by the Havana Charter, in many cases activity might be heavily concentrated on one side of the market.[18] Such considerations suggest that it might be desirable to have buffer stock agreements with longer lives than generally has been proposed.

Another important point about the simulated operation of these buffer stocks is that the magnitude of financing becomes fairly large after several years, even though there are significant advantages from pooling finances across these six core commodities. For example, the sum of purchases minus sales in the penultimate row of Table 10–3 indicates that, on the average, a total of about one billion dollars per year would be expended. Thus, in about six years the buffer stocks would exhaust the six-billion dollar fund mentioned in the UNCTAD proposal, even if only these six of the ten core commodities were included. This occurs despite a gain from pooling across commodities of about 30 percent by letting sales in a given year offset purchases of other commodities in the same year. For example, the sales of coffee in 1975 would offset almost all of the purchases of sugar in that year.[19] Large required access to financing despite such pooling may make it necessary at least politically to establish such programs initially on a shorter term basis than the considerations in the previous paragraph would indicate are desirable.

Now let us consider the impact on producers' revenues of the operation of the buffer stock programs. It is useful to break down revenue between the quantities supplied and the price received. For the quantity supplied, the results in Table 10–4 indicate initial periods of no response for cocoa, coffee, and copper. These initial periods of four or five years of no supply response reflect the relatively long gestation required to bring newly planted trees or expanded mine capacity into operation. Subsequently, however, fairly large supply responses are induced, at least for the agricultural products. Increases over 11 percent occur for cocoa and sugar, over 6 percent for cotton, and over 3 percent for coffee. Changes of these magnitudes imply that it may be quite misleading to consider the impact of international commodity agreements within a framework that assumes no supply responses. In fact, in some respects the existence of supply responses with long lags may make stabilization more difficult. For example, the simulation for cocoa indicates a fairly large supply increase in the 1970s in response to the much higher price received for cocoa because of the simulated buffer stock program rather than market conditions in 1965 and 1966.

With the exception of tin, the simulated buffer stock program has much larger percentage effects on prices than on quantities supplied. Tin is an exception because actual prices were fairly stable during the simulation period, perhaps due to the international tin agreement,[20] so relatively little simulated additional buffer stock activity is indicated. For the other five core commodities of interest, in almost every year the price is affected either upward or downward. Note that the price is changed in many years in which no buffer stock activity occurs because of the dynamic impact of past buffer stock purchases or sales. Under the particular assumptions of these simulations, the average price impact is by far the largest for sugar, in which case the average increase is 23.1 percent (see column 5 in Table 10–5).[21] For cocoa and cotton the average annual percentage increases are 4.2 and 3.7 percent, respectively. For coffee it is 1.5 percent. For the two minerals it is less than 1 percent in absolute value. It is interesting to note that in every case except for tin, however, in some years the price stabilization program leads to prices higher than otherwise would exist, whereas in other years it leads to prices lower than those that would prevail without the program.

Altered dynamic price paths induce changes in supplies, as has been noted above, and in demands. The combination of the impact on prices and on quantities results in changes in producers' revenues. In some cases, the movements in prices and quantities reinforce each other, such as in 1967 through 1970 for cotton. In other cases they are opposing, such as in the next two years for cotton, or in 1973 through 1975 for cocoa. The total effects are fairly significant revenue gains for agricultural commodities and much smaller revenue losses for the two minerals (columns 7 and 8 in Table 10–5). For sugar alone the estimated annual average revenue gain is 23.6 percent, which implies a present discounted value of additional producers' revenues of over ten billion dollars.[22] For the other three agricultural commodities the average annual revenue gains range from 2.4 percent for coffee to 6.7 percent for cocoa. The total 6.1 percent average annual revenue gain for cotton, however, implies a present discounted value of total producers' revenue gains of approximately eight billion dollars over the simulation period. Across all six commodities the total simulated present discounted value of additional producers' revenues is somewhat over twenty billion dollars. This gain is fairly substantial, with most of it accruing to sugar and cotton producers and less so to coffee producers.

On the other hand, there are simulated small losses for the two mineral products. Of course, these results are conditional on the particular assumptions discussed in the third section. They would change with different assumptions. However, it well might be the case that under any set of assumptions for a particular time period there would be some losers among the producers (such as the minerals in this case) as well as some gainers. This possibility may make it quite difficult to hold together an integrated arrangement.

These comments refer to what happens to the level of revenues. But some critics of the UNCTAD program have claimed that under reasonable assumptions increases in revenues will be accompanied by decreases in the stability of those revenues. For example, see Johnson

(1976) where this argument is made using linear supply and demand curves with additive disturbance terms and elastic price responses. However, as is indicated in Behrman (1977), whether or not there is a tradeoff between the level and the stability of revenues cannot be settled a priori. It depends upon the elasticities of the underlying curves and the natures of shifts in those curves. It is basically an empirical issue. The results in the last column of Table 10–5 indicate that only for copper is there evidence of a tradeoff between the stability and the level of revenues. For copper, the price stabilization program stabilizes revenues slightly, but with a result of a somewhat lower present discounted value. For the four agricultural commodities, revenues are increased fairly substantially, and instabilities of revenues are reduced significantly. For tin there is a slight reduction in revenues with almost no change in the degree of stability of the revenues. At least for the agricultural commodities, the strong critique that Johnson (1976) has made about the tradeoff between the level and stability of revenues does not seem warranted.

THE IMPLICATIONS OF THE SIMULATED UNCTAD INTEGRATED COMMODITY PROGRAM FOR REVENUES OF LATIN AMERICAN PRODUCERS

In the previous section we discussed the aggregate implications of the proposed UNCTAD program for the six core commodities of interest to Latin American producers. We now turn to the distribution of changed revenues for Latin American producers that would result from this program. Table 10–6 gives the present discounted values of real revenue changes that would accrue to each of the major Latin American producing countries from each of the six UNCTAD core commodities, the total present discounted additional value for each major Latin American producing country, and the ratio of that total value to the average export value in 1970–1975.

The present discounted values of gains to producers in an individual country depend upon the total present discounted value of additional producer revenues (column 8 in Table 10–5) and the country's share in world supply (Table 10–2). These simulated gains are gross values that do not include any contributions to the financing of the buffer stock operations (columns 1 and 2 in Table 10–5). If the producing countries contributed half of the net cost of buffer stock operations, the aggregate producer net gains would be from 17 to 46 percent lower, depending on the evaluation of final buffer stocks held at the end of 1975. In order not to become too complex because of alternative schemes for distribut-

Table 10–6. Present Discounted Values of Gains to Latin American Producers of Simulated UNCTAD Commodity Program over 1963–1975 Period[a]

Latin American Countries	Present Discounted Values of Additional Revenues to Producers (millions of 1975 dollars)							Ratio of PDV of Additional Producer Revenues to Average Annual Export Value in 1970–1975 (percentages)
	Coffee	Cocoa	Sugar	Cotton	Copper	Tin	Total	
Argentina				82			82	3
Bolivia						−3	−3	−1
Brazil	312	40	743	412			1507	28
Chile					−23		−23	−2
Colombia	243	3		82			328	29
Costa Rica	52						52	16
Cuba			849				849	55
Dominican Republic		7	424				431	97
Ecuador		13					13	2
El Salvador	87						87	28
Guatemala	69						69	17
Jamaica			106				106	22
Mexico	69	3	424	247	−2		741	33
Peru			212	82	−8		286	26
Venezuela		3					3	0
Total	832	70	2758	907	−32	−3	4532	16

Source: Based on the authors' computations.

[a]Calculated by distributing the simulated present discounted values of additional revenues for producers in column 8 of Table 10–5 by the proportions in Table 10–2. For the last column the total export values are from the United Nations (1976) with the OECD deflator used to convert into millions of 1975 dollars.

ing the net costs of buffer stock operations among producers and consumers and the question of how to value the final stocks, we focus here on gross producer gains without subtracting their contributions to the buffer stock operations. The present discounted value of gains net of contributions for the costs of buffer stock operations would be lower, with the amount of the reduction depending on the exact assumptions about the funding arrangements and the evaluation of final stocks.

The largest simulated gainers in absolute terms are the sugar and cotton producers (because of the large simulated overall gains for those producers in Table 10–5) and the coffee producers (because of the moderate overall simulated gain in Table 10–5 and the large Latin American share in world production in Table 10–2). The gains for the other three commodities are much smaller and negative for the two minerals.

Therefore, in absolute terms, the big simulated gainers include 1,507 million 1975 dollars for Brazil, 849 for Cuba, 741 for Mexico, 431 for the Dominican Republic, 328 for Colombia, 286 for Peru, and 106 for Jamaica. Smaller gainers include Argentina and the Central American countries. Bolivia and Chile are small losers. The total present discounted value of these revenue gains to Latin American producers is about 4.5 billion 1975 dollars.

To put these numbers in perspective, it is useful to consider them as ratios to the average annual value of exports in 1970–1975 (the last column in Table 10–6). In percentage terms, these ratios range from -2 to 97. The big relative gainers are the Dominican Republic with almost a year's export value (97 percent) and Cuba with over half of a year (55). Mexico, Colombia, Brazil, El Salvador, Peru, and Jamaica all gain from a fifth to a third of a year's export value. For all of Latin America the estimate is a gain of about one-sixth (16 percent) of an average year's export value.

Are such gains for Latin America small or large? The answer depends upon the point of comparison. A total of 4.5 billion 1975 dollars is not so small as to be irrelevant. On the other hand, to obtain it requires the operation of the buffer stock programs for a fairly long period of time. It is small, moreover, in comparison to the transfers of roughly 65 billion dollars per year engendered by the OPEC petroleum price increases. Furthermore, some of the poorer Latin American countries (e.g., Bolivia and Paraguay) would not benefit from such a program.

CONCLUSIONS

Latin Americans long have been concerned about effects of price fluctuations and downward secular trends in international primary commodity markets on the economies of producing nations. This preoccupation has led to some important policy decisions about the internal allocation of resources and international cooperation.

Recently, discussions about possible international cooperation have been very active, not only among Latin American nations, but also among other producing and consuming countries. The framework for this discussion has been set by the UNCTAD proposal for an Integrated Commodity Program for ten core commodities. These commodities account for about one-fourth of total Latin American exports, with coffee, sugar, and copper being of particular importance and cotton, tin, and cocoa less so.

We have simulated the operation of the UNCTAD buffer stock price stabilizing commodity program over the 1963–1975 period, using econometric models for each of the core UNCTAD commodities of interest to Latin America. Based on these simulations, we have a number of qualifications about the program. The financing required probably would exceed the six billion dollars mentioned in the UNCTAD proposal. It would be difficult to identify the underlying secular price trends because of long periods not on one side of the market by the buffer stocks. The producers of some of the core commodities well might lose because of the operation of any specific program in a particular time period. The gainers from such a program might not include some of the poorer nations, such as Paraguay. Even in the nations that do gain, it is not clear that the poorest part of the population will benefit.

Despite such reservations, we conclude that supporting the development of such a program possibly is in the Latin American interest. The simulated resource gain of 4.5 billion dollars is not insignificant. The development of such a program might also increase the extent of control of the Latin American economies, together with the other developing nations, over the international markets in which they operate. In the long run, such increased control may be more important than the simulated producer revenue gains from price stabilization.

NOTES

1. Lord focuses on the 1960–1975 period. From a long run point of view considerable Latin American interest in fluctuations and trends in international primary commodity markets is understandable. Brazil, for example, has received the gains and suffered the losses from a number of different commodity booms and busts for sugar, rubber, and coffee over the past decades. Throughout Latin America, moreover, previously existing worries about the dependence on international commodity markets were intensified greatly by the devastating experience of the Great Depression. According to the League of

Nations, one of the Latin American economies, Chile, was the country most negatively affected by the evaporation of international commodity markets at the start of the 1930s. In that case, export revenues dropped to less than one-sixth of previous peak levels, and total national product per capita fell to half of previous levels (see Behrman, 1976 for more details about the long-run Chilean experience).

2. For a review of events leading to the call for a new international economic order and for more details concerning the UNCTAD proposal and resolution see Lewis (1976); Hansen (1976); Barraclough (1976); Erb and Kallab (1975); Michalopoulos (1976); Behrman (1977, 1978a, 1978c); Taylor and Sarris (1977); Smith (1977); Grubel (1977); Adams and Klein (1978); and the references therein.

3. Several well-known studies look at this question, primarily on a cross-section basis. For example, see Coppock (1976); Glezakos (1973); Kenan and Voivodas (1972); Knudsen and Parnes (1975); MacBean (1966); and Maizels (1968). Lord reviews most of the relevant literature in Chapter 9. Such studies do not seem to come up with consistent conclusions. In part, this may reflect that cross-country estimates are satisfactory only under strong assumptions about the existence of equilibrium or identical lag structures and identical degrees of overvaluation across countries. A more satisfactory approach is one that integrates the producing country with a model of the international primary market. For early work in this area, see Acquah (1972). For some preliminary results concerning coffee and Brazil, see Chapter 7.

4. The measure of concentration that is utilized is the Herfindahl-Hirschman index defined as the sum of the squares of the shares of the individual commodities. The higher this index, the greater is the concentration. The maximum possible value is 1.

5. The data are from standard sources. For details, see Adams and Behrman (1976).

6. Behrman (1978b) discusses theoretical considerations for modeling commodity markets in some detail.

7. For most of the models used in this study, production is divided among developing, developed, and centrally planned nations because of heterogenous responses across these groups. For coffee, only the developing nations are significant producers.

8. In all of the regression estimates presented in this subsection, "ln" refers to the natural logarithm of the indicated variables, subscripts refer to the number of years of lags for the indicated variable (if any), t-statistics are given in parentheses beneath point estimates, $\overline{R}^2$ is the coefficient of determination (which indicates the extent of consistency of the relation with the variation in the dependent variable during the sample period), SE is the standard error of estimate, DW is the Durbin Watson statistic, and the years refer to the sample period.

9. For the centrally planned economies this variable is net material product per capita.

10. The relatively large size of the income elasticity for the centrally planned economies, however, may reflect a price response to a foreign ex-

change allocation for coffee imports in these economies; see Adams and Behrman (1976).

11. The coefficients on current and lagged demand are not significantly different from each other in absolute value, although they are opposite in sign. The response is equivalent, therefore, to a response to the first different of demand.

12. See Tinakorn (1978) for consideration of alternative specifications of inventory relations within these models.

13. The differential length of these cycles across commodities is interesting. To the extent that they originate in demand side fluctuations, fewer differences across commodities might be expected. To the extent that they originate in supply side fluctuations, longer cycles might be expected for the commodities with longer gestation periods (i.e., the tree crops and minerals). Although the estimates for the extreme points (i.e., sugar and coffee) seem consistent with such a pattern, many of the others are not. For example, except for sugar, the shortest mean cycles are for copper and cocoa (a mineral and a tree crop)—and except for coffee, the longest mean cycle is for cotton (an annual crop).

14. Actual quotas and restrictions are used to the same extent as in the sample period, since the estimates of the structure reflect the impact of any such policies.

15. Note that the use of price targets in real terms is not tantamount to indexing since the secular trend in the real price may be either up or down, depending upon changes in the long-run market forces. For a study of the implications of indexing, see Behrman and Tinakorn (1978a) and Tinakorn (1978).

16. The point of comparison for this table is a set of simulations that are identical to the simulations summarized in the table, except that no buffer stock activity is allowed.

17. This index is the ratio of the standard deviation of real revenues with the price stabilization program to the standard deviation in real revenues without the stabilization program. A value of less than 1 thus indicates that revenues are more stable with the program than without it.

18. Perhaps the failure of the cocoa agreement originally negotiated in 1970 to come into effect reflects not that the target price is so much below a long-run equilibrium value, but merely the existence of a long period in which the buffer stock would not be buying, even if the target price is related to the long-run equilibrium value.

19. This calculation of the gains from pooling depends upon the assumption that the capital markets are not perfect and that individual countries participating in the international commodity agreements could not do such pooling on their own. See Behrman and Tinakorn (1977) and Labys (1977) for further discussion of these issues.

20. But Smith and Schink (1976) suggest that the explanation more likely lies in U.S. government tin stockpile activities.

21. However, we have somewhat less confidence in our sugar model than in the others, see Behrman and Tinakorn (1978a, 1978b).

22. But see the previous note.

BIBLIOGRAPHY

Acquah, Paul. 1972. "A Macroeconometric Analysis of Export Instability in Economic Growth: The Case of Ghana and the World Cocoa Market." Ph.D. dissertation, University of Pennsylvania.

Adams, F. Gerard, and J.R. Behrman. 1976. *Econometric Models of World Agricultural Commodity Markets: Cocoa, Coffee, Tea, Wool, Cotton, Sugar, Wheat, Rice.* Cambridge, Mass.: Ballinger Publishing Company.

Adams, F. Gerard, and Sonia Klein, eds. 1978. *Stabilizing World Markets: Analysis, Practice and Policy.* Lexington, Mass.: Lexington Books.

Agosin, Manuel. 1976. "Preliminary Econometric Models of Sisal, Iron Ore, Rubber, and Copper." New York: UNCTAD. Draft.

Askari, Hossein, and John Thomas Cummings. 1977. "Estimating Agricultural Supply Response With the Nerlove Model: A Survey." *International Economic Review* 18, no. 2 (June): 257–92.

Barraclough, Geoffrey. 1976. "The Haves and the Have Nots." *The New York Review of Books* 23, no. 4 (May 13).

Behrman, Jere R. 1975. "Mini Models for Eleven International Commodity Markets." Report for UNCTAD. Philadelphia: University of Pennsylvania.

———. 1976. *Foreign Trade Regimes and Economic Development: Chile.* New York: NBER and Columbia University Press.

———. 1977. *International Commodity Agreements: An Evaluation of the UNCTAD Integrated Commodity Programme.* Washington, D.C.: Overseas Development Council.

———. 1978a. *Economic Development, the International Economic Order, and International Commodity Agreements.* Reading, Mass: Addison-Wesley Company.

———. 1978b. "Commodity Market Modeling: Theoretical Structure." In F.G. Adams and J.R. Behrman, eds., *Econometric Modeling of World Commodity Policy.* Lexington, Mass: Lexington Books.

———. 1978c. "The UNCTAD Integrated Commodity Program: An Evaluation. In F.G. Adams and S. Klein, eds., *Stabilizing World Commodity Markets: Analysis, Practice and Policy.* Lexington, Mass: Lexington Books.

Behrman, Jere R., and Pranee Tinakorn. 1977. "The Simulated Potential Gains of Pooling International Buffer Stock Financing Across the UNCTAD Core Commodities." Report for the U.S. Treasury. Philadelphia: University of Pennsylvania.

———. 1978a. "Indexation of International Commodity Prices Through International Buffer Stock Operations." *Journal of Policy Modeling* 1, no. 1: 113–34.

———. 1978b. "Evaluating Integrated Schemes for Commodity Market Stabilization." In F. Gerard Adams and Jere R. Behrman, eds., *Econometric Modeling of World Commodity Policy.* Lexington, Mass.: Lexington Books.

Coppock, J.D. 1976. *International Economic Instability.* New York: McGraw-Hill Publishing Company.

Eads, George C. 1976. "Address of Executive Director of National Commission on Supplies and Shortages Before the Section of Natural Resources Law,

American Bar Association Convention." Atlanta, Georgia, August 10, 1976. Mimeographed.

Erb, Guy F., and Valeriana Kallab, eds. 1975. *Beyond Dependency: The Developing World Speaks Out.* Washington, D.C.: Overseas Development Council.

Glezakos, C. 1973. "Export Instability and Economic Growth: A Statistical Verification." *Economic Development and Cultural Change* 21 (July):670–78.

Grubel, Herbert G. 1977. "The Case Against the New International Economic Order." *Weltwirtschaftliches Archiv* 113, no. 2: 284–307.

Hansen, Roger D., and the Staff of the Overseas Development Council. 1976. *The U.S. and World Development: Agenda for Action*, 1976. New York: Published for the Overseas Development Council by Praeger Publishers, Inc.

IMF. 1976. *International Financial Statistics.* Washington, D.C.: International Monetary Fund.

Jiler, Harry, et al., eds. 1975. *Commodity Year Book 1975.* New York: Commodity Research Bureau, Inc.

Johnson, Harry G. 1977. "Commodities: Less Developed Countries' Demands and Developed Countries' Response." In J.D. Bhagwati, ed. *The New International Economic Order.* Cambridge, Mass.: M.I.T. Press.

Kenen, P., and C. Voivodas. 1972. "Export Instability and Economic Growth." *Kyklos* 25, no. 4: 791–803.

Knudsen, Odin, and Andrew Parnes. 1975. *Trade Instability and Economic Development: An Empirical Study.* Lexington, Mass.: Lexington Books.

Kreinin, Mordechai E., and J.M. Finger. 1976. "A New International Economic Order: A Critical Survey of Its Issues." *Journal of World Trade Law* (September-October).

Labys, W.C. (1977). "Optimal Portfolio Analysis of Multicommodity Stocking Arrangements." *Oxford Bulletin of Economics and Statistics* 39: 219–228.

Labys, W.C., and J. Hunkeler. 1974. "Survey of Commodity Demand and Supply Elasticities. Memorandum No. 48, UNCTAD/RD/70, GE. 74-45107. Geneva: UNCTAD Research Division.

Lewis, Paul. 1976. "The Have-Nots are Gaining Ground in Their Drive to Gain Concessions." *National Journal* (June 5): 774–82.

MacBean, Alasdair I. 1966. *Export Instability and Economic Development.* Cambridge, Mass.: Harvard University Press.

Maizels, A. 1968. "Review of *Export Instability and Economic Development* by Alasdair I. MacBean." *American Economic Review* 58 (June): 576.

Michalopoulous, Constantine. 1976. "U.S. Commodity Trade Policy and the Developing Countries." Washington, D.C.: U.S. Agency for International Development. Mimeographed.

Prebisch, Raul. 1959. "Commercial Policy in the Underdeveloped Countries." *American Economic Review* S49 (May): 251–73.

Smith, Gordon W. 1975. "An Economic Evaluation of International Buffer Stocks for Copper." Rice University, Mimeographed.

———. 1977. *The External Debt Prospects of the Non-Oil-Exporting Developing Countries.* Monograph No. 10 (NIEO Series). Washington, D.C.: Overseas Development Council.

Smith, Gordon W., and George P. Schink. 1976. "The International Tin Agreement: A Reassessment." *The Economic Journal* 86 (December): 715–28.

Taylor, Lance; Alexander Sarris; and Philip Abbott. 1977. "Grain Reserves, Emergency Relief and Food Aid. Washington, D.C.: Overseas Development Council. Mimeographed.

Tinakorn, Pranee. 1978. "An Empirical Evaluation of the UNCTAD Integrated Commodity Program." Ph.D. dissertation, University of Pennsylvania.

UNCTAD. 1975. "A Common Fund for the Financing of Commodity Stocks: Amounts, Terms and Prospective Sources of Finances." TD/B/C.1/184. Geneva.

———. 1976a. "An Integrated Commodity Programme." Geneva.

———. 1976b. "Resolution Adopted by the Conference: Integrated Programme for Commodities." TD/RES/93 (IV). Geneva.

United Nations. 1950. *The Economic Development of Latin America and Its Principal Problems.* New York: Lake Success.

———. 1976. *Monthly Bulletin of Statistics.*

APPENDIX

Participants in the Workshop on Commodity Markets, Models, and Policies in Latin America

1. Nissim Alcabés, ESAN
2. José Nuñez del Arco, Interamerican Development Bank
3. James Burrows, Charles River Associates
4. Lander Pacora Coupen, ESAN
5. Alfredo Dammert, Banco Industrial del Peru
6. Gordon Gemmill, Business School, City University, London
7. Louis Goreux, International Monetary Fund
8. Daniel R. Hoyle, Southern Peru Copper Corporation
9. Panos Konandreas, International Food Policy Research Institute
10. Walter C. Labys, West Virginia University
11. Lizarda de las Lasas, Iowa State University
12. Carlos Amat y León, Ministerio de Economia y Finanzas, Peru
13. Ricardo Lira, Universidad Catolica de Chile
14. Montague Lord, Interamerican Development Bank
15. M. Ishaq Nadiri, National Bureau of Economic Research and New York University
16. Alembert Pacora, Banco de la Nacion
17. Lorenzo Perez, U.S. Agency for International Development

18. José Portillo, Banco de la Nacion
19. José de la Puente, Ministry of Foreign Affairs, Peru
20. Fernando Robles, ESAN
21. Romualdo A. Roldan, University of Pennsylvania
22. James R. Simpson, University of Florida
23. Interdijt J. Singh, World Bank
24. Alberto Stewart, Banco del Credito del Peru
25. Robert L. Thompson, Purdue University
26. John Tilton, Pennsylvania State University
27. Hugo Torres, Instituto Interamericano de Ciencias Agricolas
28. Jorge Torres, JUNAC
29. Javier Villanueva, Instituto Torcuato di Tella
30. Robert West, Data Resources, Inc.

Index